Icon and Conquest

To my mother and the memory of my father

Our world has just discovered another world (and who will guarantee us that it is the last of its brothers, since the daemons, the Sibyls, and we ourselves have up to now been ignorant of this one?) no less great, full, and well-limbed than itself, yet so new and so infatile that it is still being taught its A B C . . . .

Montaigne, *Essays* 3.6

Contents

The plates follow page 174

List of Illustrations

Volume and plate of the *Great Voyages* are given in Arabic numerals separated by a colon (3:15). F indicates a frontispiece.

Acknowledgments

This study, which was originally written as a dissertation for the Ecole Pratique des Hautes Etudes of the Sorbonne, has been substantially revised for general publication. In the course of my research I have incurred many debts of gratitude to scholars on both sides of the Atlantic.

Thanks to Professor Lévi-Strauss who first called my attention to the research possibilities posed by that vast compendium, the *Great Voyages,* I was able to pursue the fascinating search of the evidence of the *pensée sauvage* among those who subjugated the American Indians. I want to express my deepest gratitude to him and my great admiration for the new horizons his work opened to all of us.

My research on the de Bry collection has mainly been carried out at the New York Public Library and has benefited from the valuable support of the Wenner-Gren Foundation, whose committee I also thank.

It gives me pleasure also to acknowledge the help of Michel Beaujour and Jean-Paul Weber, whose comments on the early drafts of the manuscript have been of great value to me; of Jean-Claude Chevalier, Mervyn Meggitt, and Eric Wolf, to whom I am particularly indebted for their critical commentaries and encouragements; of Professors Etiemble and Jacques Le Goff for their attentive reading of the first draft of the text and their valuable suggestions, as well as of Mary Douglas, whose criticisms have inspired many revisions in the text.

Thanks are due to Pierre Berès, the French publisher, and to Patrick Menget, the editor, for their assistance in the publication of the French edition of this work.

Last, my thanks go to Robert Glasse, my husband, who endured the book's many metamorphoses with tenderness and good humor.

Introduction

Anthropologists, too, are notorious for studying everyone but themselves.

Sol Worth

The purpose of this book is to locate and analyze the genesis of a nonverbal mythology expressed in the European iconography of the late sixteenth century with respect to the New World. This attempt poses a challenge, because, to grasp the creation of this "conqueror's mythology" concealed within iconographic forms, I have borrowed from structural analysis the very tools forged by Lévi-Strauss for his analysis of Amerindian myths. However, the documents to which I have applied them differ drastically from oral myths, particularly Amerindian ones, in several important respects: first, in terms of their cultural area, because they come from our own past—European at the close of the sixteenth and the beginning of the seventeenth centuries; second, by their mode of communication, for here we deal with iconographic documents and not with verbal messages. Finally, and most important, they differ by their factual and historical content, absent from myths.

These documents comprise several hundred copperplate engravings illustrating the *Great Voyages*, that monumental collection published between 1590 and 1634 in thirteen "parts" or in-folio volumes by the de Bry family. The illustrated texts relate the conquest of the Americas from the venture of Columbus to the English and Dutch settlements in the early seventeenth century. The illustrations offered, then, a kind of pictorial reportage on the New World and its inhabitants to the Europeans, as well as the eventful story of the changing relations between the conquerors and the Amerindians and among the invaders themselves (English, French, Spanish, Dutch, and so forth). No wonder then that the historical events of the conquest and colonization of America combine with a totally fanciful vision of the subjugated peoples. Moreover, the publication of these volumes extends over nearly fifty years, which poses a problem of multiple historical transformations.

But the issues these documents raise from an anthropological point of view set them even more sharply apart from myths. Indeed, these artistic engravings constitute a unique ethnographic record of the way in which certain cultural groups have integrated a new object of knowledge into their mental universe: a whole continent with an unknown flora and fauna, and, moreover, culturally diverse populations. To the Europeans, this world, "unpredicted by the Sibyls" as Montaigne has said, revealed itself not only as an object of knowledge, but also as an object of greed—a land and people to be conquered. Thus any research into the conquerors' modes of perceiving America and its inhabitants at that time inevitably entails a study of the relation between their perception and the behavior they adopted toward the Indians.

In addition, our search for that order which enabled the Europeans to control an unknown external world will at the same time reveal the very chaos that these classifications tended to exorcise. By focusing on the physical portrayal of Amerindians in its numerous variations, and more specifically on anomalous figures (including the "savage with sagging breasts," the "disheveled Indian," and the "dwarf king"), we shall confirm the theories about taboo and anomaly proposed by Edmund Leach and most of all by Mary Douglas. It is precisely in the interstices between classifications, where beings and things fail to fit into a preconceived order, that symbolic thinking freely develops through the medium of graphic images.

This theoretical position may seem to extend several trends of contemporary cultural anthropology into the fields of two other disciplines: comparative literature and iconography. The image a people forms of another as seen in travel literature has for a long time been considered the almost exclusive domain of the former, while the study of themes and motifs, as expressed in text illustrations, belongs to the latter. But this multidisciplinary trend should be viewed not as an unwarranted encroachment on other fields by anthropology, but rather as the convergence of different currents issuing from all three. These currents also tend, each in its own way, to break down the old structures in terms of which *l'homme total* has been arbitrarily dismembered. It is time for them to unite.

In art history, Panofsky's work has opened iconographic study to a greater collaboration among disciplines in order to decipher the "intrinsic content" of a work beyond its aesthetic appreciation. For the author of *Studies in Iconology,* iconological interpretation, the third step in interpreting a work of art, tries to define

> those basic principles which underlie the choice and presentation of motifs, as well as the production and interpretation of images, stories, and allegories and which give meaning even to the formal arrangements and technical procedure employed. [1955, p. 38]

This interpretation tries to grasp the work of art as a document about the culture from which it emanates. A number of critics have rightly called attention to the relation between Panofsky's approach and the structural method of Lévi-Strauss.[1]

As early as the 1950s, Etiemble fought the eurocentrism, common in comparative literature, mired as it was in the descriptive study of factual and historical relations among a few privileged literatures. His books, *L'Orient philosophique au dix-huitième siècle* (1956) and *Comparaison n'est pas raison* (1963) directed comparative literature toward the study of constants—whether in imagination, in literary genres, or in images—by opening it up to non-Western literatures.

Conversely, a form of critical, at times radical, anthropology seeks to dislodge from the very postulates of the discipline a hidden ethnocentrism that makes meaningless any claim to objectivity in the study of man. Defined from a purely operational point of view, as many anthropologists in fact do, anthropology is reduced to the study of colored peoples by whites, or to "a defensive source of knowledge about the exploited of the world for those who exploit them" (Hymes 1972, p. 51). If this were so, the anthropologist should also question the cultural basis for his theories and the classifications provided by his own culture and start to study the ethnography of power, of conquerors, and of cultural and political hegemony.

This book intends to set up a few signposts along this road, using the anthropologist's conceptual tools and inviting him to consider the phenomenon of ethnocentrism at its source, at the very moment when Europe discovered the New World and prepared to occupy it. We shall uncover the formation of an ideology, still unaware of itself, masked by the hieroglyphics of the image. The problem is to understand the relation between this ideology and the Europeans' ostensible knowledge of and actual behavior toward the New World.

The study comprises three parts. The first (chapters 1 to 4), describes the network of relations through which the picture of the New World is elaborated and communicated. This will also be a means for defining those whose mythic thought we shall explore—the social groups for whom the pictures of the *Great Voyages* were engraved—and for justifying the method followed. The making of the pictures reveals in turn a technique of *bricolage*, which partly explains why conceptual tools borrowed from the structural analysis of myths may be relatively easy to apply here. In addition, the description of the techniques used by the de Bry family and the analysis of the relations between text and image set up some important guides to this end. Thus the narration of the engravings may be segmented as a message and the analysis of the picture's components then justifies the choice of the reference motif: the Indian with sagging breasts.

In the second part, the structural analysis bears on this iconographic motif which is followed chronologically throughout the contexts in which it appears in the first nine volumes of the *Great Voyages*. In doing this, I have slightly inflected the Lévi-Straussian method of myth analysis, because of the historical and iconographic nature of the material. The chronological data give a new dimension to the analysis of classification systems; they allow us to show how such structures evolved from 1590 to 1634.

As in mythology, a coherent system appears, showing the contradictions sensed by the Protestant conquerors while they settled in America and revealing a rationalization for their attitude toward the Indians. Their perception of cultural differences and of social and political relations becomes clearer when seen through a complex symbolism of the human body, whether alive and healthy, dismembered, or monstrous, and of the foods exchanged, prepared, or eaten by Amerindians and Europeans. Of course, among the elements of this symbolism, one discovers a mélange of representations, borrowed from ancient cosmologies, alchemy, and Protestant theology. But these representations overlap one another and shape themselves to respond to the concrete facts of European material and social life at that time, reflecting, for instance, current divisions of arable and waste land and existing relations between the sexes.

The increasing frequency of the "savage woman" motif, from the tenth volume onward, leads to a disintegration of the symbolic system, which gives way to a combative logic, a serial combination of elements. This logic is the subject of the third part of the book. The initial motif now joins other anomalous figures, the dwarf king, the disheveled Indian, monstrous animals. From this we can learn, thanks especially to a sociological theory of taboo and anomaly, how the symbolism of the savage woman with sagging breasts evolved in relation to the social and political dynamics of the Protestant conquest of America. The analysis of the new graphic associations reveals the treachery of visual images and denounces the conquerors' casuistry. Here, one can grasp the as yet implicit elements of an ideology that would later triumph with the settlement of New England.

1   The *Great Voyages* (1590–1634)

I speak of new lands, new customs; new plants, trees, roots, gums, liqueurs, fruits; of new routes of the sky and ocean never ventured before, and new stars sighted.
Louis Le Roy, *On Vicissitude*

The de Brys' published work is generally divided into the *Great Voyages*, describing navigations to what was called at the time the "West Indies," namely, the Americas and Oceania, and the *Small Voyages*, dealing with the East Indies, which included India, Japan, China, and sometimes Africa. Between 1590 and 1634, some thirty volumes, of both large and small folio size, appeared under the editorship first of Theodor de Bry, then of his sons Johan Israel and Johan Theodor, and finally, of Matthäus Merian, their successor. The detailed bibliographical description of these volumes may be found in the *Manuel*, by Gustave Brunet, in the work of Armand Camus, *Mémoire sur la collection des Grands et Petits voyages* (Paris, 1802), and in the 1924 study by Henry Stevens.

The circumstances of the project led de Bry to deal with the various events in other than chronological order. His first volume, acquired from Hakluyt, described the English expedition to Virginia in 1585; the second, published in 1591, described the French Huguenot expedition to Florida in 1565. At first glance, the presentation of these illustrated narratives appears unsystematic. Only by looking back at the work as a whole can we appreciate its unity and value as a representation of the New World for the eyes of the Old.

At different times, we shall return to one part or another of the *Great Voyages*, the only group we shall examine here. Appendix 1 provides a convenient reference chart for the reader.

AMERICA AS SEEN BY EUROPEANS IN THE SIXTEENTH CENTURY

In 1590, nearly a century after Columbus's discovery, the first volume of the *Great Voyages* appeared in Frankfurt. As surprising as it may seem, this work represented the first attempt to introduce in Europe and on a large scale a pictorial image of the New World as a whole. It is all the more curious because just a hundred years earlier the *Nuremberg Chronicle* had offered a vast visual and narrative survey of the world before the discovery of America. Nothing comparable to de Bry's *Great Voyages*, the imposing group of large folio volumes illustrated by several hundred copperplate engravings, yet existed;[1] only some few pictures had circulated after the publication of Christopher Columbus's *Letter* in 1492. The de Brys offered a broad view of European conquests in America and the first contacts with the Amerindians.

Copperplate engraving, appearing as a technique of reproduction at the end of the sixteenth century, prompted publishers to bring out new encyclopedias. This technique, known since the fifteenth century, had until then been neglected by publishers of illustrated books because it required twice as much work as wood-engraving: narrative and illustration had to be printed separately. Copperplate engraving, however, offered a precision of line and a clarity that were infinitely superior to wood engraving. Moreover, it made it possible to reproduce plates over longer print runs. Thus the *Great Voyages* appears as the first European panorama of America. As such, the work involves a large communication network, from the publisher to his sources of information and to the places from which the work was distributed.

To understand how Europeans received their information at the time, one has only to read the account of the news and rumors collected from day to day in Augsburg by the Fuggers, the Hapsburgs' wealthy bankers.[2] For example, the discovery of Mexico on 30 April 1599 was announced in Venice at the end of the century in this way: "The newly arrived fleet informs us also that the Spaniards have conquered a new kingdom in the Indies called Old Mexico. It is inhabited by intelligent people who are to be instructed in the Christian faith. Very rich gold and silver mines exist there also" (Matthews 1959, p. 237).

The first account about America published in England appeared more than fifteen years after Columbus's voyage. Although published works on cross-Atlantic voyages increased substantially in number during the first half of the century, they reached so limited an audience that, according to historians, the majority of the population did not even suspect the existence of another continent. Sometimes the results of the explorations were intentionally kept secret for several years by a small number of initiates for commercial or political reasons.

Yet a few Europeans had the chance to draw near and see in the flesh Indians whom the conquerors had brought back with them and who were exhibited as "curiosities" on the streets of several European cities. Thus the people of Seville and Barcelona were able to see a procession of Amerindians whom Columbus had brought back with him from his first voyage. When he went to Lisbon, the adventurous Genoese took along seven Indians captured in Hispaniola, now Haiti. The court of Charles V received Mexican entertainers offered by Cortez. Christopher Weiditz, a German, visiting the Spanish court in 1529, sketched them in a number of pen drawings, which, reproduced as engravings, circulated in several books throughout the sixteenth century. In 1550, the inhabitants of Rouen attended a triumphal feast in honor of Catherine de Medici and her court. On this occasion, some Norman sailors who had returned from Brazil disguised themselves as Indians and, with some authentic Tupinambás, performed a Brazilian dance.[3] When Montaigne went to Rouen to gather information about "cannibals," the "plain" man who helped him communicate with the Indians was probably one of those Norman sailors who had settled in Brazil even before the Protestant colonists from the Villegaignon expedition settled there. But the case of Montaigne personally going to question these Brazilian Indians with the help of an interpreter is exceptional. One may well surmise that the processions and masquerades in which the uprooted Amerindians were thus offered for exhibition scarcely let the general population gain acquaintance with the New World inhabitants as men or cultural groups. Likewise, objects brought back from America and sometimes exhibited reached only the inquisitive few. Still, Dürer deeply admired the Mexican art objects he had been able to see in Brussels: "In all my life, I have seen nothing that so delighted my heart, for I have seen some marvelous works of art there and I was enraptured by the subtle genius of men from foreign lands" (letter of 27 August—3 September 1529).[4]

Knowledge of the New World through pictures was even more limited.[5] The first representations of Amerindians were woodcuts, worked in a rudimentary way. One of the earliest known examples shows naked men and women dressed in plumed collars standing under a palm-leaf roof from which human limbs are hanging. The woodcut was probably based on a description of Brazilian Indians contained in a letter from Vespucci to Lorenzo de Medici. As late as the second half of the sixteenth century, picture books on America contained only a small number of woodcuts, rarely larger than vignettes. These illustrations were often reproduced from earlier ones. For instance, to illustrate the description of America in Munster's *Cosmographie* (1554), the editor simply took old woodcuts that had been used for illustrating Mandeville's voyage more than a century before the discovery of America. Only with the *Singularités de la France antarctique*, by the Franciscan friar Thevet (1557), does wood-engraving illustrate systematically and artistically, perhaps after Jean Cousin, a text about the Amerindians.

THE *Great Voyages* AND THE PROTESTANT WORLD

It is remarkable that this technical progress in book illustration should have developed in the midst of religious struggles. The Flemish and Dutch Jesuits had quickly understood the power of copperplate engraving. The Wiriex dynasty of engraver-publishers put out religious prints and illustrated booklets for the Counter-Reformation. Still, it was a Protestant, Theodor de Bry, a native of Liège exiled for his religious opinions, who first used the possibilities offered by illustration on copper to let Europe see the New World, its inhabitants, and its conquest, in pictorial form. And, in fact, the production of these pictures of Amerindians is completely bound up with the emotional, financial, and political interests of the parties engaged in the struggle with the Spanish in America. The majority of the texts comprising the collection of the *Great Voyages* deals with the settlement of Protestants in America and with their struggle against the Spanish hegemony promoted by the famous bull of Pope Alexander III, which divided the still-unexplored New World between Spain and Portugal. As for the accounts of the Spanish conquest written by Spanish or Italian Catholics, they were often cut and, moreover, contain violent attacks against Spanish methods.

All the texts had previously been published before the de Brys illustrated them and included them in their immense collection. A large number had even been directly planned and written to serve the interests of the great maritime companies financing these voyages, such as the English Virginia Company or the Dutch East India Company.

In the preface of another of his books, Theodor de Bry has left us one of the few documents about his life. There he describes his family as having been one of the most prosperous and most honored in the city of Liège, still under Spanish domination. In 1570, accused of sympathizing with the Reformation, he had to go into exile, robbed of all his wealth. Then it was, he said, that "of the ample patrimony my parents had left me, only art remained. Neither robbers nor thieving villains could lay hands on it. Art has given me back my former fortune and reputation and has never abandoned me."[6]

De Bry found refuge in Strasbourg, the seat of Protestantism where many refugees in flight from persecution were welcomed. The city was to become one of the great Protestant centers of the book trade. De Bry worked there as engraver and goldsmith under the influence of Etienne Delaune, a French engraver and, like himself, a Huguenot refugee. At first he did work to order for the courts and the Protestant nobility. From the beginning of this period, he was in touch with London publishers. In 1586 and 1587, for example, he went to London to illustrate a work on the funeral procession of Sir Philip Sydney. There he met the famous Hakluyt who encouraged him to launch his project of illustrated voyages to America. Actually, a number of the narratives in the *Great Voyages* are drawn from *Principal Navigations*, collected and published by Hakluyt without illustrations, on behalf of the Virginia Company. In making his collection of texts, Hakluyt drew from the archives of commercial companies, and consulted official accounts and even private letters. Thanks to his contacts with merchants, navigators, and sailors, he was able to gather oral reports. The purpose of these documents was to promote English colonization and commerce in America, a fact particularly evident in the first two parts of the *Great Voyages*.

Thus the narrative on Virginia by Thomas Hariot was only an official report on the possibilities of colonization in the newly discovered lands; Hariot addressed himself specifically to those who wanted to invest capital in Virginia or go and live there as colonists, as the title indicates: *A Brief and True Report of the New Found Land of Virginia, directed to the Investors, Farmers and Wellwishers of the project of Colonizing and Planting there.*

Hariot had been sent officially to Virginia as geographer and historian by Raleigh, the instigator of the expedition. De Bry's first book reproduced copper engravings of the watercolor paintings by John White, who had plotted maps, drawn the flora and fauna, and painted the inhabitants in their own land.

Hakluyt was also the source for part 2 of the *Great Voyages*.

Before meeting Hakluyt in London, de Bry had probably read about him in Captain Laudonnière's diary of the Huguenot expedition to Florida. Basanier, the Parisian editor of this diary, pays homage to Hakluyt, "a man truly versed in geographical history and having command of the variety of languages and sciences," for having "rescued" Laudonnière's diary "from the tomb." The erudite Englishman himself published this text in his own book, *Principal Navigations*, so closely did the Huguenot venture in Florida address the English interests of the period. In fact, Catherine de Medici was the first to dare transgress in America the "status quo" resulting from the papal bull of 1493, and Grenville's expedition to Virginia, nearly twenty years after Laudonnière's expedition to Florida, owed much to that earlier French incursion over the trail opened by the Spaniards. De Bry did not publish Laudonnière's diary itself, but rather a narrative based on that expedition. At the same time he reproduced the drawings brought back from Florida by Le Moyne de Morgues. It was also Hakluyt who put de Bry in touch, in London, with Le Moyne, a refugee who survived the massacre of the Laudonnière expedition by the duke of Alba's envoys. To these prints de Bry attached explanations which are probably Hakluyt's.

Beginning with part 3 of the *Great Voyages* in 1592, de Bry became a bookseller and publisher himself. Settling finally in Frankfurt, he published the first six parts of his *Voyages* during his lifetime. His sons Johan Israel and Johan Theodor succeeded him in the business. After the father's death in 1598, the books, published at wider intervals, were of lower quality. The elder son, Johan Israel, who died in 1611, took charge of the company. He published parts 7 and 8 in 1599, and part 9 in 1602. Three others, edited by the second son, Johan Theodor, appeared in 1619. On the death of Johan Theodor his son-in-law, Matthäus Merian, editor-engraver of famous alchemical treatises, took over the business and published the last four parts. He also reissued all the earlier volumes. The business was then handed down to one of Matthäus Merian's grandsons, Wilhelm Fitzer, a London bookseller, who came to live in Frankfurt.

Principal Navigations continued to inspire the choice of texts for the *Great Voyages* after Theodor de Bry's death in 1598. His sons adapted several reports which had previously appeared in Hakluyt's English collection relating to English voyages to America. By contrast with their father's practice, they did not acquire the texts directly from England, but rather through Dutch translations. This was true for Drake's voyage around the world, compiled in part by Hakluyt himself from a variety of manuscripts; for Raleigh's and Keymis's voyage to Guyana; and finally, for Cavendish's voyage around the world. The final volumes of the collection illustrated the history of colonization in Virginia and New England with Captain John Smith's adventures and the story of the Jamestown Colony.

After 1602, the collection consisted essentially of ships' logs kept by Dutch navigators who sailed down the coasts of South America in search of new routes to the Pacific islands and the Far East. The majority of these voyages were made on behalf of the all-powerful Dutch East India Company. Before its incorporation in 1602, Dutch voyages had been financed by various syndicates. From its inception, the Dutch East India Company held a trading monopoly in the Far East. The ships' logs of Sebald de Weert, Olivier de Noort, and Georges Spielbergen reported on the progress of their expeditions and justified the capital invested; the voyage of Le Maire and Schouten published in part 11 had been undertaken by Le Maire himself, a rich merchant from Amsterdam, without the knowledge of the Dutch Company. This account justifies the voyage and at the same time reports the discovery of a new passage to the Pacific around Cape Horn—the Straits of Le Maire.

These commercial and geographical accounts form the background against which the vision of the "savage Indians" presented in the later volumes must be viewed. They mostly concern Indians from Tierra del Fuego and Polynesians, met by the Dutch in the Pacific islands. De Bry's bias for the Protestant world that supported his enormous enterprise also accounts for the distorted vision of the New World offered to the European public. This bias can be felt in the liberty taken with the texts in translating, editing, cutting them from one edition to the next. This is particularly flagrant in the only texts originally written by Spanish Catholics: one by José de Acosta, a Spanish Jesuit, the other by Antonio de Herrera (part 9 and 11). Moreover, these texts deal merely with the description of the New World and its natural and human history, leaving aside the conquest itself or the Indian-European relations. If the texts—of Dutch origin for the most part—used by the de Brys were cut, one can easily imagine that those coming from Spanish sources were no less so. All of them show the mark of anti-Spanish sentiment. The most important one, the *History of the New World,* by Girolamo Benzoni, was written by a Catholic, but its translator, Chauveton, a Protestant theologian from Geneva, added commentary and scholia, which the de Brys reprinted in their edition. In his French translation, Chauveton included a "petition in the form of a supplication" addressed to the king of France by "the women, widows, grandchildren, orphans, and others, all relatives and in-laws of those who were so cruelly invaded by the Spaniards in the French Antarctic called Florida." Benzoni's account takes up Las Casas's indictment of the methods of Spanish colonization. At the same time, Theodor de Bry published a text by Las Casas himself, with illustrations often identical to those in the earlier parts of the *Great Voyages.* Even more than the texts, his engravings, by stressing slavery and the practice of torture, contributed to the spread in Europe of the famous "black legend," hostile to the Spanish. These pictures of Indian genocide mirrored, for the Protestant victims of the Spanish Inquisition, their own misfortune.

The same bias appears in the illustrations for the account by the German Schmidel, a mercenary on Mendoza's expedition; the Spanish are shown in the very act of cannibalism. In the *Voyage de Vespucci* (part 10), they appear not only cruel, but licentious.[7] The illustrations show them trying to seduce Indian women. One plate shows the *conquistadores,* with Vespucci leading, as slightly ridiculous beneficiaries of the native women's sexual hospitality; another shows them on the island of Curaçao trying to seduce three giantesses whom the Indians, armed with clubs, are coming to defend. By contrast, the British are seen observing all the forms of civility by sending an emissary from the governor to ask for the hand of the celebrated Pocahontas in marriage. It is clear, then, that among the innumerable accounts of voyages to America, the *Great Voyages* were made up, grouped, and selected with a bias toward the point of view of the Protestant countries involved in the conquest. It should be mentioned that the *Small Voyages,* concerning the East Indies, was put on the Index by the pope.

The *Great Voyages*: Its Public and Its Success

Beyond the Protestant world, de Bry was seeking a wider European public. To reach this public he published these volumes simultaneously in High German, which had become over the course of the sixteenth century the national literary language of the Germanic countries, and in Latin, understood in all the Catholic countries. The first volume was published simultaneously in four editions: Latin, German, English, and French. This attempt was abandoned probably because it was not profitable. The remaining volumes, then, were published in Latin and German. The de Brys' presence in Frankfurt was also certainly instrumental in successfully distributing the volumes to European booksellers.

Who was to be found on the periphery of the communication network of the *Great Voyages?* Who read and viewed these illustrated books? First of all, there were the members of the European aristocracy and in particular the members of the German courts.[8] Several volumes contain a dedicatory epistle to a prince, accompanied by his coat of arms. For instance, we find the names of Maximilian, the king of Poland; of Guillaume, count Palatine; of Christian, duke of Saxony; and of Louis, *landgrave* of Hesse. These dedicatory epistles no doubt also discharged a certain debt to the patrons who had allowed the printing or had even offered some financial support. Further, the collection reached a much broader group of readers. Widely read in the world of educated people and collectors who had early become fascinated by the voyages of exploration, it was also sought by the rising class of merchants and artisans who were beginning to buy books and art objects. If the taste for accounts of cross-Atlantic voyages lasted into the late sixteenth century, it was not only because of curiosity, but also because most people, even those of modest means, had a stake in this kind of enterprise. The maritime companies collected their capital by offering stocks underwritten by a quite large segment of the public, including even the international *petite bourgeoisie.* The Dutch East India Company, for example, sold its stock not only in its own country, but also in France—in Paris, La Rochelle, and Rouen.[9]

The fact that these works were profusely illustrated no doubt increased considerably the size of their potential market. Thus, even people of modest means who scarcely knew how to read could become interested. It was also a common practice at the time to display frontispieces in the streets for publicity purposes. The pictures of Indians that enriched them could not fail to have attracted a wide range of customers. One may also imagine that, just as religious woodcuts were shown around at fairs by peddlers and acquired by a very large clientele, the frontispieces—not to mention the illustrations—of this new type of book were introduced by itinerant vendors and encouraged browsers to buy the complete volumes for themselves.

The description of the communication network through which the Amerindian pictures were created thus leads us to discover a whole range of economic, political, and religious relations among quite diverse cultural and social groups. The process of picture production, dependent on a wide assortment of materials, expands this network over space and time by drawing on a very old tradition.

2   The Makeup of the Mythic Material: Collage and Bricolage

> *The characteristic feature of mythical thought is that it expresses itself by means of a heterogeneous repertoire which even if extensive, is nevertheless limited. It has to use this repertoire, however, whatever the task in hand, because it has none else at its disposal. Mythical thought is therefore a kind of intellectual "bricolage"–which explains the relations which can be perceived between the two.*
>
> Claude Lévi-Strauss, *The Savage Mind*

BABEL AND LEVIATHAN IN AMERICA

When Theodor de Bry began publishing the *Voyages* he was in possession of drawings that talented artists had brought back from America. John White was attached to Grenville's expedition as cartographer; Le Moyne de Morgues to Laudonnière's expedition. These drawings provided a powerful asset for launching the collection and a model for de Bry's future undertakings.

John White was sent to Virginia and Le Moyne de Morgues to Florida. Recently, some previously unpublished works by the two artists have appeared;[1] their publication makes it possible to judge both how true to his models de Bry really was and what additional attraction the copperplate engravings conferred on them. The etchings made from White's drawings in volume 1 have an outstanding documentary quality. They show us wigwam life among the Algonquian, or more precisely, among the Pamlico and Secota, the southernmost branch of the Algonquian. At that time the Secota occupied the swath of land lying between Albermarle Sound and the mouth of the Pamlico River, and in addition, all the neighboring islands, that is, on the present site of Washington, Tyrrell, Dare, Beaufort, and Hyde counties in North Carolina. Secota village, painted by White, was on the left bank of the Pamlico; Pomeiock village near the mouth of Gibbs Creek. The illustrations show Adam and Eve; some Picts (the first inhabitants of England, portrayed with their body paintings) and Bretons; and the arrival of the English in Virginia, with the natives and their surroundings. The Indian villages are fully shown: Pomeiock and Secota with their agriculture; the religious buildings—the temple of the idol Kiwa and the tombs of the Weroans—are interspersed with the totemic marks of the Virginia chiefs; a major place is also given to solemnities, festivities, dances, and games.

Cartographic landscapes, scenes of fishing and hunting, and nature plates showing specimens of animal and plant life give an idea of the topography, flora, and fauna typical of the region where Sir Richard Grenville and his colony were settled—that is, the environs of Roanoke, on the site of present-day North Carolina. The magnificent portraits of the inhabitants show the dress, tatooing, and many ornaments of the Algonquian with a wealth of detail. Some plates describe the Indians' techniques and subsistence activities: slash-and-burn technique, making canoes from a single piece of wood, smoking meat, and cooking succotash, and Algonquian dish prepared from a mixture of boiled corn and beans to which fish or meat is sometimes added.

Other plates offer a view of the Algonquian village, the inside and outside of different types of dwellings, and the layout of crops in the fields—corn, tobacco, and squash. The Indians are shown in a hierarchial order meant to acquaint Europeans with the social organization of the group but actually copied from European society: chiefs, priests, nobles, and the "common" people.

Le Moyne de Morgues's illustrations, which appear in volume 2, provide an introduction to the daily life of another tribe of the American southeast, the Timucua of Florida, an extinct tribe of the Muskogean linguistic family. Despite the fancifulness of many details, the maps of the Timucua towns and villages and the native portraits and scenes show a spirit of documentation and ethnographic observation rare in the iconography of the time. A whole native society is lavishly presented. Taken together, the illustrations describe the "scalp-hunting Timucua." We see the arrival of the French, the natives' welcome, and the construction of the fort by the invaders. The Timucua style of war is described in detail; we see ceremonial preparation for it among the Saturiba and the Outina; then the battle line drawn between the two opponents, the march of Outina's army, the treatment of the scalped prisoners, and the dances around the trophies after the victory. Hermaphrodites are used as beasts of burden. Widows petition the chiefs after the defeat and begin to mourn on the warriors' tombs. Other plates illustrate hunting techniques, leisure activities, feasts, and political organization. The plates emphasize the scalp-hunters' political and military organization and their various techniques of war: staged battle, guerilla warfare, defense of the town, cutting up the scalp and smoke-drying it, as well as all the ceremonies and rites that surround the preparation for war and the celebration of victory. Nor are other aspects of native life neglected: sowing, harvesting, cooking preserving food (smoke-drying and storing in public granaries), the technique of leaching inedible plants, panning for river gold, and so forth.

When left to himself, de Bry devised his iconography from the widest variety of techniques. He scorned no evidence or document and did not scruple to interpret or plagiarize every illustration he encountered whether it concerned the subject of his book directly or had only a distant relation to it. In this respect, the iconography of volume 3 is extremely interesting. This volume comprises two texts dealing with voyages to Brazil: the text by Hans Staden, the German adventurer, who belonged to Spanish, then Portuguese, galleons and was held prisoner by the Tamaio for nine months; and the text by the Protestant Jean de Léry, companion of Villegaignon on the expedition by the latter to Brazil in 1557.

De Bry altered Léry's text; his translation is only a paraphrase of the original. Neglecting the episodes of the Villegaignon expedition and the epic side of the establishment of the French colonists in Brazil, he focused his illustrations on Staden's captivity among the Tupinikin, another Tupinambá cannibal tribe. At the same time, he used Léry's striking narratives to support his illustration of warrior manners, cannibal rites, and the natives' religion. The first edition of Staden's narrative, published in Marburg in 1557, includes a few crude vignettes after the sketches Staden drew from life and those by one of the expedition's sailors. De Bry drew some of the motifs of his inspiration from them, especially the views of the stockaded Tupinambá village where the explorer was held. They show the treatment to which the prisoner was subjected and the progress of the cannibal rites. But de Bry borrowed the characteristics of his

Tupinambá and the details of their finery from Léry. Léry's *Voyage to Brazil*, published in 1578, was embellished with several woodcuts. The author sought to have one of his friends make drawings from life, and he tells how he posed a Tupinambá family that he wished to paint "from nature": "It is true that to complete this plate we have put near the Tupinambá man one of his wives holding her baby in a cotton scarf as is the custom, and the child, in turn, who is carried as the women carry them, hugs his mother's side with his legs" (1600, p. 121).

Several of these illustrations, drawn from memory in Europe, imitate those of Thevet's *Singularités de la France antarctique*. Léry, who pays homage in his account to the "truthful narrative" of his predecessor, Staden, also pokes fun at the Franciscan Thevet; it is thus certain that he knew Thevet's book, and understandable that he more or less imitated its illustrations. These were the first visual portrayals of New World inhabitants. Their authorship has been attributed to various artists of the Fontainebleau school, especially to Jean Cousin.

De Bry here used the text to create his iconographic models, following the authors suggestions. Thus, Léry introduces the "contemplation of a savage":

> Now first of all, following this description, you will want to imagine a savage. Imagine a naked man, well built and well proportioned of limb, with all his body hair plucked out, the hair of the head shorn in the way I have described (that is, like a monk), the lips and cheeks split, with pointed bones or fresh-quarried stones set into them, the ears pierced, with rings in the holes, the body daubed with paint, the arms and legs blackened with the paint they make from the *genip* tree mentioned earlier; necklaces made from innumerable tiny pieces of the large shell they call *vignol* . . . hung around the neck. You will imagine him as he usually is in his country, and his physical appearance is as you see him portrayed below, wearing only the highly polished bone crescent on his chest, the ornament in the hole in his lip, and, to keep himself in countenance, his loose bow and his arrows in his hands." [1600, pp. 119–20]

This Tupinambá appears on the frontispiece exactly this way, standing beside a woman who holds her baby in her cotton scarf, also as described by Léry. The same process will be used again in part 8 of the *Great Voyages*, though it is devoted to Indians from a quite different part of the Americas.

With part 4, the texts are of a quite different nature. Instead of direct narratives of previous expeditions, a historical background appears and the text often loses ethnographic values for the sake of the narration.

The narration of the Spanish conquest of the New World is combined with the personal adventures of the Italian, Girolamo Benzoni. His journeys lead the reader into the Caribbean area: Hispaniola, that is, Haiti; Borichen, or Puerto Rico; and the Pearl Coast, or the coast of present-day Venezuela and Colombia. Then he takes us to Central America—Panama, Nicaragua, and Costa Rica—and from there to Peru. The geographical range makes it hard to identify the tribes. With this volume, the illustrations do not focus on the Amerindian mores as before, but rather on the Spanish conquest and mistreatment of the Indians. In the series of plates, pictures from different stages of the conquest follow one another, with descriptions of pre-Columbian Indians placed next to those of acculturated Indians held in slavery. No attempt is made to distinguish among the different tribal or cultural groups, indiscriminately grouped together in the category "Indians." Lacking real models, de Bry reproduces earlier ones and portrays these Indians consistently naked with a strip of cotton around the loins; the men still have the monk's tonsure of the Tupinambá and the women the long loose hair of the Timucua and Tupinambá women. Some new items of clothing and some new attributes whose models are found elsewhere are sometimes added to these old elements. Thus de Bry rigs out the inhabitants of Hispaniola— thus of the Arawak group—in the garb of the Peruvian Inca: the *lauytu* or *lyawo,* the vicuna-wool turban wrapped around the head several times, topped off by the *mascapaycha*, a kind of semicircular miter of birds' feathers, and a sleeveless short tunic. As the explorers brought back no iconographic models or information, de Bry obviously used all the iconographic material available at the time. The extensive *De Civitatis orbis terrarum* by Braun and Hogenberg contains models of the clothing of all the world's known peoples. It is the source of a view of the city of Cuzco (Peru), with the figure of Atahualpa, the last Inca of Peru, borne on his litter by his entourage, outlined in the foreground. De Bry reproduced the view of

Cuzco with no change, but for the figures in the foreground, which he uses elsewhere, he substituted Indian tumblers and jugglers copied from another print, that of the jugglers Cortez brought back from Mexico to the court of Charles V, drawn by the German, Christopher Weiditz, in 1529.

Old materials going back fifty years and more are thus separated from their original settings and turn up again in new arrangements. We are, then, confronted with a sort of Tower of Babel of the Amerindian peoples. Physical types, articles of ornamentation, and hairstyles, all borrowed from different cultures appear together quite incongruously in a single plate.

In a market scene of Cartegena, a region inhabited by Caribbeans, de Bry plays, as on a keyboard, with the range of exotic clothing and ornaments he has already engraved. Especially noteworthy is a collection of native hairstyles: the Algonquian cock's comb, the narrow strip of hair these Indians let grow along the center of the head, as John White painted it; the hair drawn up and tied in a chignon on the top of the head, like the Timucua warriors; the shaven heads of other men; the hair falling in a long twist down the back of Tupinambá women; beside entirely naked individuals, others are covered with feathers or skins reminiscent of the capes of the Tupinambá shamans.

This process, which leads to infinite variations in dress, physical appearance, clothing, hairstyle, and native attributes, continues and accelerates in the succeeding volumes. Indeed, the geographic itinerary of the *Voyages* becomes more and more complicated. In the absence of new iconographic documents about America, de Bry's sons attempted to revitalize the interest of the collection by offering newly discovered lands to the reader. In the titles for the volumes they frequently pointed out the fact that they contain the first descriptions of the countries seen by the explorers. Schmidel's account, which opens part 7 and appeared in 1599, is introduced with phrases of elegant promotional pomposity, such as: "The true description of several important countries and islands of the Indies which have never before been mentioned in any chronicle and which were explored for the first time and in the midst of the greatest dangers during the navigation of Ulrich Schmidel von Straubigen."

This statement is only partly accurate, since the original edition of this narrative was published in German in Frankfurt in 1567. It deals with the Gran Chaco and the conquest of the Paraña River, in which Schmidel participated under a number of Spanish captains, including Pedro de Mendoza. In fact, his narrative is one of the oldest sources for the ethnography of these regions at the time of their discovery. It gives information especially about the clothing, physical appearance, and mores of the Timbu, related to the Guaicuru, and of the Payagua and Mbaia. Unfortunately, Schmidel returned without drawings, and the woodcuts illustrating the Dutch editions of the same date as the text, are pure fantasies, partly inspired by the pictures in earlier volumes of the de Bry collection. Ethnography is thus completely forsaken in favor of simple anecdotes about relations between the Indians and the Spanish conquerors.

The *Voyages* continue with a series of circumnavigations of the coasts of South America through the Straits of Magellan or through the newly discovered Straits of Le Maire, as reported by Schouten. The illustrations for them consist in landing incidents and show quite superficial contacts with the peoples encountered. For the most part they are devoid of ethnographic interest, with the exception of a few plates depicting Polynesians, for which the de Brys had new models at hand.

As we proceed through the collection, a greater variety of peoples comes into view, all merged under the name of "Indians," especially in the captions. Thus appear, without distinction, the inhabitants of the Canary Islands, some Africans met on the Gabon coast while the ship was in port, some Alacalufs in the Magellan archipelago, and some Micronesians and Polynesians.

Sometimes a picture of foreign peoples slips in among the Indians thanks to a digression in the text. Thus the Jesuit, José de Acosta, describing certain customs of the Aztec religion, is led to compare them with a religious practice recorded by other Jesuits living among the Japanese: the public confession of Japanese pilgrims sitting on a scales that hangs in the air (plate 9A:10). The plate illustrating this digression has an odd mixture of two different ethnic types; the penitent in his scales is, in his features and clothing, a new type, while the supposedly Japanese priests are identical to the Aztec priests who, in other plates, engage in human sacrifice.

Sometimes the description of these peoples is supplemented by the description of mythical peoples, such as the famous Inca of Manoa mentioned by Raleigh in his *Voyage to Guyana*, included in

volume 8. The de Brys show the Inca emperor being anointed with
a golden oil, on feast days, while drinking an intoxicating beverage
from a huge tankard (plate 7/8:15). Raleigh takes this anecdote from
old sources, notably from Lopez de Gomara, the author of the
Historia general de las Indias; he paraphrases it in his description of
the legendary emperor of Guyana, linked to the Eldorado legend.
Other mythical figures, inherited from Pliny and the medieval
tradition, appear on a map of Guyana, supposedly drawn by one of
the members of the crew. In it we see an Amazon and some representatives of a "race of men whose shoulders rise up along the sides
of the head so high that the face seems to be placed in the chest."
What was only a comparison in Raleigh's text is brought to life in
the de Bry map in the form of headless men with faces drawn on
their chests—a type of medieval monster called "Blemmye." The
caption identifies them as inhabitants of "Iwapanoma."

In this strange tower of Babel, specimens of no less incongruous
flora and fauna also mingle. Some give evidence of naturalistic
precision and scientific realism; others are but the product of an
imagination capable of begetting the monsters of the Leviathan. By
contrast with the naturalistic plates reproducing White's watercolors and lying next to general-purpose landscapes used as backgrounds, notably those of Virginia and Florida, we see fantastic
landscapes and animals that are reappearances of the "medieval
marvels" reworked by the Baroque imagination.

We find, for example, the tree of Iron Island in the Canaries,
"from whose leaves there is a perpetual flow of water," which the
natives caught in jugs; the water is full of monstrous man–eating
fish ready to devour shipwrecked Europeans (plate 6:28). In
another plate, a gigantic bird, a kind of giant cock, upright in a
strange boat, spreads his wings and covers two boatsmen, one of
whom is standing (plate 11B:12). In still another plate, reptiles with
dragon's bodies are chained by the feet, then roasted and eaten by
the Indians (plate 10:4).

In the final volumes the fantasy element reappears. The old literary or iconographic tradition and alchemical symbolism lend full-
ness to the narrations. Johan Theodor de Bry and Matthäus Merian
both illustrated at least two alchemical texts, *Atalanta fugiens*, by M.
Maier, in 1618, and the *Tractatus*, by Mylius, in 1620. Thus a plate
of 1598 (12:4) evokes prodigious phenomena described by Acosta

alchemical

in his chapter on "Strange portents and prodigies which happened in Mexico before the end of their empire." These prodigies were indeed strange: an immoveable stone the Mexicans tried in vain to pull with ropes, the appearance of cosmic and cataclysmic phenomena, a flame in the shape of a pyramid, a comet seen in broad daylight, an inextinguishable fire heating the lake waters to boiling, and, finally, the apparition of a many-headed monster shown in one of the traditional shapes of the Lernaean hydra. In the foreground, the engravers combine two old motifs, the one coming from the Greco-Latin tradition, the other from the biblical heritage: Jupiter's eagle transporting Ganymede in his claws, and the dream of Jacob at the foot of the ladder. This singularity illustrates the last wonder described by Acosta: a Mexican peasant dreaming that a bird carried him into a grotto where Montezuma lay sleeping, with a sheaf of aromatics and flowers in his hand; the bird brings word of the dangers threatening the kingdom.

The fantastic animals of Guatemala, drawn in front of a volcanic landscape in a different plate, also come from a variety of iconographic sources (plate 12:5). The scene of an animal carrying its young on its back and hiding them under its tail is inspired by a woodcut in Thevet's *Cosmographie universelle*. Thevet showed the *su* or *sucurath* as the best example of maternal love in the animal world. Ambroise Paré, the king's surgeon, did not hestitate to borrow this curiosity from Thevet in turn, and insert it in his book, *Des monstres et prodiges*.

At the pictorial level, a real syncretism of ethnic, cultural, zoological, mythological, and biblical forms is created that does not necessarily exist at the level of the texts taken separately. It comes into being precisely because the de Brys brought together, more or less arbitrarily, a heterogeneous assortment of narratives with a view to illustrating them. It is elaborated little by little, by the process of repeating elements borrowed at times from the Timucua, at times from the Tupinambá or Peruvians, to which are added others, drawn from other traditions completely foreign to the American continent.

This fantastic ethnography and zoology is incorporated into a history of dated facts that proceeds in a certain order. Each volume of the *Great Voyages* recounts events that, for the most part, actually took place. But they treat history no better than they do geogra-

phy. The illustrated voyages constitute a mythico-historical amal-
gam intended to introduce America's conquest and colonization to
Europeans.

A Pictorial Epic

The events portrayed by the engravings are not presented in the
chronological order in which they really occurred, but in the order
in which the volumes appeared between 1590 and 1634, at fairly
regular intervals of from one to seventeen years. We note the same
chaos in history that we have seen in the geographical itineraries.
The order of the expeditions at first moves backward in time, that
is, the more recent are described before the earlier ones. The reason
is simple: the de Brys chose their texts as they became available,
according to the contingencies of the book market. Thus de Bry
published Le Moyne de Morgues's account of the voyage to Florida
as volume 2, after the Virginia voyage, although in fact it took
place twenty years earlier, for de Bry was at first unable to obtain
Le Moyne's drawings. Only with Benzoni's *History of the New
World* (volume 4) were the early stages of the Spanish conquest
related: Columbus's voyages to the West Indies, the venture of
Cortez and Pizarro to Mexico and Peru. Yet these events were
mixed with other, later, ones, such as those Benzoni himself witnessed during his voyage fifty years later.

A similar confusion in history occurs on several other occasions.
The narrative of Vespucci's voyages (1449–1504) was published
only in 1619, while the letter to Lorenzo de Medici, the famous
Novus mundus, was translated into Latin as early as 1503. They were
published by de Bry at the same time as English accounts bearing
on the recent colonization of Virginia and New England in the early
seventeenth century.

The collection is remarkable for its heterogeneity. Written by a
variety of authors from different periods, the texts were patched
together in a sequence to be illustrated. This procedure recalls more
the way epics were made than myths. It brings to mind Bérard's
theory about the *Odyssey* and the various speculations about the
supposed authorship of the Homeric poems. In the *Great Voyages*,
we find ship's logs and narratives by navigators, some written by
the captain himself, as in the case of Raleigh on his return from
Guyana, and others written by a secretary, such as Ralph Amor, of
Captain John Smith's expedition. Some are texts by scholars, like

Thomas Hariot, author of the *Voyage to Virginia*, philosopher, mathematician, astronomer, and correspondent of Kepler, or José de Acosta, historian of the New World, who, in his *De novi orbis natura*, suggests a classification of peoples foreshadowing Lewis Henry Morgan's theory of social evolution. There are also narratives by mere adventurers, taken as mercenaries onto Spanish or Portuguese galleons, like Hans Staden, Ulrich Schmidel, or Girolamo Benzoni, later collected in works edited by priests and monks. The Spanish Jesuit, José de Acosta, leans to problems of comparative religion or theology: Léry was a Protestant pastor; Fletcher, who wrote part of Drake's voyages, a ship's chaplain. Other texts are anonymous, compiled from disparate sources by Hakluyt or Zacharias de Heynes, who, with the de Brys themselves, might be seen as Homeridae of these American voyages.

3   From Text to Picture: Decoding the Visual Narrative of the Plates

The illustrations for the *Great Voyages* depend on two different domains. On the one hand, engraving as an art draws a series of esthetic and technical conventions from the iconographic tradition. On the other hand, the narrative function of the plates uses the written text as a base. To find the semantic units in the corpus the first thing is to analyze its internal characteristics without any preconceived ideas about the nature of visual messages. Only by describing the different relations between text and picture and the organization of space within the plates, shall we be able to decide where to find the units and segments of the implicit iconographic discourse.

The grouping of the plates is the first significant link between text and picture. The de Bry collection contains groups of pictures, each of which forms a relatively autonomous whole from the point of view of the explicit meaning. To some degree, the groupings of plates depend on the texts to which they relate. Thus we can identify several types of units linking a text with a group of pictures. These units may correspond to what is called a "part" of the *Voyages aux Indes occidentales*, that is, an in-folio volume. A volume may contain a single text or several texts related by a common theme and illustrated by the engravers as a single unit. This is true of the plates of part 3, which refer equally to the two texts published in the volume (both the text of Hans Staden and that of Jean de Léry deal with life among the Tupinambá of Brazil). Or, when a single text is illustrated in several volumes, the pictures correspond to several "parts." Thus the engravings of parts 4, 5, and 6 are closely linked to the text they illustrate: Benzoni's *History of the New World*. The division into three parts corresponds to Benzoni's three books. The three different frontispieces show them as three volets of a triptych, whose subject is the Spaniards' conquest of the New World and destruction of the Indians. Yet again, the unity formed by the plates of several parts may not be due to the text, but may result instead from the organization of plates within a single volume. Thus parts 7 and 8 are frequently published as a single volume, and, though there are four different texts in all, they are preceded by a single frontispiece, the same one used to open part 3. The illustrations follow one another in a single group. Finally, the illustrations may refer to only one section of a part: by contrast with the preceding arrangement, the illustrations are grouped by the editor into several sections, each one corresponding to one of the several texts published in the same part. The plates of the various sections may even be numbered differently and inconsistently.

In this framework, other, more direct links tie one or several selected passages of a text to the illustrations. The use of a caption makes this link more obvious. Quite apart from the narrative properly speaking, most of the engravings include a short explanatory text or caption to make them more accessible to the reader. As an exception, some engravings are embedded in the text and carry no caption, unlike the captioned plates, which each occupy a full page.

In other cases, the engravings relate to no particular passage in the narrative and may even come from quite other texts: in these cases the caption is the only description or explanation available to the reader. Two kinds of plates are found in this category. First, some are reproduced in copperplate from ready-made drawings and plates, like those of parts 1 and 2; certain plates in part 11 come from another Dutch edition. In the main, these are geographical maps to which have been added figures or specimens of flora and fauna; each of these additional elements carries a letter that corresponds to part of the caption.

Second, some illustrations inserted in the collection bear no direct relation to the text published in the volume. In fact, it was common at that time use ready-made engravings that passed from book to book. A caption added by the editor would adapt the picture to the new text. Several plates of the *Great Voyages* follow this practice. One of them, for instance, depicts the triumph of Magellan as he discovers the strait that later bore his name and is matched by another showing the triumph of Christopher Columbus. Both engravings appeared in many other books before becoming part of the *Great Voyages*. That of Magellan's triumph (illus. 29) was drawn by Jean Stradan and engraved by Jean Galle on Magellan's return in 1522. Their source is given neither in the caption nor in Benzoni's text; we must go to Pigafetta, the chronicler of Magellan's voyage, for their accurate identification.

Sometimes the link between narrative and picture or between caption and text is even more tenuous. In fact, de Bry introduced some engravings that do not directly illustrate a passage of the published text, but that he considered appropriate for his own reasons. When this occurs, his commentary is the only explanation for the picture. This is true, for example, of the plates representing the myth of the Fall of Adam and Eve and that of Noah's Ark; de Bry himself explains why, in his view, the two biblical myths are perfectly relevant to the New World.

Elsewhere, de Bry illustrated some anecdote he read in a book on a subject related to the text he was publishing. For instance, he added two new plates to part 6 after reading two anecdotes he particularly enjoyed: "and because it is an amusing story, I decided to add it and ask you to write a caption for it, as well as for the story of the horse charging Atahualpa in the face" (Giuseppi, 1915–17, p. 220).[1]

But whether the engraving is based on the text published in the volume or on some other source, the added caption always introduces a new intermediary in the chain of transpositions leading from the textual account to the picture. There is, in fact, a dual transformation in meaning, from the description in the original text that inspires the artist to its graphic depiction, and from this depiction to the new description offered in the caption, which, in turn, impresses the reader with a new interpretation of the picture.

In addition to factual errors—and they are many—that slip into the captions, these captions always create a new meaning chosen from among the picture's possible signifiers. More often than not, whoever wrote the caption was as much a stranger to the making of the text as to the making of the engraving. De Bry seems to have given over this task, at least for a time, to the bookseller, Raphalengis; on sending him proofs of the engravings for part 6, he asked him to "be so kind as to write captions for each account, as usual" (Giuseppi 1915–17, p. 220).

The plates will be decoded, then, depending on the case, by following the statements in the caption, by using one or several passages from the body of the illustrated text, or by referring to a text foreign to both text and caption. In this, we shall follow Erwin Panofsky in the first two stages of his method of iconographic analysis, when decoding the meaning of a picture: identifying the objects, figures, and events depicted in a plate, availing ourselves of all the literary sources necessary, and seeing to what segment of text [énoncé] a given sign or iconographic motif corresponds.[2]

Moreover, engraving, as a means of expression, makes use of a spatial syntax and this syntax of space is what organizes and binds together the different segments of the graphic discourse. Thus, part of the decoding process consists in discovering the spatial orientation in which the plates must be read. To find out, one must know the different techniques the de Brys used to transfer the narrative's temporal relations into the space provided by the page and the book.

The engravers of the collection employed a variety of methods for expressing the temporal dimension. In spite of a constant regard for accuracy, they did not fail to introduce changes and create new relationships between the figures, objects, and landscapes they portray. These changes always followed from the need to transpose temporal and circumstantial information to a spatial framework. Most of the methods were not new; the first three date from the beginnings of illustration—illustration on Greek sarcophagi, papyri, and vases (Weintzmann 1947); the last is more recent and is peculiar to the printed book.

THE MONOSCENIC METHOD

A single action, taking palce at a precise moment, is depicted in its entirety in a single plate, thus respecting a classic unity of time and place. The engravers quite often chose this method for dramatic scenes. A certain aspect of native life appears as an entertainment performed by the Indians, which the engraving lets us attend. The presence of European spectators around the scene of an Indian ceremony, rite, or council sometimes reinforces this impression. Thus Spaniards stand watching a horrible slaughter for which they themselves have given the orders: Indians eaten alive by dogs (illus. 28).

The selection from the textual narrative of a single action concentrated in one place sometimes assumes a spatial division quite similar to that of the theaters of the Elizabethan period or the Italian Renaissance, which were bounded on three sides by houses and arcades. The parallel is evident in part 3. De Bry found the model of the Tupinambá village in the illustrations for Staden's text. The long houses or *malocas*, whose vaulted roofs are covered with palm fronds, are laid out in a square surrounded by a circular stockade. However, when the village becomes the setting for the cannibal rites, de Bry transforms its layout: he changes it to a hexagon, either bound on five sides by malocas or with only its three upstage sides visible. In fact, this arrangement re-creates the view of the stage one might have had in London's Globe Theatre, either from the top of the galleries or from the wings.[3]

We meet the theatrical influence again in the engravers' other methods of transposing temporal elements from the text to the space of the engraving. Whether transcribing simultaneity or the complex passage of time, they generally succeed in conveying the logical sequence of the events depicted using techniques like those offered to the dramatist by the skillful architecture of theaters at the end of the sixteenth century. Here, too, the text or caption dictates the reading of the plate.

SIMULTANEOUS METHOD

This method goes back to the Homeric period. A single plate portrays several actions supposedly taking place at the same time. The de Brys used this technique often and systematically when they had at hand static, ready-made portraits that told no story. In these cases—for example, in John White's portraits in part 1 of the *Great Voyages*—they add a landscape or background scene of hunting in the woods or fishing from the riverbanks. Descriptive elements that were scattered through the text are thus brought together: descriptions of landscapes, styles of life, and customs assembled in a single plate, animating a simple portrait of an Indian. In this way new links are created between the figure and his environment. This method is used also for showing group activities: a market scene, an interior scene when, during a night attack launched by the Spaniards, an Indian village is awakened and robbed; scenes of festivities combining dances, preparation of food and drink, and so forth.

The simultaneous transcription of various actions in juxtaposition sometimes leads to a complete distortion of meaning. This occurs in particular in certain plates showing a native technique misunderstood by the Europeans. For example, a plate in part 2 depicts the preparation of a Timucua feast. It brings together several groups of persons engaged in different cooking operations supposedly occurring at the same time according to the caption. As the author of the original and witness to the scene, Le Moyne de Morgues, failed to understand its meaning, neither caption nor text suffices to link the actions logically and they thus appear incoherent. In fact the Indians are engaged in leaching, a technique they used for making edible an otherwise too-bitter plant. We can discover the sequence of events as they actually occurred in sources other than the *Great Voyages*.

The engravers used two much more efficient methods to illustrate the Indians' technical activities: a cyclic method and a serial method (Bucher 1975).

ROTATIVE METHOD

This consists of bringing together in a single plate actions that really occur in sequence. Several separate actions are laid out in the space of the plate, most frequently in a circular order that reproduces, by contiguity and succession, the temporal order in which they took place and which is stated in the caption. The caption tell us in what direction the plate should be read. Thus, for example, the textual statement, "A native woman has just brought a basket of fruit to the governor," is expressed in two adjacent scenes in the same plate: in the background, to the right, we see a landscape and, coming toward us, a native woman with her fruit basket on her head; in the left foreground the same woman is seen sitting inside the governor's house, with her fruit basket at her feet (illus. 8).

The period of time separating two or more scenes thus brought together in the space of a single plate may be much longer— months, or even years. For example, an engraving in part 2 illustrates Timucua therapeutic practices: fumigation, bleeding, and the use of tobacco. Beyond the depiction of these different methods, a series of iconographic motifs expresses the Indians' belief in the efficacy of their medicine. A pregnant young woman drinks blood from the gourd in which it is collected during the bleeding of a sick person by the shaman. The caption explains that the women "believe that this will make their fruit better and their children more robust." Another woman, identical to the first, nurses an infant. Near her, two small children are fighting. Thus the juxtaposition of figures and iconographic motifs allows us to see several periods of human life in the limited space of a single engraving: pregnancy, nursing, and robust childhood (plate 2:20).

SERIAL METHOD

The most recent, this method consists in breaking up the temporal progress of the narrative into several plates, forming a series based on a theme or event, somewhat like present-day comic strips. This method can, moreover, be combined with any of the three preceding ones in any single plate, but the expression contained in each plate, even if it forms a relatively autonomous episode, continues from one plate to the next. For example, the long description of cannibal rites among the Tupinambá, described in detail by Hans Staden in part 3, covers several months, from the capture of the prisoner to the time he is eaten. The way the engravers choose to divide or group these events in one or several plates is significant in itself and implies an interpretation of the reported facts. In some cases an engraving brings different actions and details of these rites together indiscriminately, using the cyclical or simultaneous methods just discussed; on the other hand, each of several stages in the sacrifice of the prisoner—execution, preparation of the body, cutting it, cooking it, and eating it—occupies several plates, each step followed by the next, and this sequence matches the various stages of the ritual reported less systematically in the text.

One can thus see the astonishing possibilities that the de Brys were able to use skillfully in their copperplate engravings to create an episodic narrative that, like a long and successful novel published in installments, lasted nearly fifty years. These techniques allow the illustrations to express all temporal relations: simultaneity, anteriority, posteriority. Of course, to understand these temporal relations one needs an explanatory text indicating how to read the engraving, but the fact remains that with these different techniques, the engraver-publishers of the *Great Voyages* create a genuine grammar of graphic forms at the level of each plate or group of plates. This grammar of forms lets the graphic narrative develop autonomously; though supported by the written text, the message it conveys is something other than the sum of the elements that compose it.

4   *Constants and Variables in the Picture of the New World*

DETERMINATION OF CONSTANTS

The kaleidoscopic image of Amerindians as it appears over the thirteen parts of the *Great Voyages* seems to consist in an unlimited number of signifiers. Still, this multiplicity, so difficult to grasp, can easily be reduced to four major categories covering all the different aspects, and their variations, of the portrayal of Amerindians. Their portrayal in fact involves:

(1) physical appearance, expressed by means of two codes: anatomical (morphology, sex, and age), and cultural (dress, finery, ornaments, and the various attributes the figures hold);

(2) actions: their attitudes, body posture, the acts in which they engage, conveying their mores and customs;

(3) sociological relationships, binding the figures together; and

(4) habitat, whether natural or cultural, within which they are portrayed.

The problem is now to discover whether, given this series of constants, there is a systematic relationship among them. For instance, can correlations be found between certain anatomical variations of the Amerindian and the act in which he engages? With a change of body build, physical feature, dress, and ornament, do we detect changes of attitude with respect to the figures surrounding him? Is his physical appearance altered by even one element according to whether he his hunting, playing the flute, or mourning his dead? According to whether he offers the foreigners his women or attacks them with a burst of arrows? Or again, according to whether he is seen in his house, in a forest clearing, or in a mountain hollow?

If so, can a systematic order in these correlations be found that may account for all the variations comprised in the description of the pictures and thus reveal a meaning in these transformations? It is obvious that before we can seek systematic relations among these variables, we shall have to isolate other, finer, and more precise elements within these major categories.

THE PERCEPTION OF PHYSICAL TRAITS AT THE END OF THE SIXTEENTH CENTURY

One is immediately struck by the inability of the European draftsmen to grasp the physical differences that distinguish Amerindians from Europeans or other peoples. If it were not for a few items of dress and ornamentation, and other exotic details, one would think the figures came from an artist's anatomy plates, which can be found in the painting and sculpture of that time—the statues adorning the palaces of the end of the sixteenth century, the figures of antique gods, portraits of Roman athletes, Italian Venuses with long, wavy, hair; or, at the other extreme, visions of medieval monsters, grimacing and deformed witches, headless men, dwarfs and giants of the forest.

On this point, pictorial representation of Indians, especially in engravings, lags behind the descriptions of them found in the explorers' narratives. Still, even in the texts, we rarely find the Indian classified as a particular physical category, whereas the peoples of Africa were so classified much earlier. In antiquity, the Greeks, Romans, and Etruscans perfected the likeness of Negro models with their portrayal of Ethiopians in sculpture and painting as well as in engraving on pottery and medallions.[1] Yet in the mid-sixteenth century, Dürer states that there are only

> two species of mankind, whites and negroes; in these a difference in kind can be observed as between them and ourselves. Negro faces are seldom beautiful because of their very flat noses and thick lips; similarly their shinbones and knees, as well as their feet, are too bony, not so good to look upon as those of the whites; and so also is it with their hands. Howbeit I have seen some amongst them whose whole bodies have been so well built and handsome otherwise that I never beheld finer figures, nor can I conceive how they might be bettered, so excellent were their arms and all their parts. [Holt 1957, pp. 324–25]

When Columbus paraded the first Indians down the streets of Barcelona, the Spaniards were quite astonished to see that their hair was not kinky, and that, though different from Europeans, they did not resemble African blacks whom the Spaniards already had the chance to see. Moreover, Dürer's opinion reveals historical and cultural modes of perception. The face and body are perceived differently. In fact, the physical differences are easier to see in the faces. The practiced eye of the German painter-engraver marks with interest anatomical details of the bone structure, especially the joints. But the whole of the body may be perfect and, as a model, a black African may attain the perfection of the nude.

The same dichotomy of body and face is found again in the perception of the Amerindians' physical features. The narrators often note that "their faces are seldom beautiful" but the body can be perfect. Thus Vespucci stands in wonder before these men, who "all go naked . . . without covering anything, no otherwise than as they came out of their mothers' wombs. They are of medium stature, and very well proportioned." Still, in spite of their fine build, "they have not very beautiful faces, because they have long eyelids, which make them look like Tartars" (Vespucci 1894).

It would be many years before the Indian's face was recognized, and especially portrayed, with its characteristic features. In the *Great Voyages*, the first and only picture of an Indian that would allow us, in the twentieth century, to identify it as such and find it a good likeness of his face, appears only in the frontispiece of part 10, that is, in 1619, among mythological figures. Yet in this impression of the "Indian profile," it is still hard to distinguish what comes specifically from physical features and what from cultural features, such as the hairstyle (the long hair smoothed over the forehead and plaited into a braid that hangs over one shoulder) and the two rings piercing the nostrils.

Still, John White's watercolors, de Bry's first models, show an attempt to express anatomical differences.[2] In fact, White managed to put in a few of the Oriental features of the Algonquian face: the high cheekbones, arched nose, and the women's flat faces, with the eyes slightly tipped up at the outer edge. When working from White's models, de Bry mutes or entirely omits these differentiations: he rounds out the women's flat faces and makes them chubby and even corrects the shapes of the body here and there, giving the men an athletic musculature and the women shapely legs, thus sacrificing to contemporary taste and the canons of the *beau nu*.

With the passage from watercolor to engraving one major element accenting the difference is lost, namely color. White's

Amerindians have brown and copper-colored skin, decorated with paint. The same is true of Le Moyne's portraits of the Timucua in part 2.[3] This brings us to the more general problem of transferring from one code to another, not only from the code of painting to the code of two-color engraving, but also from the code of textual description to that of the graphic image. Compounding the problem of direct perception, the transfer partly governs the physical depiction of the American Indian and more particularly that of his nudity.

TRANSFER OF PHYSICAL REPRESENTATION FROM TEXT TO IMAGE

In the transfer of various—pictorial or textual—codes to the code of copper engraving, three phenomena seem to me determinant.

1. Lexical Reduction of Physical Attributes

As it is restricted to black and white, the technique of engraving must leave out one whole aspect of the exoticism of the Amerindian world that did not, however, fail to strike and amaze the explorers: the "artistically painted" colors in the ornaments of feathers or skin; body paints made from vegetable dyes (whose preparation is sometimes described by the narrators)[4] that stand out on their copper-colored skin, described by Vespucci as "red, like a lion's skin"; the dyed clothing of Mexicans and Peruvians; the magnificence of the frescoes in the Mayan, Aztec, and Inca temples and cities. Thus engraving entails the loss of a whole cultural dimension, perceived and described by the narrators, if not always understood or appreciated for its true worth. The tattoos and body paintings of the Timucua and Algonquian are converted into lines and dots so that, in certain engravings, it is often hard to decide whether they represent tattoos, paintings, or scarifications. The Mesoamerican temples and cities, radiant with color, are transformed into poor huts or scaffoldings—unless they are copies of European cities to which a few fanciful details have been added. The Mexicans' jewelry, so admired by Dürer,[5] and the Peruvians', of which Benzoni speaks so highly, are replaced by shoddy-looking objects. From this point of view, engraving degrades the image of the New World and dulls it from the outset, affecting it not only as a cultural whole but as a natural environment of tropical landscapes.

In return, what engraving loses from the viewpoint of visual richness is made up on the level of abstraction. Thus the use of black and white causes the disappearance of one criterion for the racial and racist differentiation that later develops in America: skin color.[6] Precisely because of this, engraving masks the naked Indian equal at least to the European ideal of the *beau nu* if not to the European himself. Ethnic differentiation here is purely cultural and not racial.

2. Loss of Negation as a Rhetorical Device

In passing from text to picture, still another change occurs that necessarily alters the textual information in a description: negation as a means of expression is lost. In fact, it is easy to describe the unknown, the never-seen, in terms of what it is not. The first accounts by Europeans returning from America made excessive use of this technique: Indians are what Europeans are not; their culture is defined by the absence of European cultural elements. It is a negative attitude ironically illustrated by Montaigne's "Eh, quoi, ils ne portent pas de hauts de chausse!" ["What! They're not wearing breeches!"] Negation is impossible in figurative drawing. Actually, in the graphic arts it is impossible to portray a thing by what it is not: it is present or absent, and if it appears, it is always positively, in a certain shape. Thus engraving, through the limits it imposes a medium, introduced, unbeknownst even to the artists themselves, a radical transformation in the vision of the New World, especially where Indian nudity was concerned. Indeed, it could not be portrayed as the absence of clothing. It was immediately incorporated in body lines and anatomy that must be drawn in a certain way. Lacking the possibility of negation, the engravers had no choice but to use the nude forms canonized in art: bodies of Roman or Greek statues and Italian virgins, or else medieval monsters, gaunt and hideous old women; dwarfs or giants. The differentiating elements—ornaments, items of clothing, and the attributes of war, hunting, and fishing—must be hung, so to speak, on these forms traditional to European art.

3. From Comparison to Metaphor[7]

For describing and "showing" the unknown part of the New World, the engravers frequently used a second rhetorical device, that of comparison, particularly comparison with other peoples

better known in Europe. We are told that the Indians look like
Tartars, Picts, or Jews in certain ways. Some aspect of their customs is "like" a custom observed in Europe or Japan. In terms of
the graphic image, no equivalent has been found for the syntactic
bonds that, in the verbal comparison, explicitly set up a relation
between two things (whether by a conjunction or by a comparative
adjective or verb). If, for example, the Indians of Virginia are compared to Picts because, like them, they decorate their bodies with
designs and paintings, the only way to preserve the relation of
comparison between the two is to tell in a caption why portraits of
Picts should appear among engravings of Amerindians. De Bry
explains that it is "to show that the inhabitants of Great Britain in
the past were as savage as those of Virginia." As long as the textual
commentary remains with the picture and is read, the juxtaposition
of the two different peoples is metonymical, like the comparison in
the text (they are partially comparable, from a certain aspect). But,
if the explanatory text is omitted, the portraits of Picts become
another way of portraying Indians. Thus a simple comparison becomes a substitution, pure and simple. This is what happened in
other editions of texts that copied the de Brys' engravings; Pict
figures are again seen among the Indians; this example illustrates
how a verbal comparison is transcribed directly as a metaphor
(complete assimilation of the compared term with the comparable
terms): it suffices to describe a people as having "shoulders so high
that the face seems to be in the chest," for a headless being to appear
whose face is drawn on his chest, like the Blemmyes of antiquity
and medieval times.

The transfer from a verbal code to an iconographic code, then,
imposes constraints, in the sense that one speaks of grammatical
constraints. In both cases these lead to making the pictures say
more than the words mean: by its translation whether of negative
statements or of comparisons, the picture performs a *de facto* transformation of meaning, similar to the surrealist metaphor in poetry.
In the examples given, the consequences are seen in terms of the
physical portrayal of the Amerindian. Within the limits imposed by
their technique, the engravers had a repertoire of physical shapes
and types from which to choose. This choice led to a conventional
norm by which Indians can be identified, in spite of the numerous
variations allowed by the convention. Let us examine more closely

the elements of this convention and the limits within which it functions.

The Choice of Reference Motif

Among the many kinds of cultural styles, forms, and elements with which Amerindians are endowed, in the main, the plates portray them as physically healthy and well proportioned. Apart from the infants nursed by their mothers, the children who are able to stand are depicted as little adults. Even the captions for certain plates emphasize the vigor of the New World inhabitants. Sometimes their vigor is attributed to their moderation, a trait Virginia's first colonists, influenced by a nascent Puritanism, offered as an example to the gluttonous English in part 1;[8] sometimes it is attributed to their quite bloody medicinal practices, for instance, the one used by the Timucua to strengthen their pregnant women.[9] A yet more striking feature: even when we are shown therapeutic practices for funerary scenes, the dead and the dying lose none of their robustness.

In addition, all the Indians, men well as women, seem endowed with eternal youth. Most are portrayed as young adults. Only two plates in the entire collection show "old people"; their build is then just as imposing as that of the young adults. One of them, "the noble old man of Pomeiock," stands out from the other Virginians only by cultural elements: the "winter" wear—long skin cape and the beard that the Algonquian let grow after a certain age, according to the caption. It is, indeed, another characteristic feature of the Indian of the *Great Voyages* that he is usually shown beardless. As the texts show repeatedly, the Europeans considered "barbarian" the Indians' custom of shaving off their facial and body hair, even including their eyebrows, as the Tupinambá did. Only a few plates show the Indians as bearded and hairy. But, rather than a concern for ethnographic accuracy (and the engravings are notoriously inconsistent in this domain, even if a cultural feature is once transcribed), we would see this, too, as a stylistic convention: the nude body of anatomical plates and statues is always shown without the beard and pubic hair, just as the bare sexual parts of the women are not drawn, yet no one supposes that Indian women are without sex organs; they simply resemble statues. The appearance and form of the women (and men) vary with the different styles of

wild types vs.
Indian

the period, but, whatever the style, the women are for the most part endowed with the ideal forms canonized by art.

Still, by contrast with anatomical quasi perfection and especially the fixed and neutral convention applied to the Amerindian, some types, appearing sporadically, stand apart from these norms. We see giants and dwarfs; headless men; others, wild-looking, disheveled, and bearded (unlike the smooth-skinned Indian); and above all, a type of woman who appears more frequently as the series advances and whose portrayal runs against the canon of proportions observed in the pictures of the other Indian women. She is afflicted with an uncomely appearance and sagging breasts: sometimes this trait combines with the robust youth of the other women; sometimes, on the contrary, with hideous, emaciated, old women.

I have chosen to analyze this motif because it appears more frequently than the others. Moreover, it forms an iconographic motif standardized by a whole tradition. In medieval iconography and through the Renaissance, it was attributed to maleficent women, vampires, witches, demons, the incarnation of Envy and Lust, and the depiction of Death. Thus one of Agostino de Musi's engravings, from 1518, entitled "The Skeleton," depicts Death as an emaciated woman with sagging breasts, seated on the carcass of an antediluvian monster. In Ripa's *Iconologie* we find Heresy also shown in this fashion, holding a serpent in one hand in the other a book from which other serpents crawl; again, we find Famine depicted in this way in Bernard Salomon's illustrations for Ovid's *Metamorphoses* (1553). The woodcut shows Eresichton condemned to an insatiable and eternal hunger. It is also one of the traditional forms of the "savage woman"; "A libidinous hag, disguised in a nice maiden, and when undisguised, is distinguished by shrunken flesh and long sagging breasts" (Bernheimer 1952, p. 35).

It is no surprise, then, to see her again among our Indian women. The problem is to understand why this standardized but deviant motif appears in the corpus of pictures of the *Great Voyages* at certain times and not at others. Is it a pure chance accident or can we discover beneath its recurrence a network of unspoken meaning, woven from differences between "normal" forms and anomalous forms? If, like the *bricoleur*, the engravers draw their material here and there from a repertoire of forms that they use and transform to suit the circumstance or mood, the result of this *bricolage*, the rearrangement of these heteroclite forms into a visual narrative of America, perhaps answers to an internal logic, as does myth.

In fact, as we shall see, it is no accident if the iconographic motif of the Indian with sagging breasts reappears through the *Great Voyages* over a forty-four-year period. The different variants of the same motif relate to each other through transformations organized into a coherent system, which I propose to explore.

2 The Savage Woman with Sagging Breasts

Ariadne's Thread

Tracing the iconographic reference motif through its multiple avatars leads us into a labyrinth whose passageways I have barely indicated. The definition of some methodological points and of my main terms will be taken as our Ariadne's thread.

DIFFERENTIATING ELEMENTS, PERTINENT FEATURES, OPPOSITIONS

I shall base my analysis from the outset on the search for differentiating elements in the signs constituting the pictures. Beginning with the first plate in which the motif of the woman with sagging breasts appears, I shall try to note the elements that differentiate it from canonical norms. These differences may relate to other aspects of the figure's physical appearance, actions, sociological role, and so forth. Among the differences thus marked, only a certain number have a distinctive or oppositional value and constitute "pertinent features." We shall say that an element is "in opposition" to another element when the differentiation fulfills a specific function in a given context and leads to a difference in meaning.

The process of identifying pertinent or oppositional features among the many differentiating elements imposes a special requirement on the form of my presentation. Certain descriptions may appear to be digressions because they fail to lead directly to a conclusion. In this study, the reader can check the method only if he is shown how some differentiations may assume an oppositional value or be judged pertinent while others are free variations and nonessential differences whose expression leads to nothing, that is, which have no function.

PARADIGMATIC AND SYNTAGMATIC OPPOSITIONS

With this criterion of pertinence, we can isolate significant oppositions as linguists do. Paradigmatic oppositions are those that exist between the elements present in a chain of the discourse (whether contained in a single plate or in a series of plates), and elements that are not present in it. The visible elements are considered as a choice made among possible choices. On the other hand, when these oppositions occur between elements of a single context they are "syntagmatic." The segmentation of the iconographic discourse is dictated by the internal organization of the plates, by the relationships among the plates, and by the relations of narrative to picture discussed in chapter 3.

TRANSFORMATIONAL SYSTEMS

The notion of transformational systems is the keystone of the analysis. It was expressed as early as 1945 by Lévi-Strauss, in an article on split representation in art,[1] elaborated in a chapter of *La Pensée sauvage* (1962), then applied in *Mythologiques*. In my opinion, this is what allows the study of nonlinguistic messages to become more independent of the phonological model, from which, in the long run, it need borrow only a few conceptual tools, such as pertinence and opposition. In the iconographic field, as in the field of oral mythology, only through transformational systems can we unravel the hidden meaning of a graphic discourse that, at first glance, appears impenetrable or meaningless. They also let us show the dynamics of structures which, in this case, have evolved over a period of nearly fifty years. These systems of transformation appear, of course, only if one considers a vast enough corpus within which recurrent elements can be found.

COMBINATORY VARIANTS AND VARIATIONS

Each recurrence of the chosen motif is a variant. In the majority of cases, a being (woman or monster) with sagging breasts can easily be distinguished from the other figures. One may wonder, however, in borderline cases, what criteria to adopt for distinguishing the "normal" from the "aberrant." Thus, as I introduce each new variant of the motif, I shall emphasize the many variations of its appearance in new contexts, and shall show how a new figure is indeed a combinatory variant of a single sign: sagging breasts.

Each variant is examined in the order in which it appears within the corpus. Not until volume 3 of the *Great Voyages*, devoted to the cannibal Tupinambá, do we find the iconographic motif isolated in a single plate. As I analyze the differentiating elements between anomalous Tupinambá women and the other Indian women of this volume and learn their function, we shall be led to discover a whole network of implicit meaning: the meaning for Europeans of the cannibalism they reject, and which, paradoxically, they portray in an abundance of pictures.

The second variant is found in a plate of the subsequent volume, in the first volet of a triptych whose subject is the damage inflicted on the Indians by the Spanish Conquest. This broad context provides a new sequence within which the differentiating elements between the anomalous figure and the others have their function. But, this time, a first set of transformations can be specified between this variant and two other plates that show Indian idols and the Christian devil with sagging breasts. This first set of permutations brings to light the transformational structures linking the first variant to the second. Subsequent variants lead us to part 9 of the *Great Voyages* and close the cycle of variants of the savage woman.

A select group of those [women]
who engage in courtesies
not otherwise than for pleasure
talked among themselves as connoisseurs
of what most appealed to them
among the meats.
Cabinet Satyrique, 1550

Part 3 of the *Great Voyages*, in which the motif of the savage woman appears for the first time,[1] is devoted to the cannibal tribes of Brazil, the famous Tupinambá.[2] This name is used to refer to the Indians of the Tupi-Guarani language who lived in the sixteenth century on the Brazilian coast between the mouth of the Amazon, to the north, and Cananea, in the southern part of São Paulo State. Hans Staden, one of the authors of the texts illustrated by de Bry in this volume, was held prisoner for nine months by the Tupinikins, one of the Tupinambá tribes occupying the region between Camamu and São Mateus. He thus reports at first hand in detail on the prisoner of war's changes of fortune before he was ritually sacrificed then cut up and eaten.

The first variant of the Indian woman with sagging breasts appears in the middle of one of the profusion of cannibal scenes engraved by the de Brys. At first glance one might think this radical change in the gracious appearance of the Indian women reflected a sudden change of attitude toward the Indian world that occurred between parts 2 and 3. As we have seen earlier, the first two parts offer a somewhat idealized image of Indian life among the Algonquian of Virginia and the Timucua of Florida. But in the third volume, the Indians are depicted as aggressive, bloody, and savage: they set traps for the Europeans using "barbarian" guerilla tactics, rob them of their clothing, engage in massacres between neighboring tribes, and indulge a meticulous butchering of recently killed victims. In addition, unlike the Algonquian and Timucua of the earlier volumes, they are shown as lacking social hierarchy and agriculture. This last trait is, however, ethnographically incorrect. The de Brys even eliminate from their iconographic models (the woodcuts from the German edition of Staden's text) a scene in which the women are seen returning from their manioc fields carrying their baskets on their backs.

In spite of these contrasts, it would be inaccurate to explain the anatomical variations of the Tupinambá women in terms of moral symbolism, and their anatomical misfortune as the sign of their cruelty. In fact, in part 2, the noble Timucua, whose bodies are majestic and perfect, though they are gracious to the Europeans, "marvelously" well organized under powerful chiefs, imbued with authority, and expert in engineering, agriculture, and hunting, nonetheless indulge in rites judged extremely cruel and idolatrous by the Europeans: sacrifice of newborn infants, scalping of the enemy, exemplary punishment, animal worship, and axing a Frenchman to death.

However, their physical appearance is not affected by this in the least. The same is true of our Tupinambá, men as well as women. In spite of their blood-thirsty mores, they keep their handsome anatomical proportions; there is even a certain irony in seeing these attractive, long-haired maenads engage in the most immodest actions, for example, pushing a stick into their prisoner's anus or treating one another to bits of human flesh with coquettish gestures. In this series, a contrast with the graceful Tupinambá appears in only one plate, where women afflicted with physical ugliness and signs of decrepitude are portrayed.

The brusque change in the physical portrayal of cannibal women is by no means unrelated to cannibalism. But the relation between the action committed and the physical misfortune is not a direct relation of cause and effect. Rather, it takes place within a network of correspondences between the elements of the physical depiction of the Tupinambá men, women, and children, and the many details of the cannibals' cooking. By their very anomaly, the strange figures of cannibal women with sagging breasts draw attention to the physical differences and elements of the man-eating rites that are chosen, reconstructed, and imagined by the Europeans, in a series of plates depicting the most startling scenes. Indeed, these plates strive to transcribe the eyewitness narrative by the poor Staden, an observer all the more concerned for feeling that he himself was in great danger of being eaten. But, beyond the distorted perception of the narrator himself, the engravers have amply interpreted and have even reconstructed the process of the cannibals' cooking in their own way: after the preliminary ceremonies and the festivities, the preparation of the prisoner and of the sacrificial club, and the ritual execution, they offer us the cleansing of the corpse following Staden's description. Cutting up the victim, cooking and eating him are the subject of three plates, but only in the last one is the fine appearance of the Tupinambá women spoiled. In the first, the victim's body is quartered and certain parts are boiled in a pot; in the second, women and children share the boiled parts; finally, the third shows the cooking and eating of the roasted parts (illustrations 2, 3, 4, and 5).

With this series of engravings, then, we have a unique document on the manner in which cannibalism, this major taboo for our culture, may have been conceived, perceived, and portrayed at that period. The graphic portrayal made by the Europeans itself implies a very interesting paradox from the viewpoint of historical modes of perception and their unconscious manifestations. The problem, in fact, for the Protestant engravers, was graphically to recreate an object of horror. Cast by the European mind both out of nature and out of culture into the domain of diabolical abominations, it was the crime imputed to witches suspected of dealing with the devil; it was the feature of savagery and barbarism par excellence.

By seeking the distinctive value of the iconographic motif of the savage woman in this first context, we can show the Europeans' fanciful vision of Tupinambá cannibalism and the unconscious structures upon which it rests. Far from diving into the depths of the Freudian libido, these unconscious structures bind the symbolism of the human body, whether of the guests or of the dismembered victim, to the social body, by the mediation of classificatory systems linking together microcosm and macrocosm.

A Meal among Brazilian Anthropophagites

Men, women, and children, surrounding the wooden grill on which the quarters of human flesh are roasted, share the cannibal feast. However, among the four women who participate, only one has the familiar features of the Tupinambá women portrayed in this volume: young, with the body and profile of a statue, the breasts high and firm, the long hair drawn smoothly across the forehead and falling behind the shoulder, a "vignol" shell in her earlobe, and strings of large round pearls around her neck and wrist. The three other women, on the contrary, have lost their physical charms: their breasts hang down, their brows are wrinkled, and they are stripped of all ornaments; their hair, parted in the middle and drawn straight back from each side of the forehead, rather than smoothed across it, hangs in disheveled wisps to their shoulders (illustrations 4, 5).

Along with this unexpected transformation in the physical appearance of the old Tupinambá women another detail can be observed: all three of them are licking their fingers greedily, whereas the young and graceful cannibal woman of the foreground bites into a human limb as do the men. The explorers find this feature of the old Tupinambá women particularly striking. Léry, especially, describes them gathered around the grill "to catch the fat that drips down the sticks of these high, wide wooden grills, licking their fingers and saying, 'Ygatou,' that is, 'It's good'" (Léry 1578, p. 245). Thevet, for his part, reports that as soon as the executioner made the victim's head fall, "the blood from the victim and what flowed from the head were scarcely on the ground before an old woman scooped it up into an old gourd, and as soon as she had collected it, she drank it raw" (Lussagnet 1953, 1:281).

Fat or blood, the old women's evident taste for the juices draining from the human flesh may be explained by their difficulty in chewing, as they lack teeth. One of the three old women depicted in this plate, while she licks one hand brandishes in the other one of the victim's legs that she is going to (or cannot) eat. Be that as it may, we can see that the use of the motif of the woman with the sagging breasts, in this first context, can not be interpreted as an opposition between benevolent woman and malevolent woman, for our young cannibals of the statuesque bodies and Roman profiles appear equally demonic and sinful as the old women who have lost their charms. In a certain degree even, their voracity is even greater, as they devour the human flesh without restraint, while the old women, more discreet in their pleasure, are satisfied to collect the drippings from it. It is necessary to look elsewhere for the meaning of the differences between the two types of native women.

If beauty is not set in opposition to the monstrous and to age as good to evil, the fact remains that within a single sin, the transgression of a food taboo, a distinction is introduced between two types of gluttony, both of which are evil and impious: one for roasted human flesh, the other for the juices that flow from it.

Although the iconography of the capital sins, particularly that of gluttony and lust, often borrows the traits of an old woman with a sagging bosom,[3] it is certainly not from a fixed iconographic tradition that the de Brys drew a ready-made difference between such subtle modes of committing a sin considered as an abomination as eating roasted human flesh or savoring its juices.

As for Christian theology, it does not give any special place to cannibalism among the capital sins. Cannibalism is considered a sin by virtue of the corollaries "Thou shalt not kill," and "Thou shalt love thy brother as theyself," and, in this sense, it appears as the antithesis of charity. It is also the corollary of gluttony, to which are joined hate and lust. Lust is linked with gluttony "because it leads to the incontinency of the eyes and ears which require unwholesome food" (Tanquerey 1924, p. 550).[4]

These three vices clearly combine in the portrayal of cannibal rituals: the combative and hostile atmosphere of a large number of the scenes depicting daily life in the Tupinambá village; the aggressive gestures of the men, even more pronounced among the women, biting their nails with envy at the sight of the prisoner, whom they force to shout, "I am your food." To this must be added the vaguely erotic gestures made by two figures of women: one caresses her companion's sexual parts during a ritual dance they perform around their victim, a gesture recalling one of the familiar motifs of Tantric sculpture; another does the same thing to herself, during a cannibal meal, while biting the nails of her other hand, at the sight of the intestines the women and children share. This motif seems to establish a similarity between masturbation (auto-eroticism) and cannibalism, although the anthropophagy of the Tupinambá was purely exocannibalistic and portrayed as such in the text as well as in the engravings, where all the victims are prisoners of war.

In any case, for Christian theology, there existed no gradation of sin according to whether the object of gluttony was flesh or blood, roasted or raw. The only distinctions made by the theologians, from the time of the Scholastics to the beginning of the twentieth century, concerned the different ways of committing this sin. No mention was made of cannibalism. The different modes were as follows: *propere*, eating before the need has been felt, between meals, from pure gluttony; *laute et studiose*, seeking delicacies for the pleasure one takes in them; *nimis*, consuming immoderate quantities of food; *ardenter*, eating with avidity or greediness (Tanquerey 1924, p. 550; Bellarmine 1619, p. 234; Toleti 1649, p. 795).

These four categories of gluttony refer respectively to excess in frequency of eating, in quality, in quantity, and, finally, in table manners. In each case, it is an *immoderate* love of the pleasures of the table,[5] beyond the bounds of etiquette. From this point of view, the Tupinambá, young or old, men or women, sinned equally by these four kinds of excess or violation of the rule, which would suffice to categorize them simultaneously as "sinners," "pagans," and "savages," unlike the Indians of Virginia and Florida of the earlier volumes, who were noted for their moderation.

Neither in theology nor in the iconographic tradition is a special value placed on these slight differences in the transgression of this food taboo of cannibalism. Still, over and above this "conscious model" of gluttony, we shall discover a meaning for these differences within a system of classifications developed from a logic of physical qualities. These qualities make apparent a whole cosmological symbolism of the dismembered body, linked with the social body by a network of interdependencies, rooted in very old cosmologies.

THE ROAST-EATING BEAUTIES AND THE BLOOD-SUCKING HAGS

At the level of differences, the anatomical variations in the cannibal women correspond to an opposition of two types of gluttony, one for roasted meat (or, more precisely, meat grilled on a wooden grill),[6] and the other for the blood and melted fat that drips from it. This is an opposition made familiar by the *Mythologiques* between different degrees in the cooking of food: the *grilled*, a kind of cooking closest to *raw*, which appears at the top of the culinary triangle; while the dripping, not yet coagulated juices (blood mixed with melted fat), collected from the pieces of grilled flesh are further yet from the *cooked* and thus more nearly raw. Moreover, the juice appears as a food waste with respect to the flesh. Thus flesh and juices stand in opposition as the whole to the part, the container to the contained, and are in a metonymic relation. Still, from the point of view of the consistency of the various human parts on which the cannibals feast, the elements of this relation arise from the passage from a solid state (that of flesh) to a liquid state (that of the juices): from the *dry* to the *moist*.

We can also link the distinctions in the body parts selected for eating to variations in the physical appearance of the cannibal women. Between the *wolf-women*, meat-eaters, and the *vampire-women*, blood-suckers, the pertinent oppositions lie along two axes: the axis of age (youth/old age), for which the signs are the anatomical variations between firm breasts/pendulous breasts and smooth forehead/wrinkled forehead; and the axis of ornamentation, which joins to aging a deprivation at the cultural level by the adorned/nonadorned opposition. In fact, the young Tupinambá are naked, but they are adorned with native ornaments and their hair is carefully done, by contrast with the old women, who are disheveled and totally lacking in ornaments.

The differences in ornamentation thus mark a contrast between two stages both close to the *naked* category: an adorned nakedness and a "savage" or monstrous nakedness. As in the case of cooking, we can situate these differences along the sides of a triangle, with *naked* and *clothed* as two of its points. Like the points of the culinary triangle, *naked* and *clothed* stand in opposition, in their European culture of the time, as nature to artifice, or, to use Lévi-Strauss's terms, as the elaborated to the nonelaborated, and the third term represents a corrupted state of the other two. The two triangles may be put side by side:

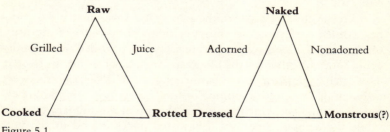

Figure 5.1

The appearance of the three old women among the typical young and handsome Tupinambá thus sets up a relation of equivalence, seen in three different codes, between physiological deterioration caused by aging, a natural process, and dual cultural regression, one from a culinary mode close to nature on the *cooked* (grilled) side to a yet more nearly raw state, but on the *rotted* side, and the other, form a nudity adorned with cultural elements to an even less elaborated state in which nature, stripped, does not appear intact but in a state of decrepitude or corruption.

This way of conceiving the "savage" state as the aging and deterioration of a more perfect state is the contrary of all the ideas of the original goodness of nature and the "savage." It is also opposed to the traces of these ideas that survive in our vocabulary, as when we refer to "young nations," as contrasted with "developed" civilizations. In turn, it reflects exactly, at an unconscious level, a theory accepted at that time for explaining cultural differences between Christian peoples and the others: the theory of natural decay. Before we move to the analysis of the other variants of our iconographic motif, we should pause for a moment to indicate, with respect to these ideas, the position of the editors of the *Great Voyages*.

PHYSICAL DECREPITUDE AND THE THEORY OF NATURAL DECAY

It is no accident that the collection opens with a dual portrayal of the mythic ages of mankind: the Fall of Adam and Eve from the earthly paradise, and the departure from Noah's Ark of the animals saved from the Great Flood. Both are attempts to inscribe the existence of the Amerindian and the newly discovered lands into the biblical schema of the common origin of man (the monogenetic theory) and to use it to account for cultural diversity. The first makes of the Amerindian an Adamite, that is, a human creature endowed with both a soul (thus able to be converted) and a mind letting him build tools. In his *Epistle to the Benevolent Reader*, illustrated by the plate of the earthly paradise, de Bry explains it in these terms: "Although because of Adam's disobedience, man was stripped of the gifts he had received at the creation, as we shall see in the folllowing narrative on the life of savage tribes he kept enough knowledge to be able to provide for his wants and to make all he needed for life and health, excepting only the health of his soul."

Then, the caption for the plate of Noah's Ark explains that the Indians are probably descendants of Ham, the wanderer, one of Noah's sons, and presumed ancestor of the Asiatic peoples and the Saracens. This belief, moreover, makes these peoples victims of an additional curse, by contrast with the other Adamites. Ham was cursed by his father for seeing him naked when he was drunk; whereas his two brothers, Shem and Japheth, [who fathered] the Africans and Europeans, walked backward to cover the drunken Noah with a cloak.

Thus this second myth could be used to account for cultural differences starting from the biblical monogenetic conception of man's origin. As Margaret Hodgen has shown (1964), the geographical remoteness of the descendants of these Hamite wanderers provided an explanation for the difference in cultural levels, for the "backwardness" of the American Indians by contrast with the Europeans, and for their idolatry and their ignorance of the Christian God. Geographical distance, added to the flow of time from generation to generation since the origin, caused a break in communication between the Indian and the "source of truth" and set off the process of his decay. This decay appeared all the more inevitable because, following one of the main themes of Renaissance thought, any change was viewed as necessarily related to evil. According to Hodgen, this conception found support in many writers of the period and was as widespread and all-pervasive as is at present the idea of progress.

We also find this idea among the texts of the *Great Voyages*, especially in Léry's discussion of the Tupinambá themselves in part 3. The French voyager, wondering whether the Indians were indeed descendants of Ham, concludes that "in any case, they are a wretched people, born of the corrupted race of Adam" (Léry 1578, p. 292). He goes on to say that their superstitions and idolatry result from the fact that they "lack any sort of writing; it is difficult for them to retain things in their purity" (Léry 1578, p. 278). The metaphors used to express this conception of natural decay take up the same types of categories—biological and physiological—as do certain attributes in the engravings: the world is "old, almost dead, rotted"; "it is now nothing but an old carcass." These elements belong to the physical portray of the old cannibal women who suck blood (category of the *rotted*) and whose chests are bony (motif very often associated with that of pendulous breasts). But these correspondences between human anatomy and physiology, the generations, and a cosmic time refer to a larger system of correspondences between microcosm and macrocosm.

After Greco-Roman antiquity and ancient China, all the European Middle Ages took pleasure in viewing the human body as a "little world," reproducing the order of the cosmos on a smaller scale. A system of classifications thus links, by a network of influences and interdependencies, the various temporal rhythms of nature (signs of the zodiac, seasons, ages of life) to spatial divisions (four elements, the cardinal points) to which correspond a hierarchy of physical qualities (hot, cold, dry, and wet) and densities (liquid, gas, dense, and solid) and a classification of man's humors and temperaments. Figure 5.2, reproduced from *Survival of the Pagan Gods* by Jean Seznec, is an example of these classifications. It is borrowed from Antiochus of Athens, an astrologer of the second century A.D. But these systems inherited from the pagan world, particularly from Neoplatonism, were incorporated by the Church Fathers into the Christian curriculum as a means for attaining knowledge of divine things.

The permanence of these beliefs in Western thought is attested in the study of alchemy and astrology from antiquity to the present. The correspondences between human anatomy, the paths of the stars, and the signs of the zodiac, go back to the Greek principle of *melothesia*, or the localization of astral influences on the human body. These correspondences gave way to a whole divinatory pseudo science, "somatomancy," which assumed great importance in the sixteenth and seventeenth centuries and claimed to predict individual destiny.

Medieval iconography abounds—be it only in the illustrations for the *Très riches heures du duc de Berry*—in images showing the distribution of the signs of the zodiac over the parts of the human body. As Marie-Madeleine Davy has shown (1964), these theories constituted the keystone of Romanesque symbolism. Later, the Reformation, in spite of its battle against Church superstitions and every form of pagan vestige in Christianity, scarcely broke with these beliefs, if we are to believe certain confessions of Melanchthon and Luther. Fervent Protestants, the de Brys themselves lent their art to alchemical treatises relying on the same system: Johan Theodor, then Matthäus Merian, his son-in-law, for instance, illustrated the *Atalanta fugiens*, by the famous alchemist Michael Maier, sometimes using figures from the collection of the *Great Voyages*.

Without attempting to identify alchemical symbols in these portraits of cannibals, we shall see that the European engravers' reconstitution of Tupinambá cannibal cooking relied, in its every detail, on a similar system of correspondences. In fact, three axes

Signs of the Zodiac	Seasons	Ages of life	Elements	Winds	Qualities	Conditions	Humors	Temperaments	Colors
Aries **Taurus** **Gemini**	Spring	Childhood	Air	South	hot-moist	liquid	blood	sanguine	red
Cancer **Leo** **Virgo**	Summer	Youth	Fire	East	hot-dry	gaseous	yellow bile	choleric	yellow
Libra **Scorpio** **Sagittarius**	Autumn	Maturity	Earth	North	cold-dry	dense	black bile	melancholic	black
Capricorn **Aquarius** **Pisces**	Winter	Old Age	Water	West	cold-moist	solid	phlegm	phlegmatic	white

Figure 5.2 Correspondences between microcosm and macrocosm according to Antiochus of Athens (from Seznec 1961, p. 47).

systematically link the ages of life, the various body parts eaten by the cannibals, and the physical appearance of the female participants, leaving aside the other individuals who also engage in cannibalism, that is, men and children. Still, the depiction of the cutting up of the victim and of the cooking and eating of the body parts fills three other plates from which the old women are omitted (illus. 1, 2, 3). It is, then, essential to take them into account insofar as this series of plates concerning cannibal cuisine forms the syntagmatic chain into which the ambiguous figure of the Amerindian woman with sagging breasts fits. More precisely, the sharing out of the victim's body parts among old and young men is only part of a larger system of classifications, establishing relations of interdependency between the cutting up of the human body, the ways of cooking the cut parts, and their distribution to the assembled company according to sex and age.

A Disintegrating World

The cutting up of the prisoner follows three major divisions: the peripheral parts (the limbs and the head), the central parts (the trunk), and the internal parts (the heart and intestines). The peripheral parts are cut with a stone blade, described by Staden, to which the engravers add an ax and a knife like those of European butchers. The trunk is split down the middle along the spine. Then the internal parts—heart and intestines—are removed.

Two types of cooking follow the dismemberment: the central and peripheral parts are cooked by the men on a wooden grill; the internal parts are boiled in a pot by the women. The head, one of the peripheral parts, is boiled with the intestines. This apparent anomaly corresponds to a European classification of animal meat: the head, when edible, actually belongs with the organ meat for butchered meat, or with the giblets in the case of fowl, and it is never roasted. It also occupies an ambiguous position whose function lies in the division of the victim according to the kind of cooking.

The quartering of the parts intended for grilling creates subdivisions: the trunk is cut across the diaphragm, thus separating the thorax from the pelvis, each part being cut into quarters. These are not pertinent divisions, however, as all these pieces of the trunk are grilled and eaten by the men and there are no noticeable differences among them, whether they eat part of the thorax or part of the pelvis. The limbs are grilled and eaten whole, with the exception of one severed hand on which a male child feasts. The peripheral parts are thus subdivided into two categories: limbs—the arms and legs; and extremities—the hands and head.

The distribution of this impious feast among the guests according to age and sex corresponds no better than does the cutting up of the body to enthnographic observation of cannibal rites among the Tupinambá. The little information we may gather on the subject from the texts of the explorers at the time suggests quite another distribution and system. In the first place, the engravings omit many organs, the genitals in particular, which must have had a special place in the ritual sacrifice of the prisoner. According to Claude d'Abbeville, they were reserved for the women, the tongue and the brain for the young people, and the skin of the head for the adults. Moreover, the kinds of cooking clearly differ. Men ate the boiled parts, women drank the meat stock, and other parts were grilled and given to prominent guests for later consumption (Métraux 1967).

In de Bry's engravings, the distribution of parts according to the guests' age and sex is organized quite otherwise. Two categories of body parts reflect a division by sex: the trunk, eaten exclusively by men; the viscera and the head, eaten exclusively by the young women and by the children of both sexes. The limbs fall in an intermediate category and are eaten by both men and women. Thus a parallel is set up between the anatomical cutting up of the body into three parts, and the sociological division of the adults according to sex. It can be seen in figure 5.3.

On closer examination, trunk and viscera stand in morphological

	Sex man/woman	Age youth/old age
Edible parts of the body	trunk/viscera	flesh/juice
Spatial relations of the parts	container/contained *external/internal*	container/contained *external/internal*
Consistency	firm/soft	firm/liquid

Figure 5.3   Relation of sex and age to the body parts.

opposition as container and contained, for the viscera lie within the trunk. A relationship of equivalency is thus implicitly supposed between the sexual division and this spatial division: man is opposed to woman as container is to contained. From the point of view of consistency, moreover, the trunk is opposed to the viscera as hard is to soft. The same type of relation accounts for the difference between the young and the old cannibal women.

Figure 5.4 shows different degrees of consistency in the parts of the human body, the object of cannibalism. The flesh eaten by the young women comes from the grilled limbs. Its consistency must, then, be classed with the flesh from the trunk eaten by the men. For the moment the series is reduced to three stages, which can be organized as follows:

Consistency	Firm	Soft	Liquid
Kinds of cooking	Grilled	Boiled	Bloody (juices)
Sex ⎫ of ⎬ cannibals Age ⎭	Men and women	Women	Women
	Young adults	Young adults	Old women

Figure 5.4

A dual dialectic of solid and liquid, of container and contained, allows us to pass from differences in age to sex differences. Not only do men and women stand opposed as container to contained, but also as solid to liquid and youth to old age. Childhood, the third point of the division by ages, and the body extremities—the head and hand—in the cutting up of the body, remain to be incorporated into this preliminary draft of a system.

The mediating function of the head now becomes clear: simultaneously container (by the skull and the face) and contained (by the brain, tongue, etc.), it is composed of both hard and soft parts. Its function is thus synthetic with respect to the trunk and viscera. It also has a synethetic function with regard to the viscera, with which it is boiled. According to butcher's classifications, in fact, the brain belongs, with the intestines, to the "white organs," whereas the other component parts of the head—the neck and the facial flesh—belong with the heart, among the "red organs." In addition, though it is cooked with the intestines, no one is ever seen eating the head. It is simply used as an ingredient of the soupstock drunk by young women and children. Whereas the limbs belong to an unmarked category from the point of view of the sex of the eaters—for the consumption of the limbs *includes* both men and women—by contrast, the head, being inedible, in fact *excludes* both. The parallel between the cutting up of the body and the distribution by sex becomes more specific. It leads to defining three types of sociological relation between sexes: disjunction, conjunction, and exclusion.

			Peripheral Parts	
Parts of the body eaten	Trunk	Viscera	Limbs	Head
	Container of viscera	Contained by the trunk	Neither container of viscera nor contained by the trunk	Container and contained
Sex of cannibals	**Men**	**Women**	**Men and Women**	*Neither men nor women*
Sociological relations	**Disjunction of sexes**		**Conjunction of sexes**	**Exclusion of sexes**

Figure 5.5   Sociological relations involved in the eating of various body parts.

With respect to the central parts, the cutting up of the body generates a type of pertinent opposition: the oppositions between outside and inside, between container and contained, correspond to a sociological division of the sexes. With respect to the peripheral parts, by contrast, the sociological division is not pertinent. What counts here is the age of those who eat. Whereas the distinction between flesh and blood corresponds to young and to old cannibal women respectively, head and hand are linked with childhood.

In fact, on two occasions, the head, still uncooked, is held by a male child. The first time, while the adult men ready themselves to cut up the prisoner's trunk and his limbs are already roasting on the grill, a child plunges the victim's head, severed from the trunk, into a stream of water, holding it by the hair as if to show that a different treatment is reserved for it: water rather than fire (illus. 1). In the second case, another male child carries a head in his arms toward the pot in which the young women are going to boil it along with the viscera (illus. 2).

We see this male child again tackling another of the prisoner's extremities, the hand. This sends us back to the reference plate, where the old Tupinambá women lick their fingers dripping with the victim's blood. As they do so, the male child bites into the fingers of a severed hand, the only time the hand appears separated from the arm, which we see being grilled and eaten whole by the adults of both sexes. The extreme difference in age and sex (old women/male child) corresponds, then, to an opposition between the use these figures make of the fingers as a lateral extremity of the human body: in the first case, they provide a means for cannibalism, for they serve more or less as an instrument for drinking blood; in the second, that of the male child, they are the very substance of cannibalism. As a means, the fingers are opposed to the bowl, a cultural element par excellence, from which the young women and the children of both sexes drink the soupstock. As a substance, the fingers represent the boniest of the edible parts of the body, and from the viewpoint of consistency, are opposed to the blood in which the old women delight,[7] or to the soupstock (considered as cooked blood): the first are the hardest, the others the most liquid.

The anatomical cutting up of the human body here reveals another kind of cutting up, not in terms of morphology but of biochemistry. In fact, division of the body was organized by spatial categories (central parts/peripheral parts; internal/external). With the categories of bone and blood, we move from form and space to substance. We can now place the body parts according to their degrees of consistency between the two extremes of bone and blood: the flesh (that of the trunk and the grilled limbs), then the boiled viscera, both composed of soft substances. Is there a relation, according to sex and age, between these physical qualities of cannibalized substances and the culinary taste of those who eat? A figure of correspondences for this other kind of division suggests that there is (fig. 5.6).

The dismembering and ritual consumption of the prisoner thus sets up a parallel between a three-step age gradation (childhood/ adulthood/old age) and the progressive liquefaction of matter. The semantic value of the old cannibal women appears even more

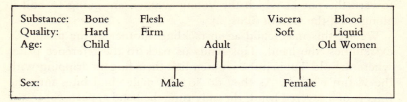

Figure 5.6   Relation between sex and age and types of food eaten.

clearly if one considers that they are at the end of both the age chain and the sex chain. In the series that leads from the hardest substance to the most liquid, from the formed to the formless, the male pole precedes the female pole.

We should not be surprised by the belief that woman comes from man as old age from adulthood and adulthood from childhood. Does not the biblical story of Eve's creation from one of Adam's ribs follow the same principle, that of a metonymic transformation passing from the whole to the part? Aquinas defends this wonderful act of creation in terms perfectly fitting the "sexist" spirit of the classifications underlying the vision of Tupinambá cannibalism: "It was right for woman to be made from a rib of a man. First, to signify the social union of man and woman, for the woman should neither use authority over man, and so she was not made from his head; nor was it right for her to be subject to man's contempt as his slave, and so she was not made from his feet" (*Summa theologica* 1, question 92, article 3).

Ambroise Paré, surgeon to the king of France, considers the problem of hermaphrodites and individuals who change sex during their lives. In the end he succeeds in keeping man's priority over woman in order to explain the opposite process, when women change into men, whereas "we find no case in history of a man becoming a woman." The reason is simple. It proceeds from a "natural law that always tends toward what is the more perfect and not the contrary, that that which is perfect should become imperfect" (Paré 1964, p. 197). Here is how this marvelous transformation works:

"Women have as much hidden within their bodies as men show outside: the only difference being that they have not enough heat or ability to push to the outside what the coldness of their temperature holds within, as if bound. Thus, if with time, the dampness of childhood that prevented the heat from accomplishing its duty, is mostly exhaled, the heat becomes more robust, bitter, and active, it is not unbelievable that, aided chiefly by some violent motion, it might push outside what was hidden within" (ibid.).

In addition to the relations of inner and outer, of container and contained, thus set up between the sexes, Paré links age and sex to what are called "qualities" at that time, that is, to atmospheric conditions: childhood to dampness, man to heat, woman to cold. These conditions refer us back to the system of correspondences between microcosm and macrocosm that associates childhood with dampness or, more exactly, to the warm and damp, "cold" with maturity and old age. Thus Paré's explanation of sex change implies that this wonder is not enough to disturb the order of nature, which functions, even in anomaly, according to the laws of the cosmos. In this, the author of *Monstres et prodiges* remains a disciple of Pliny the Elder, like his contemporaries, for whom the history of the "pretergenerations," or the history of monsters, belongs to natural history. The same is not true of the system of correspondences that we have detected behind the portrayal of cannibal rites among the Tupinambá. In that portrayal, old age appears to be congruent with a softening and finally with a liquefaction of substance—the opposite of the system in which microcosm and macrocosm are interdependent, the system that governs the harmony of the world, and in which the gradation of ages is congruent with a solidification of substance (fig. 5.7).

Such is, short, the conceptual model of cannibalism governing the graphic portrayal of the Tupinambá rituals in these engravings created from imagination, using the scanty graphic and literary facts as a base. It is scarcely surprising to see cannibalism, condemned by society and thus belonging to the area of the strictest taboos, conceived by part of European society of the sixteenth century as the motor of a regressive process moving against the order of the universe and dragging it toward a progressive and ineluctable destruction.

It is more surprising to see that these concepts and the system of classifications they imply account for variations in the physical appearance of the cannibals—as fantastic as they may appear at first sight—and, generally, govern in the slightest detail the choice of motifs and even the organization of forms. Beyond this rigorous logic, linking together a whole system of quite complex relations, it

Harmonious world	**Childhood** liquid	**Youth** gaseous	**Maturity** dense	**Old age** solid
World of cannibalism	hard (bone) **Childhood**	firm (flesh) **Adult**	soft (viscera) **Adult**	liquid (blood) **Old Age**
	Male	**Male**	**Female**	**Female**

Figure 5.7   Comparison between cannibal world and harmonious world.

is important to stress the economy of means used in its construction, in spite of the apparent wealth of fantastic details brought forth by an unbridled imagination. The system functions with a minimum of signifiers, organized into binary divisions (two sexes, two kinds of food preparation), ternary divisions (three ages of life), and quadripartite divisions (anatomical cutting up of the body, qualities of matter). This numerical progression can not fail to remind us of Pythagoras' tetractic addition (1 + 2 + 3 + 4 = 10), which, for alchemists, corresponds to the philosophers' stone. For some of the alchemists, the philosophers' stone is composed of four elements, three principles, two seeds, and one essence (Read 1959, pp. 104–8). The representational system of cannibalism is organized by the same numerical principle, even though it is presented as a reversed phenomenon of the philosophers' stone, for the latter embodies the principle of the unity of matter, and the former leads to its liquefaction and to chaos.

The Indian Woman from Cumaná Province

Let us leave our voracious Tupinambá women for the moment and turn to another figure whom we recognize as one of the variants. This figure appears in volume 4 of the *Great Voyages*, which illustrates the *History of the New World*, by Girolamo Benzoni.[1] Like the old Tupinambá women, her wrinkled forehead is framed by disorderly locks and her breasts hang heavily from a bony, emaciated chest. She is the wife of a *cacique*—an Indian chief—and probably Caribbean, for the Spaniards meet her on the Pearl Coast (to the northeast of present-day Venezuela).

Benzoni, who was a witness to the scene, reported that, on the arrival of the Spaniards, an "Indian lady," wife of one of the principal chiefs, brought a basket of fruit to Pierre Errera, the provincial governor.

We see her in the distance carrying her basket on her head, then again, seated on a bench in the foreground facing the Spanish conquerors, her basket at her feet. De Bry found a ready-made model for engraving her in the woodcuts illustrating Benzoni's original text. He clearly drew his inspiration from it, partially retaining the composition of the original scene. But he completely transformed the Caribbean woman's appearance, notably by removing her Indian profile and tattoos and transforming her into a monstrous old hag. That is, the engraver rejected the image at hand, preferring to start from the textual description, which he followed rather closely, and to recreate her from his imagination. Why? We must first read Benzoni's description of her:

> She wore no clothing or covering other than a narrow cloth over her private parts, as is the custom throughout this country. She was quite old and her whole body was painted black; her long hair hung to her waist. Her ears stretched down to her shoulders, as a hound's (the ugliest and most hideous thing it is

possible to see), and the many holes pierced in them were filled
with a variety of ear-rings and ear-pendants made of a certain
light wood that is called *cacoma* in their language. It was the
ugliest and most hideous sight I have ever seen; she appeared
more like a monster than a human being." [Benzoni 1579, p. 8]

The engraver retained two cultural traits from this portrait: the
strip of cotton that conceals the sexual parts of the Caribbean
woman, and the wooden rings, hung from the large holes pierced
in her ears, excessively enlarging the earlobe and distending it to the
shoulder. In fact, Caribbean women let their hair grow quite long
and float around their shoulders, cutting it only across the forehead
above the eyebrows. They wore nothing but a tiny cotton apron to
cover their genitals. They would pierce their ears and nostrils and
fill them with ornaments made of bits of wood, bone, or fish, and
pendants of stone or feather. Léry's earlier narrative about the
Tupinambá also gives a description of ornaments deforming the
ears, but the engravers do not use this detail in portraying the
cannibal women.

Caribbean women were, however, even more adorned than de
Bry's portrait suggests. In particular, they fastened bracelets so
tightly around their ankles that they swelled up, a detail overlooked
by the Europeans, at least if one is to believe Benzoni's description.
They also painted their bodies. In the woodcut illustration of the
Italian voyagers' original text, body paints are awkwardly transcribed on the woman's body by means of a lattice. The engraver
dropped this feature that would no doubt have changed too markedly the image of the savage woman with sagging breasts, a motif
not mentioned in the text.

De Bry also gives her the face of the old cannibal women of part
3, modified, however, by ornamentation—rings in the nostrils and
earlobes. In addition, the nails on her fingers and toes are long and
pointed, like claws. This purely invented detail repeats a cultural
feature of the Timucua Indians as they were portrayed after Le
Moyne de Morgues in part 2. In fact, this practice appears mostly in
the ornamentation of chiefs or certain dignitaries, for example,
sorcerers.

The textual description of a monstrous native woman fails, then,
to account completely for her graphic portrayal. Yet on the other
hand, if we consider her as a variant of the old Tupinambá women,
we note that, here, she is a figure without evil intent. On the

contrary, she appears kind and generous by bringing fruit to the foreigners as a sign of welcome. Here again we can attribute no intrinsic significance to this iconographic motif, because it may be linked with moral monstrosity, sin, as well as generosity. The objection may be raised, however, that her generosity is only a pretense and that her monstrous appearance signifies and reveals, by contrast, the true nature of her act, as in medieval legends we see the spell-binding temptress transformed, like Ariosto's Alcine, into a hideous and senile old woman. For this reason, it is necessary to see this plate in the context of the *History of the New World* from which it was extracted, and in the context of the other illustrations accompanying this narrative. As in the case of the "cannibal" variant, the paradigm of the Indian woman with sagging breasts can take on meaning only within this new sequence.

THE *History of the New World* AND THE MIRROR OF THE SPANISH TYRANNY

The three volumes of Benzoni's narrative, constituting parts 4, 5, and 6 of the *Great Voyages*, are very much alike. Urbain Chauveton, a Protestant theologian from Geneva, translated the work from Italian into French and Latin, and it is this Latin translation that de Bry published with the translator's commentary.

Benzoni, an adventurer in the service of the Spanish, voyaged from Seville to the Antilles, then along the Pearl Coast and the Gulf of Urabá, now Venezuela; on reaching Central America he went south as far as Peru.

In the *History*, Benzoni's own adventures often disappear behind the narrative of the Spanish conquest, from Columbus's voyages to Pizarro's conquest of Peru, which Benzoni undertook to write. Thus several perspectives overlap in the text, all intended to bring out the conquistadors' cruelty and the havoc they inflicted in the Indies wherever they went. The illustrations, which follow the text quite closely, constantly reflect this dual viewpoint, and, for the first time in the collection, the Amerindian is placed in the historical perspective of the times before and after the conquest. A striking opposition is created between the native, free at the time the Spanish arrived, and the Indian subjugated by his conquerors.

Many details in Benzoni's documentation of events he did not witness coincide with the narratives of the Spanish conquest written earlier by Pierre Martyr, Oviedo, and Gomara. Chauveton, moreover, often notes comparisons with these authors in the margins. But most of all Benzoni's text includes a true indictment of the methods of Spanish colonization, inspired by Las Casas's indictment and reinforced by Chauveton's commentaries.

The de Brys, apart from their work on the *Great Voyages* and at about the same time, published an illustrated edition of a text by Las Casas, translated into German as *Der Spiegel der Spanische Tyrannie* [The mirror of the Spanish tyranny] (Frankfurt 1598). The original text appeared without illustrations. In his own edition of Las Casas's text, de Bry added copperplate engravings some of which he later used in the *Great Voyages* to illustrate Benzoni's narrative. When first published in Venice in 1565, Benzoni's text had small, crude woodcuts for illustration. The large prints by the de Brys thus played a capital role in the visual diffusion of Las Casas's indictment of Spanish colonization in America. Beyond de Bry's own experience in the Netherlands,[2] one can seek his sources of inspiration in the large plates in the *Evénements remarquables*, by Perissin and Tortorel, published in Paris several years earlier, which recall with a gripping realism the massacres of the wars of religion.

By contrast with the enslaved and martyred Indian, the image of the Indian as the Spaniards first meet him, free and nonacculturated, is quite ambiguous. Unrestrained and light-hearted, as in the plates that show them dancing, they are idolatrous and also exhibit certain cultural traits of the Tupinambá, that is, of cannibalism, whereas the Indians of Hispaniola, or Haiti, did not practice anthropophagy. Still, the image of their "barbarous" or "savage" manners is eclipsed by the fierce barbarity of the Spaniards, whom de Bry depicted in the very act of cannibalism. The whole arsenal of tortures familiar to the Inquisition appears in his engravings: flagellation, garroting, water torture, strappado hanging, burning at the stake, burning of village, massacre of women and children, the casting to the dogs of "sodomites" to be eaten in sight of their tormentors, forced labor, ransoming for gold, pillage of the towns, rape.

The Spaniard appears infinitely more diabolical and monstrous than the Indian. Even when the victims in their turn subject the conquerors to torture, it is not from cruelty: sometimes they are rebelling, sometimes testing the Spaniards' immortality by a forced drowning, which at least shows evidence of a spirit of experimentation. Again, if they pour melted gold down the throat of a conquistador, it is, as the legend explains, to punish him for "avarice," and—with Dantesque humor—"to satisfy his thirst for gold."

In this context, the scene of gift-giving by the savage and monstrous but generous old Caribbean woman brings us to the very heart of the problem of the Europeans' plundering of the Indian. A native figure, an autochthone, brings, in all good faith, in a gesture of welcome, some of the fruits of her land to the foreigners. In return she will be expropriated, tortured, and reduced to slavery. The basket of fruit, as a gift, thus takes on value as a sign or portent of the fall and destruction of the Indian; it recalls the biblical symbolism based on a play of words in Hebrew between "ripe fruit" and "end." In fact, it is by this symbolism that the fall of Israel is foreshadowed in the book of Amos:

> Here is what Yaweh made me see:
> It was a basket of ripe fruit
> And he said, "What do you see, Amos?"
> And he said to me,
> "My people of Israel are ripe for their end."
> [*Bible oecuménique* 1965, p. 550]

Finally, we must clarify why the Indian woman as gift-giver and as future slave of her guests should have the appearance of a "monster" woman, in the original meaning of this term, whereas, on the one hand, this element is absent from the biblical symbol of the fruit basket, and on the other, this vision of the native is as aberrant with respect to the other engravings of this group as the old cannibal women were with respect to the other Tupinambá. Whether savages or martyrs, the Amerindian women of this part are only variants of the iconographic models of the first three volumes.

The chosen motif appears again in part 4 as an attribute of the idols worshiped by the inhabitants of Hispaniola. The Indians of this island are also victims of Spanish brutality, as can be seen in several other plates of this series. Here they break another European taboo, idolatry, which, along with cannibalism and nudity, is part and parcel of the concept of savagery and barbarism in the Christian consciousness of the period. In these idols it is easy to recognize the Europeans' fantasies of the devil, zoomorphic and androgynous, familiar in medieval and Renaissance iconography. Two of the idols, half-man, half-woman, are endowed with one of the specific attributes of the Christian devil, sagging breasts, and thus combine

Caliban — idolatry

androgyny with their various animal features. Of the three idols, one has a snake's tail, another a rooster's spurs, and the third, a goat's feet. The idol at the left is made from a profusion of different parts: it has a stag's head as well as heads of Cerberus and the head of a bird of prey. An owl's beak covers its genitals.

This projection of traits of the Christian devil onto the portrayal of an Amerindian rite leads us more deeply into the symbolism of the human body parts, here closely linked with the animal world and to physical and moral monstrosity. As in the cannibal plates, this symbolism leads us to discover, behind the iconographic motif under analysis, a whole network of social and even political relations. At the same time, it leads us back to the theological problem of sin and of the breach of a taboo, more specifically, to original sin and the myth of the Fall. But first let us evaluate the error of ethnocentric perception committed by the Italian, Benzoni, in his interpretation of an Amerindian rite as idol worship.

THE WORSHIP OF ZEMIS AMONG THE ARAWAK

This plate fits a description in Benzoni's narrative (illus. 6). It aims to demonstrate that the Indians love the devil and that their idol worship is inspired by him: "some are made of clay, others of wood, or gold, or silver; and in Peru I have seen them in the shape of birds, tigers, stags, or other sorts of animals, and I well remember having noticed some with a long tail dragging down to their feet in the same way you see demons painted over here" (Benzoni 1579, 285).

The precise description that corresponds to de Bry's engraving is a commentary by Chauveton. Benzoni's translator cites Oviedo who had had direct contact with the Arawak of Hispaniola before their religion was entirely destroyed by the monks:

> Among these peoples I found no older paintings or carvings nor anything more devoutly revered than the abominable figure of the devil. They paint it and carve it as hideously as possible, not tied down by chains or sprawled on the ground as we paint him, at the feet of Saint Michael or Saint Bartholemew, but with pontifical dignity, sometimes seated in a tribunal, sometimes standing, and in other ways . . . . You will see some with five or six heads and as many tails, large teeth, enormous ears, and the eyes flaming like dragon's eyes, and in other ways, of which the most attractive must frighten those who look at it."
> [Benzoni 1579, p. 290]

alcohol

These fantastic figures reproduced by de Bry, as well as the ceremonies surrounding them, have an ethnographic basis: they refer to
the Arawak worship of *zemis*, which Oviedo calls *"cemis."* The
Handbook of South American Indians (Steward 1963, 4:24, 536–37)
gives an account of this form of worship based on Oviedo.

De Bry's depiction of the zemis in terms of the fantastic style in
Europe varied, in reality, according to the dream visions of the
Indians (probably the Taino). The substance and shape of these
statues depended on an individual's vision, induced by a series of
ritual practices, often with the aid of drugs. A chief's body might
also be preserved as a zemi, after the intestines were removed and
the body dessicated. The religious ceremony itself, which the engraving lets us watch, corresponds to a type of worship, actually
practiced by the Taino of zemis kept in the chief's house and worshiped collectively. The chief led the procession of men and women
together to the temple that housed the idols. He beat the drum then
sat down on a wooden footstool at the entrance.

Inside, the chief's assistants prepared the statue, hanging
necklaces around its neck and laying bouquets of flowers on the
pedestals. These assistants wore a specific type of dress setting them
apart from the other participants. They wore a long chasuble open
on both sides over the twisted cotton strip wrapped around their
hips, also worn by the rest of the audience. We recognize the assistants as the figures of the frontispiece, both by their costume—the
chasuble of the officiating priest and a pointed hat that pick up
elements from the Inca costume as it appeared in the iconography
of the period, where de Bry found his inspiration[3]—and also by
their attributes. These are the necklaces, the bunch of flowers
offered by a man wearing a chasuable in sign of welcome to the
Spanish conquerors whose boats approach the shores, and finally,
the chief's staff.

Each of the other participants, on entering the "temple," had to
make himself vomit as a sign of purification. They put a stick down
their throats, as do the figures in one of the groups at the feet of the
principal idol: one holds the emetic stick in his hand, another
thrusts it into his throat, and finally, a woman vomits. After this,
the text continues, "they all sat down on their heels and . . . sang
some more songs" (Benzoni 1579, p. 290).

In the engraving, a native woman, looking like a beautiful young
Tupinambá, distributes some bread from the basket in her hand to
the group, seated tailor-fashion. The bread, intended for the zemis,

and laid at their feet, is then shared by all (Rouse 1963). Oviedo noted the resemblance between this ceremony and the Christian rite of the consecration and distribution of bread. After presenting it as an offering to the idol, "the priests took the bread and, after blessing it, shared it among all; and everyone kept this blessed bread as some holy relic" (Benzoni 1579, p. 290). It is true that the Arawak believed that if they failed to provide their zemis with food, the owner would fall ill. The purpose of the collective ceremony here portrayed, concerning the zemis of the chief, was thus to insure the prosperity and health of the entire village.

What is the relation between this ceremony and the scene examined in the preceding chapter where the Caribbean woman with the fruit basket greets the Spaniards? Although the sagging breasts motif is here linked to an idol of half-animal and half-human form rather than to a human being, it is important to take account of the context in which it appears. With this new variant of the motif, we may now further define the role the protagonists play in it and moreover relate this variant to a new one ("the Garden of Eden"), which, at a superficial reading, one would not think relevant.

Earlier I questioned the value of the Caribbean woman's offering in the context of the Indian-Spanish relations and wondered whether the ambiguity of the figure, both monstrous physically and generous in her behavior, did not spring from the gift itself. In this case, the motif is an attribute of an idol, a supernatural figure rather than a human being, and it is again linked with an oblation, not of fruits this time but of bread and flowers. The Amerindian once more assumes a position of gift-giver, but his physical appearance has changed; certain details of costume suggest these handsome men and woman are a variant of the handsome men and beautiful women of the Tupinambá. But in this plate it is the gift-takers, that is, the idols, who assume the traits of diabolical monsters with old women's attributes. If one compares the two plates from the point of view of the narrative they contain, we discover in them the following transformations in the respective positions of the ambiguous beings, Indian or idol: a monstrous old woman makes an oblation of ripe fruits to foreigners in the first, and in the second men and women offer bread and flowers to monstrous idols.

This reversal of roles from one plate to another places the gift-taking Spaniards in a position congruent to that of the monstrous idols in the scene of zemi worship. This homology appears more explicitly in a comparison of the three frontispieces of parts 4, 5, and 6, which form a triptych illustrating the three books of Benzoni's *History of the New World*. In the frontispiece for part 4, we can see the troupe of Arawaks dancing and singing in a bucolic setting, their idol standing on the mountain-top. The frontispiece for part 5 replaces the pagan idol by the Christian cross and the bucolic scene of the free Arawak gives way to a scene of Calvary. The cross replaces the idol, and the Indians, their backs marked by whip-lashings, serve the Spanish as beasts of burden. Finally, in the third volet of the triptych, the Indians excavate a mountain for mining.

The idol in the first frontispiece clearly differs from the zemis in the other plate: it is again a traditional portrayal of the devil, with horns, goat's feet, the face of an animal disguising the sex organs, and a pitchfork as attribute. At the foot of the mountain, symmetrically with the idol, a marine landscape shows the Spanish caravels off the American shores; on both banks we can identify the two main actors from the offertory rite with the zemis—the chief with his staff of authority and his turban, and the priest, wearing his chasuble and holding out, as an offering, this time to the foreign ships, the necklace and bunch of plants that he offers to the zemis in the later plate (illus. 6). The roles of the conquistadors are therefore interchangeable with the roles of the idols. The indigene stands in a position of gift-giver to a diabolical being, while his doom and degradation are imminent. His only transformation is anatomical.

The problem is thus to understand why the "monster" figure with pendulous breasts, among other elements, stands in a position of gift-taker in one case and of giver in the other. Let us extend the analysis to a new variant of the sagging breasts motif. It is this time not an attribute of Indian women, but of a supernatural being, the Christian devil (illus. 9). The theme of this plate is the myth of the Fall of Adam and Eve. The Tempter is represented as a hybrid child with sagging breasts, which is indeed one of the traditional images of the devil. By placing the biblical myth at the beginning of the collection, de Bry was also following a more recent tradition for travel books about America. Even the earliest ones frequently contained a woodcut on this theme. Its repeated recall remained closely associated with the enigma posed by the origin of the Indians and the biblical beliefs about man's origins. The graphic portrayal of the part-child, part-animal, part-man, part-woman devil, like the "idols" worshiped by the Indians, allows a deeper exploration of the network of relations that Europeans established at the time between the origin myth and the conquest of America.

In the picture of the Fall, we quickly recognize the same pattern as in the two previous instances of offerings by Indians: one from a generous Caribbean woman to the tyrannical Spaniard, the other from the Indians of Hispaniola to their demoniacal idols. Here a monstrous character offers a fruit, which is also a sign of imminent fall, that of Adam and Eve who will be driven out of the earthly paradise and, after them, all of mankind. As we move from an ambiguous human being to a nonhuman monster, the cosmological symbolism of body parts associated with food offerings will bring out the European perception of the Amerindian world and its conquest, in the light of the Judeo-Christian myth of the Fall. For this, we must examine more closely the transformation system which allows us to pass from one group of plates to another.

The Indian's Fall and the Expulsion from Eden

The Indian woman of Cumana province and the Tempter in paradise are interchangeable in two respects: first, through their common physical ambiguities that make them "monstrous" or anomalous creatures (that is, outside the norms considered "natural" at the time), and, second, as fruit-givers. As in the plates dealing with cannibalism, three codes remain constant: the anatomical, the sociological and the alimentary. Unlike the first plates, however, the code of physical appearance ties the sagging breast motif to parts of animal, hybrid bodies and to nonhuman figures; the food code changes its natural domain from meat to vegetable, and, on the sociological level, cannibalism gives way to the gift.

But before linking cannibalism with the fateful gift, leading, in Paradise as in the New World, to catastrophe, we must first establish that the Old Caribbean woman is indeed a combinatory variant of the devil in the Garden of Eden and that indeed the two plates are related through transformation. In fact, by means of homologies set up among the three codes, these transformations clarify the view of the Spanish conquest in light of the myth of the Fall and, conversely, the picture of the Spanish conquest shows a special interpretation for the origin myth thus transformed.

It should be stressed that the following interpretation of the conquest as a transformation of the myth of the Fall is not subjective. It

[handwritten margin notes: Devil → New World / Eden / Monsters]

follows from the system of equivalence between the various codes; the analysis helps us only to decipher them. If, in addition, it sometimes leads to one or more theories (one in particular concerning the relations between the sexes, exchange, and the gift), I make no claim that these theories were accepted as such at that time. On the contrary, I suggest that unlike what is expressed, written, and conscious at a given period, these graphic images contain a message not expressed by speech, one that is pictorially diffused and giving us the unconscious model of an ideology in the making.

A closer comparison of the two physically anomalous figures reveals significant differences. The monstrous appearance of the Caribbean woman sitting by her basket reveals a series of ambiguities. In terms of age, the facial wrinkles and the distortion of her breasts denote decrepitude and old age. By contrast, the powerful musculature, the perfectly formed body, and erect young manner of her walk mark the prime of life.[4] Sexually, her buxomness contrasts with the masculinity of her face, of the muscles of her arms and legs—an exclusive trait of the men in the collection—and her height. Further, the body distortions resulting from her ornaments and finery (the rings in her earlobes and nostrils) give her animal traits, perhaps canine traits in particular. This corresponds to traditional iconography in which Lust is shown with hanging breasts and dog's ears (pointed, if not hanging, as in this plate). Moreover, the verbal images in the text also suggest the canine appearance: the ears of a "hound," nostrils widened by the rings, and finally nails sharpened like claws. As for the Tempter with Adam and Eve, and half-animal and half-man, he has a serpent's tail, bat's wings, and claws on his hands. Sexually, he exhibits the same ambiguity: the breasts of an old woman and the viril musculature of the arms. As to age, the child's face contrasts with these masculine and feminine adult features and the connotation of old age suggested by the pendulous breasts.

From this point of view, the transformation of the monster from the devil in the earthly paradise into a woman in the New World is marked first of all by maximum differences in age and sex, in spite of the ambiguity they share in this respect. A monster with the face of a male child is transformed into another monster with an old woman's face. On the other hand, their respective hybridity (half-animal, half-human) proceeds either from natural, constituent elements (wings, serpent's tail, and appended animal parts) in the case of the demon, or, in the women's case, from cultural elements

perverted order

which "make her look like" an animal: the artificial distortion of the earlobe, greatly enlarged by the weight of the wooden rings worn by Caribbean women, the excessive separation of the nostrils for the same reason, and the nails sharpened to look like claws.

Our two ambiguous figures then both represent degraded and corrupted states, one of creation, the other of society. In the heart of the earthly paradise and thus of innocence, before the Fall of man, the monstrosity of the devil, in his graphic portrayal, is "natural" as it is marked by a confusion of several natural orders—of sexes and animal/human species. On the other hand, the animal ambiguity of the Caribbean woman comes from elements of ornamentation and is, then, "cultural," although it appears unnatural and barbarous and thus "outside nature" for the Europeans. As Montaigne observes with respect to the problem of monsters and strange customs that haunts the consciousness of the period: "We call contrary to Nature what comes about contrary to custom; nothing whatsoever exists which is not in accordance with her" (*Essays* 2:30). Whether this corruption springs from nature or culture, the two ambiguous, monstrous figures, the devil and the "savage woman," represent a perverted order [*la Dé-nature*] in the schema of moral categories linked to the Fall of man.

Considered sociologically, these two anomalous characters engaged in gift-giving stand in opposition to those who accept the fruit, who are "normal," sexually differentiated figures: In paradise a man and a woman, Adam and Eve; in the New World, men only, the conquistadors. They show the same attitude toward the gift: they accept it. But the role of the protagonists and the nature of the gift are transformed and reversed. In paradise, those who accept the gift are the autochthones facing an intruding devil; conversely, in the New World, those who accept are foreigners who later act as intruders and usurpers, facing a benevolent autochthone. On the other hand, the acceptance of the forbidden fruit leads in the first case to the expulsion of those who take it (Adam and Eve), and in the other, to the dispossession of the Indians, that is, the gift-giving autochthones, by forbidden visitors, who, if they legitimately accepted fruit from the old Caribbean woman, later behave improperly, as the whole text of the *History of the New World* shows, by acting like destructive tyrants instead of reciprocating. In this, our enigmatic figure of the old Caribbean woman, congruent with the demon through her physical anomalies and her offering, is at the same time congruent with the primordial couple in that, as an inhabitant of the New World, thus an autochthone, she stands in the position of a hostess greeting the Spanish intruders.

The New World conquest, then, reenacts the temptation that precedes man's Fall, but here the terms are reversed. The passage from one to the other takes the form of a chiasmus: the autochthonous gift-takers in the earthly paradise become the intruders in America; inversely, the intruding monster giver in Paradise becomes an autochthonous giver in the New World and their moral roles are transposed. A dual arrangement can be seen in this transformation. One involves the relations of benevolent or overly tolerant autochthones and brutal intruders, that is, politico-economic relations. In both cases, food-giving brings about the expulsion or plundering of the autochthones, whether givers or takers, which thus involves problems of territoriality and ownership. From this standpoint, the substitution of elements from one plate to the other is symmetrical and inverse: in one case, we find autochthonous givers, in the other, intruders as takers. On the other hand, when it comes to the sexual nature of the protagonists, the permutation between the two plates show a curious asymmetry. On the side of the food-receivers, we find a man and a woman (Adam and Eve) or only men (the conquistadors)—in both cases sexually differentiated figures. In this respect, the permutation Eden-America leads to eliminating woman from the gift cycle among the receivers, and thus involves sociological relations between sexes. As opposed to this, on the side of the food-givers, we find two sexually ambiguous beings with hybrid characteristics (the demon and the Caribbean woman), both *monsters with sagging breasts*. The differences between them bear upon their physical appearance (detail of ornamentation, body parts) and age (child/old woman), as can be seen in figure 6.1.

MARCEL MAUSS IN THE GARDEN OF EDEN

In two essays on Genesis, Edmund Leach (1969, 1970) has emphasized the relationship between the myth of the Fall and the Oedipus myth. Both deal with androgynous monsters—the Tempter and the Sphinx—and with the problem of man's autochthony and the primordial incest the two myths try to solve. Leach bases his argument upon an analysis of the biblical text itself from which he identifies a series of binary oppositions, of recurrences in several

	Eden ⟶	America
Offering (fruit)	forbidden *transgression* on the tree/unripe	permitted *legal acceptance* basket/ripe
Givers (anomalous)	demon child intruder	Indian woman old autochthone
Takers (normal)	man and woman (Adam and Eve) consanguines	men (conquistadors)

Figure 6.1   Transformations of the fateful gift.

episodes of Genesis and the relative positions of the figures to one another.

The situation here is different. The print picturing the biblical myth was not the starting point of the analysis. It became part of it only as a transformation of another plate dealing with the arrival of the Spanish in America. The hermaphroditic nature of the demon, which Leach deduces from the structural argument,[5] is, in our case, supported by iconography. But it is chiefly the moral, political, and sociological aspect of the myth that is reinterpreted and given new meaning by the people of the late sixteenth century, by projecting it into contemporary historical events. This interpretation expresses itself by ways that indirectly communicate a message both apparent and implied. The logic of the transformations between signs from one plate to another is only the means by which the message is expressed.

What do these transformations in fact say? As in the plates of the cannibals, they set up a system of correspondences between the cosmic world and the social world, the normal flow of time (aging of the anomalous figure and ripening of the fruit) and the social order. The age of the Caribbean woman by contrast with the Tempter first accompanies a reversal in the respective positions of the two figures from a socio-political viewpoint. The child-faced demon is intruder, the old Caribbean woman a generous autochthone. From paradise, to the New World, we actually move from the transgression of a taboo to a licit gift of fruit legitimately possessed, from an Indian woman to the foreigners. This substitution also affects the fruit offering in the food code. In paradise, the fruits of temptation are offered for eating from the tree; in the New World they are presented in a basket. This distinction remains strongly marked in our culture by the moral association of eating fruit from a tree with the eating of forbidden fruit or transgressing a taboo; hence the frequent connotation of "green" or unripe fruit [in French, the unripe corn, *le blé en herbe*, stands in opposition to the sheaf of corn, *le blé en gerbe*]. On the contrary, the image of the fruit basket connotes ripeness and is here associated with the generous gift of something legitimately possessed. Structurally, then, although we cannot see if the fruit on the tree is green or ripe, the distinction between fruit on the tree and the basket of fruit may be schematized by an unripe/ripe opposition. All that matters is the temporal (and cultural) difference between fruit still on the tree and the fruit offered in a basket, implying a selection of the ripest and most beautiful fruits, perfect for eating. Thus by moving from mythic times before the Fall to the historic time of the Spanish conquest, the presence of the anomalous figure reverses the consequences of the Fall. With a new network of relations between the social world and the cosmic world as intermediary, the transformation from one variant to the other sets up a congruence between the two orders: we shift from the offering of the usurping demon, giver of forbidden fruit, to the foreigner, and this double transformation on the sociopolitical level follows the normal flow of time on the level of the cosmic order: maturation of the fruit, aging of the giver.

In light of these transformations, the New World, at the time of the Spanish conquest, appears as still untouched by the consequences of the Fall, in a state of original innocence. As Benzoni's *History of the New World* shows, the responsibility for bringing original sin to the New World falls on the Spanish, who played the role of the devil, not a tempter this time, but an ungrateful figure: in response to an innocent and generous gift, the Spanish come as intruders and provoke the Indians' ruin, their fall from grace. Their fall, unlike the fall of the first man and woman, is expressed not as an expulsion but as the usurpation of their goods and their lands, and as their destruction.

The transformations of the gift-takers in the two situations (Adam and Eve on the one hand, the Spaniards on the other) go still further. They also involve the relations between the sexes and the rules governing them by means of the symbolism of the gift of fruit. The interdiction that strikes the fruit of the Tree of Knowledge is associated with the transgression of a sexual taboo in the Bible. At first Adam and Eve live in ignorance of sexuality. It is only after eating the forbidden fruit that Adam "sees" Eve's nudity and they both hide their nudity with leaves, in keeping with a common theme in Christian iconography. The sociological relation between Adam and Eve is ambiguous in the extreme. As the first human beings, without parents in this world, they were created from the same flesh, Eve from one of Adam's ribs. According to our social conventions and those of the Renaissance, this extraordinary relation of the whole to the part would make their sexual union an incestuous relation between consanguines, equivalent to incest between brother and sister. Edmund Leach uses these terms to summarize the paradox that the myth of original sin, like that of Oedipus, tries to solve: "How was it in the beginning? If our first parents were persons of two kinds, what was the other kind? But if they were both of our kind, then their relations must have been incestuous and we are all born in sin" (1969, p. 10).

Christian theology, and particularly scholastic philosophy after Aquinas, has been sensitive to this problem. The interpretation given by Aquinas of Eve's creation emphasizes the fact that God creates her from one of Adam's ribs in order to show that "there should be a social relation between them" (question 92 [1]), an interpretation that rejects the idea that their relations are incestuous.

If the forbidden fruit is indeed a metaphor for the incest taboo, conversely, the transformation of the illicit offering into a generous gift made by an autochthone to the foreigners implies permissible sexual relations between Indian women and Spaniards. From this transformational system it follows, in fact, that the autochthone may legitimately be in a position of giver (the old Caribbean woman) in relation to foreigners (Spaniards), but not of taker (Adam and Eve); conversely, the foreigner must not give what does not belong to him as does the hermaphroditic devil, but may receive, as do the Spaniards. According to whether they sin against the rules or respect them, those who receive are either a man and a woman with ambiguous sociological relations over which hovers an incest taboo, or simply men facing an alien woman.

On the other hand, as the literary and iconographic context of the Caribbean variant condemns the Spanish, not because they accept the Indians' gift, but because as guests they behave abusively, rendering bad for good, the transformational system also supposes that the lawful, generous gift entails an obligation to return, which is precisely the principle of Mauss's concept of reciprocity.[6] By a metaphoric association between a fruit offering and a sexual relation, this principle of reciprocity is set up both at the level of goods and at the level of women. Nor should we forget that at the time in Europe, any prescription of sexual relations between men and women brought with it a de facto prescription of marriage, for any sexual relation outside marriage was prohibited both by religion and by social convention. Thus it implicitly included marriage. Hence the confusion often decried by ethnologists between incest prohibition, which bears on sexual relations, and exogamy, which bears on marriage. Be that as it may, this principle of reciprocity, in our case, conceives miscegenation as permissible, and alliance, whether purely sexual or sociological, is set up structurally as the reverse of the prohibition of incest between Adam and Eve. Thus these new transformations of the motif of the Indian woman with the sagging breasts project an image of the Spanish conquest into the mythic past before man's Fall, a past in which the relations with the Indians, still untouched by original sin, might have been idyllic, if . . . This accusatory "if" makes the Spanish to blame for the New World's loss of innocence. As we shall see in the next chapter, with new variants of the motif, the ground is laid for justifying the later relations between Indians and their Protestant conquerors.

Moreover, a dialectic appears between the flow of time, evil, and the relations between the sexes (the problem of the hermaphrodite and the exchange of women). Ethnographic literature brings out numerous examples of this triple connection, linked with several forms of ritual. Rigby's study (1968) of purification rites among the Gogo will lead us in a later chapter to abandon the European beliefs temporarily in order to examine European behavior toward the Indians. At present, we shall compare these plates of the "fateful gift" with the plates of cannibalism, as it is now possible to see the relations between them.

FROM OBLATION TO HOLOCAUST

The paradigmatic ensemble obtained by a system of transformations linking the Caribbean variant with the myth of the Fall takes up point by point a segment of the chain in which the Tupinambá variant is incorporated and which stands in opposition to it. The substitution of the offer of fruit on the tree for the basket of ripe fruit repeats a type of difference seen earlier in the scenes of cannibalism between flesh grilled for eating and the juices that drip from it. That is, the different degrees of ripeness, a natural process, in the *offering* of fruits (vegetable food) recall the different degrees of cooking, a cultural process, in the *consumption* of human flesh (meat food). Then too, the shift from vegetable food to meat food involves the change from offering to consuming, thus leading us back to the problem of evil and the Fall. The theological aspect of the sin involved in cannibalism will thus be clarified in the light of the myth of the original sin and Spanish conquest.

In the scenes of cannibalism, the differential function of the analyzed iconographic motif consisted in making a distinction, shocking from the theological viewpoint, between various degrees of corruption and evil in the consumption of human flesh. This distinction became clearer within a system of correspondences between microcosm and macrocosm. The old women, in their role of vampires, were placed at the end of a long syntagmatic chain where the age and sex of the cannibals was systematically organized according to the parts of the body that were eaten. Thus cannibalism appeared as a sort of antimatter, a phenomenon leading ineluctably, by a slow gradation of small differences, toward the dissolution of the cosmic and social world.

The European vision of cannibalism created by this system of correspondences seemed totally to abandon the Christian theology of sins in favor of old cosmologies, for, unless one were as irreverent as Voltaire, who could ask whether it is better to eat your man boiled or roasted? Considering that the Protestant public viewed the Spanish conquest as a transformation of the myth of the Fall, it is easier to understand how ancient cosmologies and Protestant theories weave into the Protestant perception of cannibalism.

Let us compare the Eden–America transformation with the sequence of the cannibal feast. The variants dealing with offerings provide a choice between what is permitted and what is forbidden, in other words, between the rule and the lapse from it (the transgression of a taboo). This distinction between types of offerings corresponds, on the theological level, to the choice implicit in the act of temptation. Two monsters, one of them, the Caribbean, innocent, the other, the devil, guilty, represent the tempters. In the

Tupinambá variant, on the contrary, there is neither choice nor temptation, but simply different degrees of corruption in the perpetration of evil.

These two positions, before and after the lapse (speaking theologically), correspond, on the level of the alimentary code, to an opposition between a natural process and a cultural process implicit in the opposition separating the maturation of fruit from the cooking of meat:

$$\text{T1} \quad \begin{array}{c} \text{maturation of fruit} \\ \text{natural process} \end{array} \quad \longleftrightarrow \quad \text{T2} \quad \begin{array}{c} \text{cooking of meat} \\ \text{cultural process} \end{array}$$

Between the two groups, the ages of the figures, tempters and consumers, are reversed:

(a) T1   (unripe → ripe)   ≡ (childhood → old age)
(b) T2   (raw → cooked)   ≡ (old age → youth)

In the first transformation, the maturation of fruit, a shift from forbidden to permissible corresponds to a shift from childhood to old age, that is, to the flow of time. In the second, where evildoing occurs through cooking, that is, culturally, the flow of time is reversed: the transformation from the most raw to the most cooked is like the return from old age to youth, that is, a reversal of the cosmic order. The flow of time (youth → old age) is congruent with a "denaturalizaton" and a deculturalization of the old "monster" women with the sagging breasts in contrast to the beautiful, naked, young cannibal women devoid of ambiguity.

This reversal reflects a specifically Protestant interpretation of the consequences of original sin. In fact, for the Protestants—Calvinists and Lutherans—nature herself has been corrupted in her essence by the Fall; contrary to Catholic theology, for which original sin simply robbed man of the preternatural gifts God granted him at the Creation but did not spoil his nature, which remains unchanged, that is, weak. Against this Catholic credo, Luther claims that "those who say that the natural forces remained intact after the Fall speak as philosophers, impiously, contrary to theology.... Also those who maintain that man is capable of choosing between good and evil or life and death, and so on. All those who speak in this way fail to understand what man is and know not of what they speak" (*Disputatio de homine,* Suess 1969, pp. 102, 103).

In the same vein, Calvin writes, "By the eternal counsels of God, it came to pass that Adam fell from the normal state of his nature, and by his fall swept all his posterity in a just condemnation to eternal death. The difference between the just and the damned depends on this same decree, because God has embraced some for their salvation and has destined others to eternal destruction" ("Articuli de praedestinatione," in Boisset 1964, p. 135). This interpretation of the Fall profoundly marks the Protestants' attitude toward the newly discovered peoples. In a system where man appears as essentially corrupt in his very nature, the distinction between different degrees of corruption allowed Protestant colonists (as in the case of the English Puritans in North America) politically to take the highest place in the hierarchy of men and thus to justify the dispossession of the Indians, marked with the sign of the damned. Margaret Hodgen summarizes their attitude on the subject thus: "every man is corrupt, but the Indian far more so." And Luther writes: "Meanwhile, man is in sin, and day by day he is further justified or tainted."

The distinction between two degrees of sin in cannibalism that appeared shocking at first becomes more understandable. But Protestant theology, which accounts for the cultural differences between Europeans and Indians by attributing "corrupt" and "savage" manners to the Indians, finds itself in contradiction with the image of the Indian as martyr of the Spanish tyranny, this view being dictated not by theology but by historical and political realities experienced by the Protestants in European countries. Sometimes the Indian is likened to the Protestants, martyrs of the Spanish occupation (of the Netherlands, in particular), who receive from the autochthones but give them nothing but blows and tortures in exchange; sometimes he is demoted in the scale of beings to the rank of "monster," or at least a variant of the medieval monster. The image of the anomalous Indian with her anatomical and cultural ambiguities is a mediator between these two interpretations of the Amerindian world.

The reappearance of the motif in three plates executed at different periods, of dissimliar subjects and contexts, shows that they all partake of the same group of transformations. These three representations in fact explain the cause of three forms of "fall" or "regression" of which the primordial couple and the Amerindians are successively victims. The causes for these three forms of fall are themselves in a relation of transformation. The expulsion of Adam and Eve takes place because they accept fruit from a stranger; the plundering of the Caribbeans, because they give fruit to a foreigner; the cultural regression of the Tupinambá, because they eat the stranger.

The first two narratives reverse the poles of the gift that provokes the Fall, but in both cases, the autochthone is the stranger's victim for having been too benevolent toward him. In the third, on the contrary, regression comes from an opposite, aggressive, attitude toward the foreigner: using him as food, as the Tupinambá do, who eat their prisoners of war. From this standpoint, cannibalism appears as the inverse of food prestation. In the plates of the *gift*, an offering of fruits brings about the expulsion of the autochthones; in those of Tupinambá cannibalism, the consumption of human flesh depends on the capture of the stranger. The capture of the enemy, the inverse of the expulsion of the autochthone, is the condition for the act provoking the native's degeneration, that is, for cannibalism. Now, in subsequent plates of the de Bry collection (part 9), new variants of the savage woman related not to the consumption of human flesh but to an offering, involve at the same time the capture of a stranger.

7   *Fuegian Variants*

THE FIERCE INHABITANTS OF TIERRA DEL FUEGO

Part 9 of the *Great Voyages* contains three series of engravings corresponding to three different texts. The first text is a work by José de Acosta, a Spanish Jesuit, called *Historia natural y moral de las Indias*, and the first fourteen illustrations of this volume relate to it. They show the customs, especially the religious customs, of the Indians of Mexico and Peru and provide a survey of animal life and resources in the Andes as well as an outline of the legendary story of the Aztecs. No women are portrayed in them.

The two other texts in this volume concern Dutch expeditions. First, Sebald de Weert's and Simon de Cordes's voyages in the regions around the Strait of Magellan and Tierra del Fuego, that is, among the coastal nomads of the tip of South America, between 1598 and 1600. With Olivier de Noort's circumnavigations around the world (1598–1601), the third narrative takes us to the same parts of America, but then moves on along the Chilean coast where the Araucanians farm and raise llamas, and beyond South America on to the Pacific islands as far as Borneo and Japan.

The peoples met by the Dutch explorers in the archipelago of the Strait of Magellan were probably the Alacaluf and perhaps also the Chono, to the north. The Yahgan were not discovered until a few years later, in 1624, by Jacques Lhermite. They appear with quite different features in part 13, which illustrates Lhermite's voyage.

The engravings portray the Fuegians[1] with a number of cultural traits of the coastal tribes of the "marginal" regions. Most likely, the woodcuts in the Dutch original texts, which inspired the de Brys, were drawn after sketches made from life. In particular, boats shaped like Venetian gondolas were common to the Chono, the Alacaluf, and the Yahgan, that is, to all the coastal tribes in the region of the Strait. The Alalcaluf used a harpoon for hunting sea lions like the harpoon held by one of the figures on the map of Tierra del Fuego (illus. 11 and 12). Both men and women wear an animal skin cape on their shoulders, a garment typical of these tribes.

On the illustrated map of Tierra del Fuego and of the Strait we see specimens of plant life as well as two native couples referred to as the "fierce inhabitants of the place" (illustrations 11 and 12). We recognize variants of our heroine in the two women portrayed. They reappear in several other plates, including the frontispiece, so that, in this group of variants, the anatomical particularity whose traces and transformations we are following appears to be the norm, typical of the appearance of the Fuegian women and not an isolated case.

But many other elements distinguish them from the variants analyzed in the preceding chapters. Those figures were of two types: "supernatural" or fantastic beings—the biblical devil and the Arawak idol, and savage women. The savage women, Tupinambá or Carribean, unlike the young and healthy Fuegians, were old and hideous. Moreover, the Caribbean woman showed hybird characteristics expressed partly by deformities due to cultural elements such as ornaments, characteristics lacking in the old cannibal women who displayed only an unattractive, but purely human, nudity. The Tierra del Fuego variants are different. Young and without animal ambiguity, their cropped hairstyle relates them to the little-boy aspect of the Tempter. Like the Caribbean variant, they wear cultural elements (clothing, ornaments, hairstyles), but unlike her they have no hybrid traits though they retain her sexually ambiguous character.

Are such differences significant? And especially, should we link these new Indians to the preceding group simply by the index of the shape of their breasts, which, in fact, could be considered as a realistic, nonidealized view of female nudity? As we have shown, this anatomical element is not monstrous in itself. It characterizes a figure of mythic or symbolic value which is inserted in a group of graphic narratives making up a system. Through this system we can once again perceive, behind the image of the conquest of Indians, their cannibalism, and their idolatry, the drama of the Fall of man and his regression in a perspective disclosing the Protestant ethic.

Certain constants now appear to govern these transformations brought about by the metamorphoses of the leitmotif figure. The figure may change either in age, going from young to old, or in physical make-up. In this case, it is either purely human, like the old cannibal women, or hybrid, participating in both man and animal. Their hybridity may be natural, like the devil with the serpent's tail, or cultural, like the Caribbean woman whose ears are artificially distorted. The transformations from one variant to the other are, then, governed by the following principle: if the anomalous figure changes in age, its specific (human or hybrid) nature does not change; inversely, if the specific nature of the figure changes, its age remains unchanged.[2]

From the gluttonous cannibal women to the generous Carribean woman of the same age, we shift from human to hybrid:

(old → old) ⟷ (human → hybrid)

From this gift to the first fateful gift, made by the devil in the earthly paradise, the transformation is:

(old → young) ⟷ (hybird → hybrid)

From this, we can deduce a third possibility of which we have seen no examples as yet and according to which

(young → young) ⟷ (hybrid → human)

The new variants of the figure appearing in part 9 happen to correspond to this possibility and verify this rule of transformation.

THE WOMAN WITH THE SHELL NECKLACE

Variant A: The Mother and the Raw Bird (illus. 10)

In the Strait of Magellan, Sebald de Weert and his crew came across a woman whose appearance and manners puzzled them. They captured her. The plate shows the Dutch watching her as she gives an unplucked bird to her two children to eat. One of them, who bites into the bird's neck, has the same position and attitude as one of the young Tupinambá who chews a bit of human viscera his mother gives him. In the background, the scene reproduces the disembarkation of the Dutch. They chase the natives—men, women, and children—who flee over the rocks along the shore at their approach.

Here again we find two food-receivers related to each other as are Adam and Eve, who received the apple from the devil. Like the first man and woman, the Fuegian's two children are consanguines, brother and sister, in fact and not through a miraculous act of creation. But the sociological relations linking the giver to the taker have changed from the most distant (between the intrusive devil and the first men) to the closest kinship relations (between mother and children). This sociological reversal is coupled with a radical transformation in the giver's physical appearance. Her portrayal more or less matches Sebald de Weert's description: "She was of medium height and ruddy complexion, with a great sagging bosom and a wild air; her hair was cut just above her ears; she wore snail shells around her neck and on her back a skin of sea calf attached by a gut string. The rest of her body was naked; her breasts sagged; her mouth was large and her nails were very long" (Renneville 1725, p. 330).[3]

In spite of her sagging breasts, this young captive does not look at all monstrous in the engraving. Her costume and hairstyle identify her as an inhabitant of Tierra del Fuego. If we compare her physically to the devil in the earthly paradise, that other giver of food to two siblings, her appearance is young and slightly ambiguous sexually. Both have the face of a young boy. On the other hand, she lacks its hybrid character. On the anatomical level, this transformation between the figures of the two givers corresponds to the operation deduced earlier:

$$(\text{young} \rightarrow \text{young}) \longleftrightarrow (\text{hybrid} \rightarrow \text{human})$$

Identical to the devil in age, the Fuegian retains an ambiguous aspect with androgynous connotation but loses the elements of animal monstrosity.

She derives her sexual ambiguity from her cropped hair, a cultural element. The other Indian women wear their hair long, floating over their shoulders or drawn into a coil. In this, they clearly contrast with the men in each group represented, whether the men's hair is cut in a "cock's comb" like the Virginian Algonquian, drawn up in a chignon like the Timucua, shaven, as certain Peruvian types in part 6, or finally, tonsured like the Tupinambá. With the appearance of the Fuegian women in part 9, the masculine and feminine poles are reversed in terms of hairstyle, with the men's hair worn long and loose and the women's cut short.

As to the shape of her legs and heels, the only anatomical anomaly, though quite unobstrusive, it may actually correspond to a peculiarity of the seafaring nomads of this coastal region, accustomed to walking barefoot over the rocks in search of shells. A contemporary ethnologist (J. Emperaire) who has observed the peoples of Tierra del Fuego also notes this physical trait: "Their feet are short and wide, with a salient instep and a prominent heel; the toes are curled under, short and spread out, with a big toe set apart that can, if necessary, be used for grasping. The arch of the foot is flat, which gives the Indian his characteristic kind of walk" (Emperaire 1955, p. 110).

Even more than her physical appearance, the woman's culinary habits strike the Dutch explorers on the de Weert expedition: "As she would not eat cooked meat, we gave her the birds that were in the boat . . . and having plucked its longest feathers, she opened the birds with clam shells, first scraping behind the right wing, then above the stomach and between the legs. Then she emptied the gizzard, turned it inside out, scratched the inside with twigs two or three times, and after heating it a bit, ate it" (Renneville 1725, p. 320).

This Fuegian custom of eating raw meat is reported by several explorers, but it seems to be an inaccurate representation of the facts. The peoples of the archipelago of the Strait eat meat and fish "barely" cooked, after putting them briefly into the fire; indeed, this is done by the young mother described by Heynes, the author of this account, for, as he says, she eats it "after heating it a bit." Even now, according to Emperaire, the Indians of these regions "do not eat meat absolutely raw; it is always warmed and, at least on the outside, begins to cook" (Emperaire 1955, p. 142).

Nonetheless, for the Dutch, the spectacle of this meal suggests barbarous and bloody manners: "She tore the rest of the bird into pieces with her teeth, biting into it so that the blood ran down her breasts. The children did the same, and ate the birds raw. One of them was a four-year-old girl, the other was not more than six months old, but he already had a number of teeth and could walk by himself. They remained quite serious while they ate, and the woman showed not the slightest smile in spite of the sailors' outbursts of laughter" (Renneville 1725, p. 321).

The nature of the food eaten here enlarges the semantic field of the offering. The raw bird, being flesh, brings us back to the old cannibal women. In the first group of plates, the distinction between vegetable food and animal food (human flesh) corresponds to an opposition between a food offered and another food consumed by the figure. Here, however, the bird is offered by the woman with the sagging breasts and is consumed by her children. What has happened?

The woman gives meat and not fruit: this act is incorporated into a sociological relation whose nature has changed, for, as an act of nurturing, it is evidence of maternal love and not a prestation of food from one stranger to another; it occurs, moreover, after the invading foreigners have captured the woman; finally, this giver who feeds her offspring has herself refused the food, overcooked for her taste, offered her by the invaders: "as she would not eat cooked meat, we gave her the birds that were in the boat" (Renneville, 1725, p. 320).

In this sequence of events we again find the reversal noted in the plate of the cannibal women. In the plates showing a vegetarian diet, prestation of food offered to strangers entails the expulsion or subjection of the autochthones. In the group of plates showing a meat diet, on the contrary, the capture of the prisoner of war or the capture of the autochthones by the Europeans is followed either by the anthropophagic consumption of the prisoner, or by food-sharing among family members.

A second Fuegian variant showing the same transformation
$$(\text{young} \rightarrow \text{young}) \longleftrightarrow (\text{hybrid} \rightarrow \text{human})$$
introduces a new possibility into the system of offerings. A meat food (fish) is again offered by a native figure, a new variant of the woman with the sagging breasts, but the food is refused.

Variant B: The Servant Woman with the Fish Platter

Recognizable by her cropped hair, typical nudity, and the animal-skin cape that hangs down her back and is attached at the neck by a necklace of shells, this figure also exhibits the bowing of the legs and the deformation of the heel noted in variant A (illus. 13). Yet she seems even younger and more slender than in variant A, with the face of a young boy. She is holding a square container in which she carries some fish she has just served to Captain de Weert, entertained by an indigene "king."

This plate brings together several episodes of the narrative, which the caption below the engraving summarizes with several changes. First of all, the meal does not take place among Indians, but somewhere in Guinea, on the route between Rotterdam and the Strait of Magellan, on 9 November 1598, according to the Dutch ship's log. Although the narrator stresses the fact that they are "Negroes" and even tells that the king ties to hide his "blackness" by powdering his face with ashes (ibid.), nonetheless, from the viewpoint of graphic representation, this plate belongs with the iconography of the Amerindian. In fact, none of the figures in these two plates (9:A18 and 19) has Negroid traits. The fish-server, described above, is no different from the other Fuegians in this volume, either physically or in her dress, except for a few variations in details. Another female figure who will be described later (variant C), borrows her features from the old women of the Tupinambá cannibals. Finally, the caption for the engraving presents these figures as "Indians": "via *ab Indiis* obsessa, nolens volens apud barbaros pernoctare coactus est" (author's italics). Iconographically, then, the fish-server constitutes a "Fuegian variant" of the savage women.

Here is the series of events as it is told and shown in these two plates. After holding conversation with the king and indicating, through an interpreter, that the Dutch have come to trade with the Guineans, de Weert is led by the king into his palace, "which was a little less attractive than the stables we have for our cows" (Renneville 1725, p. 287). There, the king gives the captain a goat and some bananas in exchange for a few pieces of canvas and iron.

The de Brys draw their inspiration for this scene from a woodcut of the original edition of the Dutch text, but they place it in the background of the events that follow. The different segments of this plate must be read in the following order:

1. In the background, to the left, the scene of exchange between the king and the Dutch captain. The captain unrolls the canvas he is giving in exchange for the goat.

2. The frugal meal: the servant (in the Latin caption) or the king's wife (in the text by Heynes) brings some smoked fish "of which the king ate moderately and the captain yet more moderately, being unfamiliar with these kinds of dishes" (Renneville 1725, p. 287). The captain, "who had not eaten for a day and a half" (ibid.), is still hungry and takes offense: "This moderation displeased S. de Weert and surprised him all the more, for seeing that the king was physically strong, healthy, and better fit than one usually finds among those who live with abundance and who have all sorts of food" (ibid.).

Once the platter is removed, de Weert calls for some provisions to be brought from his boat: "a bit of bread, a little smoked meat, and some cheeese" (Renneville 1725, p. 287) and a bottle of Spanish wine that he offers his parsimonious host. Unlike the captain who disdains the food offered him, the king does great honor to the captain's food; so much so that having overdrunk and overeaten, he must retire to his room to sleep.

3. In the background, to the right, the Dutch are prevented from leaving the city. While the king sleeps, they want to look around, but when, at nightfall, they prepare to go back to their launches, they find their way barred by "a great troop of blacks, armed with bows and arrows" (Renneville 1725, p. 288).

When de Weert asks them the reason for their conduct, they tell him that one of his men has committed some violence in the town; but for the narrator this is only a pretext, and in reality they were incited by the fear that their king or they themselves might be carried away by the Europeans, a common practice on what is called the "Slave Coast" (located to the north of this region, if the bearings given in the text are accurate), and which these Guineans had quite likely already experienced. Regardless of the cause of the incident, we find the following logical sequence in the series of events portrayed in this engraving: for refusing the food offered by a welcoming native, the foreigner becomes the captive of his hosts. The capture of the foreigner appears to be the consequence of refusing and not of accepting the food offered. Thus the Dutch captain's adventure bears a relationship of transformation with the plate portraying the myth of the Fall. In the plate depicting the Fall, Adam and Eve are expelled from paradise for having accepted a fruit offering from an intruder, the devil, an ambiguous being.

Considering the physical appearance of the woman who gives, this variation reflects the transformation

$$(\text{young} \rightarrow \text{young}) \longleftrightarrow (\text{hybrid} \rightarrow \text{human})$$

Moreover, when the cause of the Fall changes from expulsion to capture, when the acceptance of food becomes refusal of food, the nature of the food also changes: the vegetable becomes meat, and the rawness (short of maturity) of the unripe fruit is replaced by the cookedness (beyond cooking) of the smoked fish. The first is not ripe enough, the other overcooked or too dried out, at least for the captain's taste.[4]

The consequences of the refusal are completed by yet another event following the capture of the Dutch. The narrative proceeds to describe an unexpected encounter, which, transcribed in the foreground of this plate, shows in the very middle of the scene a new variant of the woman with sagging breasts.

Variant C: The Horrid Old Woman and Pandora's Box

The following day the captain left the house in which the king's soldiers had kept him confined (illus. 14). A "horrid old woman," entirely naked, "with a fierce and meancing air," came up to him. She resembled the old Caribbean woman, although the Caribbean woman wore ornaments and this old hag, like the old cannibal women, was completely lacking in cultural elements. She raised the lid of a round box and held it out to the Dutch captain. According to the caption the box contained ashes, and the strange old woman, after circling three times round the Dutchman, knocked three times on the lid, sending ashes flying in all directions and covering de Weert's clothing with them.

Why does the hideous image of the old cannibal women of part 3 reappear here, nine years later, beside the dwarf king of Guinea and the Fuegian woman with the cape?

It is hard to know what rite the Guinean woman is performing with respect to the foreigner, whether curse, insult, or exorcism, or perhaps simply a joke, because, according to the narrator, "the captain and the blacks laughed about it and made fun of it" (Renneville 1725, p. 290). The same element of ridicule reminds us of the episode of the raw bird eaten by the mother and her children: "They remained quite serious while they ate, and the woman showed not the slightest smile in spite of the sailors' outbursts of laughter" (ibid., p. 321).

The text, however, gives a quite different description of the box containing the ashes: "She carried a leather-covered container which was loosely held together by leather gussets and could be pulled open and shut" (Renneville 1725, p. 290). Instead of this purse-shaped container, the illustrators substitute a round box whose lid is lifted by the woman who carries it. This same interpretation appears in the caption rewritten to suit the engraving. Thus it seems that the transformation of the box is brought about by the common iconographic motif of Pandora's box from which escape all the evils of mankind. In fact the text does not say that the woman raised the lid, but that, turning three times around the captain, "she knocked on the leather of the box from which flew ashes or dust that settled on the body of de Weert" (ibid.). Moreover, this episode does not appear in the model which inspired the de Brys' depiction of this landing in Guinea.

Now, as we know from Dora and Erwin Panofsky (1962), the sixteenth century experienced a revival of iconographic and literary interest in the old myth of Pandora, after undergoing several transformations. Throughout Europe, the antique vase (*pythos*) containing all of mankind's ills gave way to the familiar "box" (*pyxis* or *dolium*) whose lid Pandora, by analogy with Psyche, imprudently raised. At the same time, the parallel drawn in the Middle Ages between the ancient myth of Pandora and the Christian myth of Eve shows up again: like Pandora, Eve is the involuntary cause of the ills afflicting humanity, and, like her, the first woman. Oddly enough, certain medieval mythographers, Boccaccio in particular, made Pandora into a hermaphrodite.

Panofsky attributes to Eramus the revival of the ancient Pandora myth under the adage, "Gifts from enemies are not gifts." This moral assigned to the myth agrees with the moral of the gesture made by the grimacing old woman as she bars the captain's way. The box she holds out to him replaces the food offered to the foreigner by the other variants of the figure, and thus it appears as an antifood, for it holds ashes, just as Pandora's box holds the ills that will befall humanity. Moreover, the act of casting ashes on someone could, at that time, be interpreted as a spell. In the beginning, scattering ashes over the fields or animals was considered to be a fertility charm, but after the Church's prohibition of performing this "pagan" rite, this practice was considered maleficent. It was said to be "pour faire manquer les fruits de la terre" ["to make the fruits of the earth fail] (Murray 1963, p. 160).

Between the young servant with the cape whose offering is rejected, and this hideous old woman, shorn of every cultural ornament, casting ashes on the captive guest, we again confirm the relation

$$(\text{young} \rightarrow \text{old}) \longleftrightarrow (\text{human} \rightarrow \text{human})$$

This transformation occurs through a deculturalization in terms of costume.

The opposition set up between the food offered and the ashes cast on the guest, and act that might be considered a defilement, works by a shift from the smoked (fish) to the burned (ashes), that is, progressively, to the extreme limit of cooking. A dialectic of defilement thus opposes two types of antifood, one connoted by the moist—human blood and fat dripping from the grill—on the near side of cooking and thus of culture, and the other, connoted by the dry, the ash, on the far side of culture by excessive cooking; on one side, the blood collected from the prisoner's dismembered body and ingested by the old woman variant of the savage, on the other, the ashes cast by the same figure over a live captive.

Thus these plates indeed form a cycle which, begun with a series of food offerings between foreigners, closes with a curse, consisting in covering with antifood a bad-mannered guest, a foreigner guilty of refusing a meal too frugal for his taste. This cycle systematically uses three different codes:

1. An anatomical code having as its central figure a being recognizable by its sagging bosom and who assumes the traits, in turn, of a grimacing old woman, of a hybrid being composed of various animal species, or of Indian women adorned with exotic ornaments.

2. The second, of a politico–economic or sociological order, introduces relations between hosts and guests, foreigners and autochthones, and, using the language of alliance and kinship, evokes problems raised by the conquest and colonization of the Amerindians.

3. Finally, a food code, expressed by different type of food (fruit, human blood, bird, fish), marked on the culinary level according to its degree of maturity or cooking.

Strangely enough, among the Fuegian variants in part 9 of the *Great Voyages* a last one lacks the food code. Though the anatomical and sociological elements persist, no food is offered or eaten in the engravings in which she appears. Before approaching the problem confronting us in this aberrant case, let us survey this first series of plates, and show the relations among these three codes. To prove the homology of the three codes, the method will follow that presented by Levi-Strauss in *From Honey to Ashes* (1973, pp. 267–95). I shall first relate the food code to the sociological code and then to the anatomical code, and finally, the anatomical code to the sociological code. In the process, we shall be led to introduce cosmological notions of the alchemists, and other theological and political notions more specifically attached to the Protestant world; notions without which the underlying structures of the graphic representations would remain a dead letter or a pure assemblage devoid of meaning.

THE NONFLAMMABLE WORLD OF BLOOD AND ASHES

The Indian woman with the sagging breasts has thus far belonged to a sequence in which a food is exchanged, refused, or eaten, so that the initial code, the anatomical one, has always been linked with a food code. These foods govern a third code, that of sociological relations between Indians and Europeans. Before relating these three codes to one another, we must examine the internal organization of the food code including the latest variant. Although this new one ends the list of foods with an antifood (ashes), it nevertheless fits in the food code through the culinary category of the burned.

If we consider the elements of the food code—fruit, human blood, bird, fish, and ash—we see that ashes and human blood clearly differ from fruit, bird, and fish. These represent botanical or zoological species, whereas blood and ashes are part of a whole: the juices dripping from the grill (blood and fat) are the residue or waste of the species man, and ashes the residue of undetermined species, as in the process of burning they lose their properties and become inorganic, like a substance from the mineral kingdom. Thus, as cooking waste or residue, the juices dripping from the cannibal's grill are akin to ashes. Human blood and ashes are nonfoods, food taboos, and belong to a diet we may call "excremental," in keeping with its sixteenth-century meaning of "that which is rejected."[1] D'Aubigné uses it in this sense when he evokes scenes of cannibalism during the religious wars in France:

> In vain you fear that the devoured flesh
> will be disputed: nature creates
> no confusion among the elements
> she can distinguish in the *excremens*
> the order that is hers . . .
>
> [*Tragiques* 7:347–51]

This classification implicit in the recurring sagging breasts motif emphasizes the ambiguous and tabooed character of cannibalism. Objectively, human flesh and blood participate in organic substance, and cannibalism implies a meat diet. This fact was unacceptable to the moral conscience of people who reduced anthropophagy to the rank of "abominations" cast out of both nature and culture. Similar to ashes in its character as cooking waste, the juices of human flesh are also reduced to the inorganic mineral kingdom. Thus the differentiating function of the motif of the sagging breasts among the cannibal women becomes clearer as well as the fact that the connotation "licking one's fingers dripping with juices," and not that of biting into human flesh, brings about its presence. The metaphorical assimilation of blood to the mineral kingdom also appears in other domains in the sixteenth century. The alchemists call blood "the mineral spirit in metals, principally in the sun, the moon, and mercury."[2]

The food code is based on five elements (fruit, bird, fish, human blood, and ashes) related to the figure with the sagging breasts. The five elements form a three-part classification in terms of food diets (fruit, meat, and excrement) and natural kingdoms (vegetable, animal, and mineral). Other constants can be added: first, the way food is prepared for consumption. Each element is presented in a certain stage of maturation or cooking (natural or cultural process): raw/smoked; rotten/burned. Second, the various foods come from different kinds of activity—the fruits from gathering, the bird from hunting, the fish from fishing, and the waste from war, for Tupinambá cannibalism is practiced on the prisoner-of-war, and the ashes cast on the foreigner previously taken prisoner mark aggressive relations toward him.

The problem is now to see how these *armatures* of the food code fit together. They may be arranged according to an arithmetic progression according to the number of elements they contain, syntactically related to the figure with sagging breasts. Between the kinds of food (five elements) and the modes of preparation (two), we can, in fact, insert the three types of diet and the four modes of acquisition.

As we examine figure 9, we see that the binary division (maturation/cooking) makes a clean break along the nature/culture axis between the frugivorous diet on the one hand, and the other two kinds of diet, meat and antifood on the other. Among the modes of

Five kinds of food	Four modes of acquisition	Three natural kingdoms	Two modes of preparation
Fruit	Gathering	Fruit (vegetable)	Maturation
Bird	Hunting	Meat (animal)	Cooking
Fish	Fishing		
Human blood	War	Antifood (mineral)	
Ashes			

Figure 8.1   Arithmetic progression of the food code.

acquisition, it also sets up a break between food–gathering, on the one hand, and hunting, fishing, and war on the other. Does this mean that the division along the nature/culture axis neutralizes the differences between two categories—meat and antifood—that appeared distinct? What about the differences within these two groups, between the different degrees of cooking, also marked by the nature/culture opposition (raw/smoked, rotten/burned)? Likewise, among the modes of acquisition, what is implied by the break between gathering and the three other modes?

This progression bears a striking resemblance to the systematic way in which the cannibals divided the prisoner's limbs among themselves (see p. 59). We must again turn to alchemy to understand the organization of the food code, now that it includes all the plates syntactically related to the figures with sagging breasts. A similar progression governs the different stages alchemists believed would lead them to rediscover the unity of matter, by making the philosophers' stone or an elixir known as "tincture." This progression reproduces the tetractic addition of Pythagoras (4 + 3 + 2 + 1) from which is derived the number ten assigned to the philosophers' stone (Holmyard 1957) (see figure 8.2.).

The classification of the three principles of matter or *tria prima* by Paracelsus and his adepts lets us understand how the three natural kingdoms and the three types of diet can be organized with respect to cooking. The three principles, sulphur, mercury, and sophic salt, which, for the alchemists represent qualities of matter (and not the chemical elements they usually designate), create a sort of elementary triad from which the entire universe proceeds. The alchemists define this triad by how its elements react to fire. Mercury—metal,

Four elements of God	Three principles of nature	Two seeds of metals	One fruit of art
fire air water earth	sulphur salt mercury	masculine feminine	tincture

Figure 8.2.   Pythagorian tetractic addition.

liquid, and flammable—cannot be transformed by fire; sulphur—volatile and flammable—can be transformed by fire; and salt, "which is found in ashes" (Read) as the disciples of Paracelsus said, is therefore already transformed by fire, burned, and nonflammable.

Similarly, in the food code, the classification of three types of diet correspond to the three natural kingdoms. Their respective reactions to cooking fire meet the same principle as the alchemists' elemental triad: the fruits—vegetable kingdom, frugivorous diet—like mercury, are as flammable but nontransformable by the cooking fire because they do not need it in order to be edible; they become edible by the natural process of maturation. Thus they correspond to a preculinary state. Meats—carnivorous diet, animal kingdom—are, like sulphur, flammable and transformable by fire, for, at least in the European culture of the time, they need the cooking fire in order to be edible. The food wastes, like salt, also presuppose cooking, but the blood dripping from the grill where the human limbs are roasting reveals by that very fact its resistance to cooking, and as for ashes, they result from excessive cooking and thus become nonflammable. These last two elements, being unsuitable for consumption, at least in the contexts in which they are found, are antifoods and fall outside cooking.

Here again we meet the old cannibal women who suck blood, this time in the company of the old woman who casts ashes, at the end of a regressive system that includes not just the syntagmatic chain of the cannibal women of part 3, but a paradigmatic ensemble drawn from many plates in different volumes depicting women as givers of fruit or meat. Whatever variations may yet be added to it, the mythic system of the Indian woman with sagging breasts, through the dynamics of its transformations, ranks cannibalism at the far end of an apocalyptic view of mankind and the universe. This is also the place reserved for it by the apocalyptic visions in the Bible, taken up again by Protestant poets during the wars of religion. Thus d'Aubigné, witness to the massacres perpetrated in France, renews the curses expressed in Deuteronomy, where blood unjustly spilled falls again as a rain of ashes making the earth sterile:

> Cities drunken with blood and still unquenched,
> which thirst for blood and are drunk with blood,
> you will feel the terrible hand of God:
> your lands shall be iron and your skies brass,
> sky which instead of rain sends down blood and
> powder,
> land whose corn expects only lightning.
> [*Tragiques* 7:287–92]

If we are to believe the same poet, scenes of cannibalism did take place in the French countryside when it was in the grip of famine, "quant Nature, sans loy, folle se dénature." This is the fulfillment of the curses in Deuteronomy, whose prophecy the French poet paraphrased:

> And thou shalt eat the fruit of thine own body, the flesh of thy sons and of thy daughters, which the Lord thy God hath given thee, in the siege, and in the straitness, wherewith thine enemies shall distress thee:
> So that the man that is tender among you, and very delicate, his eye shall be evil toward his brother, and toward the wife of his bosom, and toward the remnant of his children which he shall leave;
> So that he will not give to any of them of the flesh of his children whom he shall eat.
> [Deuteronomy 28:53–56]

European thought, whether in poetry or its graphic representation, thus rejected cannibalism, considering it as cast both out of nature and out of culture. The dynamics of the transformations of the food code within the iconographic system of the woman with sagging breasts, makes us shift from nature (the maturation of fruits) to culture (the cooking of meat) and from there to a "denaturalized" state, that of cooking wastes. Thus we can classify these three poles with the three poles of the abstract culinary triangle (raw/cooked/rotten), which here correspond simply to the presence or absence of cooking and not to the modes of cooking, as was the case for the triangle in which the juices were set in opposition to the bits of grilled human flesh.

The "Mesnage des Champs" and the Limits of Alliance

This leads us to relate the terms of the food code to those of the sociological code, and first, to determine the correspondences between changes of diet and sociological relations (fig. 11).

In the first group of transformations, the frugivorous diet corresponds, in the sociological code, to a food offering accepted between foreigners. This group forbids incest between siblings and stipulates a positive reciprocity between Indians and Spaniards, whether in the form of exchanged goods or of relations between the sexes.

In the second group, on the contrary, when we move from fruit to meat, the sociological significance of the food code is reversed. In the two variants, the food prestation is refused after being subjected to a form of cooking. The fish refused by the Dutch is smoked; the Fuegian woman captive at first refuses the cooked and prepared food offered her by the Dutch, before sharing a feathered raw bird with her own children.

This second group thus stands in a relation of complete inversion to the first. The raw food goes from mother to children according to filiation within the group, no prohibition being attached to it other than the disgust felt by the Dutch for these "barbarian" manners. Conversely, the smoked fish offered by the autochthones to the Dutch are refused. In opposition to the first group, then, the permutations in this group of transformations indicate that sexual relations are permitted according to filiation within the ethnic group, a sort of endogamy within the wide family known by the Europeans as the "Indian" category. Exchange and alliance through women between Indians and Dutch are, in turn, impossible and mutually rejected. The transformation thus affirms mutual incompatibility between the two peoples and a taboo of miscegenation and intercultural marriage.

In the third group, that of antifoods, the corruption of foods corresponds to a complete deterioration in European-Indian relations. It is no longer a question of accepting or refusing a prestation of food; in the absence of real food that might serve to mediate them, relations between foreigners are marked either by an exces-

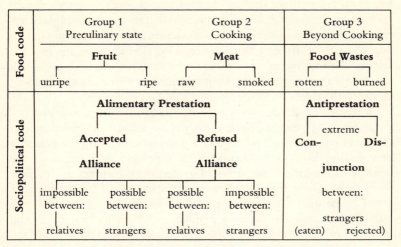

Figure 8.3   Correlations between food code and sociological code.

sive conjunction that consists in drinking the prisoner's blood, or by a disjunction in which the prisoner, covered with refuse, is rejected as waste.

The relation of equivalence between the food code and the sociological code thus undergoes a three-stage transformation revealing a progressive degradation of relations between Indians and Europeans. The maturation of fruit corresponds to a possible alliance; the cooking of meat to the reciprocal refusal of alliance; and finally the wastes of cooking to destructive relations.

In the preculinary state, the two degrees of maturation of the offered fruit (unripe/ripe) are associated respectively with prohibited and prescribed sexual relations. We shift from the food and sexual taboo to the permissible by means of temporal relation involved in the fruit's maturation. At the stage of meat and cooking, a smoked food (fish) offered by the Indians is disdained by the Dutch, "the captain being unfamiliar with this kind of food."

What is eaten within a kinship group (composed of the Fuegian mother and her children) appears too raw to the Dutch, who mock their barbarous manners. Between the raw and the smoked, there is no point of perfection that would correspond to ripe fruits, just as, in the sociological code, there seems to be no mediation possible between different cultures, between Fuegians and Dutch. The temporal relation we find in the first group gives way to a spatial relation in the second. The sociological distance signified by the refusal of the offering corresponds to two modes of cooking characterized by their distance from the cooking fire: the raw, because the feathered bird is not even exposed to the heat; the smoked, because it represents a technique of cooking by the slow work of smoke alone, far from the flame.

On the other hand, when it comes to food wastes, situated beyond cooking, the opposition on the sociological level between excessive conjunction and excessive disjunction (eating the prisoner or rejecting him) is associated with a reverse opposition in the degrees of cooking. The juices of grilled meat imply a disjunction from the cooking fire, for they come from animal substances that prove to be unaffected when presented to the fire. The juices run out of the roasted meat as a residue and thus participate in the category of the rotten. Conversely, the sociological disjunction indicated by the act of throwing ashes over the foreigner corresponds to the category of the burned, the result of an excessive conjunction with the cooking fire.

The iconographic system of the leitmotif figure is thus associated with the problem of the deterioration of Indian-European relations. This deterioration appears to be parallel, and thus necessarily linked, to a shift on the plane of cooking from a fruit to a meat diet, and from meat to the wastes of cooking.

Fruit-gathering is intimately associated with the state of innocence in which Adam and Eve lived before the first sin, as God, according to the Bible, gave them as their only food the fruits of the garden, with the exception of the fruit of the Tree of Knowledge. In his *Summa theologica*, Aquinas, treating the relations of man and animals before the Fall and the way our earliest ancestors fed themselves, states:

> In the state of innocence man would not have had any bodily need of animals: neither for clothing, since then they were naked and not ashamed, for there were no inordinate notions of concupiscence—nor for food, since they fed on the trees of paradise—nor to carry him about, for his body was strong enough for that purpose. But man needed animals in order to have experimental knowledge of their natures. This is signified by the fact that God led the animals to man, that he might give them names expressive of their natures. [*Summa Theologica* 1, question 96, article 1]

The fruit diet corresponds, then, to a state of innocence in which man has no need for his survival to murder animals or men, nor to have tools for acquiring his food whether by hunting, fishing, or farming, nor to build a fire to make them edible. In this sense, the myth of man's Fall is both a myth of the origin of cultural arts and of man's break with his natural environment and animals. The plate depicting the temptation and the Fall of the first couple in a "moralized landscape" clearly indicates, in the same terms, the break caused by their expulsion.[3] Before the temptation, Adam and Eve see the animals mingling together at their feet, even the most harmful and the most dangerous, like the rat and the lion, and the most inoffensive, like the rabbit. After the Fall, by contrast, Adam breaks up the earth with a digging stick, a cow indicates animal husbandry, and Eve nurses a child; three images evoking three of the basic aspects of what we call "culture" (farming, animal husbandry, family) (illus. 9).

But these notions of nature and culture must be put back into the ecological context in which the Europeans of the time imagine the relations between man and nature. Modern anthropologists would also give the name of "culture" to a gathering economy, even a purely vegetarian one (if indeed a so-called gathering society could be found that did not at the same time live from hunting or fishing). As seen in both the etymology of the word and the iconography, the image of paradise implies an already domesticated, civilized, organized nature, according to the traditional image of the enclosed garden, the *hortus inclusus*.[4] What was meant, then, by the different modes of acquisition of food (horticulture, hunting, fishing, and farming) in Western Europe, at the close of the sixteenth century?

The exploitation of agrarian resources remained characterized in large degree by a series of practices and customs established throughout the Middle Ages and the Renaissance. As Glacken emphasizes in his monumental study of the notions of nature and culture in European thought, this body of customs and traditions forms "the medieval counterpart of the modern concept of culture" (Glacken 1967, p. 323).

Since medieval times, the different ways of getting food and using the land have been organized into three major categories corresponding to different types of sociological relations. At one pole, the enclosed garden (*courtils* or *verchères*), around the house and thus fertilized with domestic waste, continually cultivated without letting the land lie fallow, represents a private island, exempt from collective servitudes and the lord's demands. At the other extreme lies rustic nature, formed of uncultivated land, forests, heaths, undergrowth, swamps, rivers, and sea. This rustic nature provides the peasants with the products of food-gathering (wild berries, roots, and nuts), hunting and fishing. Farming and animal husbandry fit in and often supersede these two poles, the one fertile, private, family-owned (the enclosure of the orchard and vegetable gardens), the other uncultivated and collective, where gathering, hunting and fishing take place (cf. Duby 1962, vol. 1, chap. 1). They are practiced alternately in the same agricultural space, part of the year reserved for farming (mainly cereals) and protected by fences. Then, after the harvest, the fences are taken down to allow the herds to graze. This agrarian territory therefore contained in rotation both terms of the opposition garden/communal land.[5]

Figure 8.4 shows the implicit system of oppositions underlying the practical organization of the land and the way in which medieval man experienced his relations with nature.

Domesticated Nature	**Rustic Nature**
Enclosure	*Free, open space*
private	collective
familial	communal
Horticulture:	**Gathering:**
vegetables	roots, nuts (for animals)
aromatics (flowers)	wild berries and fruits
medicinal herbs	
fruits (orchard)	**Hunting and Fishing**
continuous fertility	untilled

	Agricultural Space	
	Seasonal rotation between:	
Agriculture		**Animal husbandry**
fertility		fallow land
enclosed		open
private		collective
plowed		natural fertilizer
(labor, tools)		(animal manure)

Figure 8.4   Organization of agricultural land in Europe.

Between medieval times and the beginning of the seventeenth century, many economic and social changes occurred that affected in some measure man's relations with nature: a tendency to extend private property with its permanent fences over lands previously uncultivated in order to grow cereal crops; the efforts of the lords to limit collective rights and keep the forests as preserves of forest and wildlife for the needs of the hunt, a prerogative of the nobility. But, even in the middle of the seventeenth century in France, as evoked by La Fontaine's familiar fable "The Gardener and His Lord," the garden "adjoining the enclosure," where the delicate plants grow, fertile all year round, well planned and surrounded by a hedge, continued to exist in opposition to the two other main surviving categories: uncultivated collective lands on the one hand, and on the other, farming and animal husbandry, major activities in the subsistence economy. Thus, in his *Théâtre d'agriculture*, Olivier de Serres draws attention to the privileged character of the garden over other plots of land in these terms: "The garden excels over any other part of the arable land, even in this particuliar property that it produces fruit every year and at all times; whereas anywhere else it may be, the land yields only once a year, or if twice, it is so rare that it should not be taken into account" (Serres 1619, p. 455).

For his part, Robert Mandrou notes that even in the seventeenth century, "this sense of a kind of rural communism, which found expression in the maintenance of undivided common lands (ponds and streams, woods, and wastes) and in naïve evangelistic dictums, was a permanent feature of peasant mentality. Everyone knows the most famous of such dictums: 'when Adam delved and Eve span, who was then the gentleman?'" (Mandrou 1961, p. 128).

In the ecological context of the time, the transformations linking the alimentary code to the sociological code assume a new meaning.

The fruit group, grown in the orchard, partakes of domesticated, ordered nature, and is subject to the law of private property. It also belongs to exogamy, for it condemns incest between blood relatives and prescribes sexual alliance between Spaniards and Indians. The meat group comes from the rustic and primitive nature of uncultivated and unfenced lands, which man controls by destructive tools killing animal life (as in hunting and fishing, for plant-gathering is not represented anywhere in the collection). Hunting and fishing correspond to a break between Indians and Europeans

(Dutch), as expressed by the mutual refusal of exchange and alliance. Between these two extremes, there is no mediating activity, such as farming and animal husbandry in the European economy.

The following scheme summarizes the equivalences between the food code and the sociological code in the three groups of variants:

Group 1	ordered nature (orchard)	possible alliance
Group 2	rustic nature (uncultivated lands)	impossible alliance
Group 3	excremental world (refuse dump)	aggressive relations (war)

A striking fact appears in these transformations. We move from domesticated nature to rustic nature by a qualitative leap: a difference between two natural kingdoms (vegetable/animal) and a qualitative change of modes in food preparation (maturation/cooking) which require essentially different means, the sun and the fire. But from the second group to third we move by degrees and nearly imperceptibly. That is, we pass from uncultivated and rustic nature to a state both out of nature and culture, located outside every arable and workable area, and which, if we seek some equivalent in the divisions of land, would correspond to what was called, in the cities of the Middle Ages, *le trou punais*, a sort of dump where natural wastes and the residues of slaughter-houses and kitchens are heaped. We move from one group to the other by quantitative differences. Human blood and flesh, ashes and food, whether animal or vegetable, are related as the part to the whole. Again, considering the different modes of cooking, we move by slow degrees from raw to the rotten and from the smoked to the dried (burned).

The homology between the food and the sociological codes thus clearly shows the degradation of European-Indian relations as the ineluctable consequence of a break with "naturally domesticated nature," that of the earthly paradise, a break accomplished after the Fall, in the state of "rustic nature," that of the first cultural arts (hunting, fishing, and cooking). We can see in this qualitative leap after the Fall an unconscious justification of a taboo against miscegenation, and with it, of marriage between Indian women and Europeans: the stage of rustic nature in which the Indians live is close to a break in communication and exchange between them and the Europeans; whereas imagined in the mythic setting of a new earthly paradise, associated with the European dream of the enclosed, private, and "naturally fertile" garden, this alliance appears not only as possible but also as prescribed.

In these qualitative differences between the period before the Fall and the period following it, we again see a typically Protestant interpretation of original sin, with man's Fall provoking a radical break between nature and grace and corrupting his nature.

In Catholic theology, man loses, by his transgression, no more than the "preternatural" gifts which God bestowed upon him without impairing his nature.[5] As opposed to this, in Protestant thought, Adam, according to Calvin, is fallen from the normal state of his nature.

Finally, we meet again the theory of natural decay linked with the distinction between various degrees of corruption, a theory we first met in the engravings devoted entirely to cannibal rites. These rites led us to a vision of a world doomed to liquefaction by the same process of metonymic transformation, of container to contained. This view of cannibalism is, this time, incorporated into a wider range of variants of the iconographic motif and combined with the image of the woman casting ashes. It appears as the inevitable consequence of a cultural regression from which the Amerindian, remaining at the stage of rustic culture, is not able to raise himself, as did the Europeans with their farming and animal husbandry.

This is all the more striking because, in the first volumes, these two modes of subsistence appear to provide a vital part of the food supply for certain Indian tribes. For example, the Algonquian painted by John White in part 1, and also the Timucua of Florida in part 2, were both farmers and hunters. Several plates show the cultivated fields of corn, squash, and tobacco in Virginia, or the Timucua preparing the ground for sowing.[7] These early parts of the *Great Voyages* present an idyllic view of life in America, where the fertility of the soil and the technical ingenuity of the Indians combine with their friendly welcome to the Europeans, specifically the English and the French Huguenots. Their appearance is harmonious and the savage woman motif does not appear. Later we find no trace of farming, except in one plate of part 9, which gives a summary view of a village, probably an Araucanian village on Mocha island off the coast of Chile. There we see fields under cultivation, as well as lamoids on leashes, a sign of domestication.

The disappearance of the postneolithic modes of subsistence in the de Bry engravings does not correspond to any ethnographic reality; it implies that the illustrators unconsciously eliminated them from the texts. The cannibal Tupinambá, for example, lived partly from farming, which provided their staples: manioc, corn, sweet potatoes, several species of beans and peppers, and pineapples. Thevet, Staden, and Léry briefly describe growing and preparing manioc. Moreover, in the woodcuts illustrating Staden's narrative, which de Bry often used for inspiration, we find a view of the manioc and tobacco fields around the Tupinambá village, with the women coming home carrying the day's harvest on their backs. This theme is systematically eliminated by the de Brys, and significantly so.

We find here one of the traits that was to contribute to the ethnocide of the non-Western peoples: Europeans deliberately ignored their knowledge of the neolithic arts and reduced the peoples to the rustic state of nomadic hunters living off the wilds.[8] The English Puritans in North America used a similar maneuver to account for the dispossession of the Indians. Washburn, after studying the documents justifying this dispossession in the archives of the first English colonies of North America, reduces their arguments to three main ones, all supported by the Old Testament. According to the colonists, and in particular the sermons of the pastors, God made room for a people in three ways: legitimate expulsion of pagans by a war willed by God, purchase, or gift. In fact, God lets a foreign people negotiate with a native people to buy a land or receive it as a gift. This was the way Abraham acquired Machpelah's fields and Pharoah gave away the land of Goshen to the sons of Jacob. Finally, a foreign people may occupy empty lands to cultivate them or raise livestock, for "where a land is empty, there is freedom for the sons of Adam and Noah to settle, although they have not bought it nor asked permission" (Washburn 1959, pp. 102–4). This principle derives from a "natural law," said the Puritans; this law, written in the "charter" given to Adam and Eve, renewed after the flood with Noah, orders them to people the earth and bring it into subjection.

The English literature of the time reveals a whole campaign against nomadism and hunting peoples in favor of sedentary peoples—farmers and raisers of animals; in particular, Thomas

More, in his *Utopia*, justifies the expropriation of nomads and hunters for "moral" reasons as follows: "When any people holdeth a piece of ground void and vacant to no good or profitable use: keeping others from the use and possession of it, which, notwithstanding, by the law of nature, ought therefore to be nourished and relived" (book 2, chapter 5).[9]

Thus we see the importance assumed by the absence of farming and animal-raising in the ecology of the system. The choice of types of food is no accident. It emerges from a system of classifications and correspondences that played a key role in the conquest and colonization of America by Protestants, and thus for the destiny of the Indians in this part of the continent.

OF MONSTERS AND MARVELS

The correlations between the food code and the anatomical code reveal another aspect of the implicit mythology of the savage woman (fig. 8.5). In the set of fruit-offering, the figure is presented as a monster, composed on the one hand of hybrid features from different animal species, either through natural anomalies, as the devil, or through cultural ones, as the Caribbean woman. On the other hand, they exhibit features borrowed from both sexes, thus displaying an androgynous connotation. Still, one of them is young and without clothing, the other is old and adorned with exotic ornaments.

At the stage of meat food, the women providing meat (bird or fish) lose all their hybrid features but retain a certain sexual ambiguity with their masculine hairstyle. In addition, they are young and dressed as Fuegians, that is, their shoulders are covered with a cape and their hair is cut quite short.

Finally, in the third group, that of antifoods (human blood and ashes), the two hideous old women paradoxically lose every ambiguous feature (hybrid or androgynous) and, at the same time, every cultural element. Purely women, but stripped of feminity; purely human, but without artifice, their nudity is without attraction and offers the image of a humanity fallen both physically, through aging, the traits of old age, and culturally, by the complete lack of ornament. The regression observable in the food code (from fruits to antifoods, from preculinary innocence to the total corruption of the cooking wastes) corresponds, in the anatomical code, to a gradual transformation of the monstrous to the human, from the

	Group 1	Group 2	Group 3
Food code	Short of cooking **Maturation** (nature)	Cooking **Cooking** (culture)	Beyond cooking **Cooking Wastes** (outside nature and outside culture) **Inedible**
Anatomical code	**Monster (hybrid and androgynous)** **(young/old unadorned/adorned)** **Corruption of nature and culture**	**Human (androgynous)** young adorned culture	**Human** old unadorned nature

Figure 8.5   Correlations between food code and anatomical code.

most "outside nature," albeit by means of native ornaments, to the most naturally decrepit and "deculturated." The physical transformations of the anomalous figure proceed by the elimination of ambiguous elements from both anatomy and costume.

In this system, then, we see a gap between the function of clothing and that of food preparation, cultural elements par excellence; native ornamentation may even share in the monstrous, "outside nature," as in the case of the Caribbean woman, whereas pure and simple nakedness, stripped both of youth and of cultural elements, appears congruent with food wastes. In fact, in the food code, the inedible wastes or nonfoods express synthetically, in one set (group 1), the negation of the edible foods, fruits and meats, expressed analytically in two separate sets (groups 2 and 3). In terms of the anatomical code, the fruit-givers, hybrid monsters, assume the same function as the wastes. These figures express synthetically the reverse of the relations expressed analytically by two separate types of women, the providers of meat and the "foul" figures.

What is the explanation for this reversal? First, why do we find in the anatomical classification an Amerindian woman wearing exotic ornaments brought together with a hybrid devil made up of different zoological species at the very heart of the state of innocence connoted by the function of a fruit-giver? What is there in the Caribbean woman's appearance that is more "monstrous" than in the native ornamentation of the Fuegian women, ranked in the most "rustic" aspect of culture? What are we to make of the link between the burned and rotten world and the hideous image of destitution and the most complete nudity in the third group?

Here we reach the borderline between the natural world, the monstrous world, and the artificial world, as they were conceived at the time in Europe. From this viewpoint, the classification of the anatomical code meets the one formulated at the beginning of the seventeenth century by Francis Bacon. Modeling his analysis after the *Historia naturalis* of Pliny the Elder, Bacon distinguishes between "natural history," that is, history in which "the works and acts of nature" are recorded, and "civil history," which reports "the works and acts of men." He divides natural history into three parts, a classification, he goes on to explain, that has nothing arbitrary about it, as it rests on the "state and condition of nature," which is found in three different states, and is more or less subject to three kinds of conditions:[10]

1. The history of generations, where nature is free and develops in its normal course, as in the skies, in the animals, in the plants, and in everything that nature offers to our eyes;

2. The history of pretergenerations, where nature is "obstructed by some stubborn and less common matters, and thence put out of her course, as in the production of monsters";

3. The history of arts, finally, in which nature is "bound and wrought upon by human means, for the production of things artificial." (Bacon 1902, p. 95).

The first corresponds to what is considered "normal" and "natural"; the second, to "monsters and marvels"; the third, to what Bacon himself calls "mechanical and experimental history" (Bacon, ibid.).[11] In this sense, the complete nakedness of the old native women belongs to the normal course of nature, total deprivation, old age, natural decay; the figure of the Tempter belongs to the monstrous, to nature "put out of her course"; the artificial, what is made by "human art and industry," corresponds to the cultural elements that contribute to physical appearance, that is, ornaments and occasional articles of clothing, such as the loincloth and cape.

In what way do the old Caribbean woman's ornaments, which testify to "human artifice," cause her to belong to the category of "monstrous," to nature "out of her course," whereas the Fuegian women, adorned in a different way, belong to the artificial, thus cultural, world?

At that time, books devoted to monsters, marvels, and "curiosities" abounded. Included was a disorderly array of anatomical malformations, legendary beings, and strange customs of exotic peoples. For a long time, barbarians, savages, and monsters were confused with one another. In this book, *Des Monstres et Prodiges*, Ambroise Paré, while critical of the superstitions of the period, adds to the marvels described by Pliny those reported by Thevet from his voyage to Brazil. Certain of the woodcuts that illustrate Thevet's *Cosmographie universelle* were taken up again by Paré: they are the very ones that Theodor de Bry must have used for his illustrations of Staden's and Léry's voyages to Brazil. Among the monsters, Paré mixes cripples (the blind, one-eyed, and hunch-backed), those with hereditary defects, hermaphrodites, and all those whose physical traits differ from the canons of beauty at the time: flat noses or "thick, inverted lips."

In this we can see how non-European physical features, Negroid traits, for example, are identified as monstrosities, such as having six fingers on one hand, wens, or skin blemishes. Thus the Caribbean woman with the fruit basket "appeared like a monster to us rather than a human being," as Benzoni said (Benzoni 1902, p. 4). What is cultural about her is limited to the inlaid ornaments causing parts of her body to be distorted; the rings piercing her nose and earlobes deform them, and her long nails look like claws to the Europeans and are considered to be malformations. By contrast, the Fuegian women have practically no distortion and all their attire consists in an animal-skin cape; their ornaments, such as the shell necklace, are attached and not inlaid. But they are more exposed than the old Caribbean woman, as they wear no loincloth.

What distinguishes the native costume of the Caribbean variant from the Fuegian costume is that the pieces are fastened into the skin rather than removable. That is, they differ by their means of attachment to the body. We may now show the pertinent features of the anatomical code as a clothing triangle like the culinary triangle earlier used to show the physical differences between the "beautiful women, eaters of roast meat" and the "old blood-sucking hags" among the cannibals. But this time we are better equipped to characterize the three poles of this triangle, knowing the values they assumed at that period (fig. 8.6).

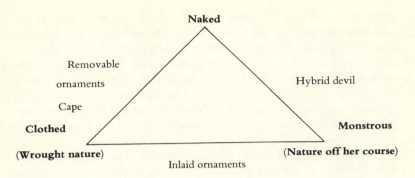

Figure 8.6   Clothing triangle.

At the same time, the anatomical and sociological codes are also transformed. From the anatomical point of view, the shift is from a hybrid monster, young or old, adorned or not, to a human being still endowed with ambiguous sexual features, but young and adorned with native ornaments, then to purely human old women, entirely naked and decrepit. This three-fold transformation marks a progression from the monstrous to the natural, but the natural made decrepit by a very rudimentary culture. At the same time, the transformations of the sociological code take us in three stages from a prescription of alliance to a reciprocal refusal of alliance between Europeans and Indians, and finally to destructive relations, whether between Indians and Europeans or between Indians themselves.

This seemingly paradoxical parallel reaffirms a Protestant conception of human nature. When the cultural element, however rustic it may be, disappears, human nature decays and becomes decrepit, as it becomes after the Fall when not corrected by culture; and this lapse into nature combines, on the sociological level, with an apocalyptic image of the human race, depicted by two types of emaciated old women, those who lick their fingers dripping with juices of human flesh, and those who cover their enemy with ashes. This aspect of Protestant thought regarding nature has been repeatedly mentioned. Considering nature as essentially corrupted, this notion leads, in turn, to a "salvaging of all human values,"[12] and thus of cultural values.

We may further inquire how well the transformations in attitude toward the Indians, revealed in this sytem, correspond to the historical evolution of relations between Indians and Europeans

(Spaniards, Dutch, English, French, and Germans). Let us recapitulate the order of the plates and the chronology of the different parts of the *Great Voyages* in which they appear. Those of the first group correspond to part 1 (1590) and part 4 (1594); those of the second group to part 9 (1602); those of the third group to part 3 (1592) and again to part 9 (1602). The description of the idyllic relations between the Indians of Virginia and the English and between the Indians and the French Huguenots, in the first two volumes, often concealed the actual tensions, battles, and refusals of the Indians, weary of feeding the newcomers. The main reason for this favorable image was to attract English colonists or other possible emigrants for the benefit of the large colonization companies. Actually, not a single campaign described in the *Great Voyages* occurred without some blood shed, prisoners captured, or war waged.

On the other hand, the nationality and religion of the Europeans appear as important factors in the changing relations between Indians and Europeans portrayed in these engravings. Earlier, we placed the scene of the offer made by the Caribbean woman in the context of Benzoni's indictment of the Spanish tyranny. This indictment, now incorporated into a wider range of variants, becomes imbued with a political bias against the Spaniards, which pervades the whole corpus. The possibility and even the prescription of alliance between Indians and Europeans, discerned in the first set of transformations, puts the blame for the loss of the ideal state and the deterioration of Indian–European relations on the devilish Spanish.

This obligation of alliance disappears where other European Protestants are concerned—the Dutch, for the plates of part 9, the Germans, like Staden, among the Tupinambá, or the French Huguenots, like Léry, participating in the Protestant expedition of Villegaignon to Brazil. The Amerindian woman, while losing her animal ambiguity when viewed with the Dutch, appears in a new light, at best as a barbarian or an object of curiosity with strange manners in terms of dress or culinary practices; at worst as an evildoer performing maleficent rites against the foreigner, whether eating him or casting ashes over him like a medieval witch, and in this case she becomes physically human, too human in her hideous nakedness.

The reappearance of the figure in the illustrations of the Dutch voyages to South America, and more specifically the old cannibal woman turned into the woman casting ashes, justifies the fact that, after all, the Dutch scarcely treated the Indians with more humanity than the devilish Spaniards, with the exception of torture, of which the Dutch offered no examples.[13]

In the landing scenes of part 9 we see the Dutch harrassing the Indians with rifle shots, including the women with children in their arms, and again, slaughtering men, women, and children captured in a cave. Elsewhere, as a group of Micronesians paddle their canoes loaded with fruit to welcome the incoming ships, the Dutch drive them away with gunshots on the grounds these people are thieves (hence the name of "Ladrones" given to their islands). The same is true in later parts, which abound in scenes of Indians shot dead by the Dutch and English. Still, the narrators do not disapprove of it in the least. The contradiction is thus glaring and pervades the unconscious background of the mythic system of the "savage woman."

The whole system, built on sets of transformations, explains why the Amerindian must be brought into subjection (by a law of "nature," the law itself a consequence of a theological conception of sin) by the European newcomers. The possibility of an alliance based on exchange between Indians and Europeans, rejected in the mythic times before the Fall of Man, is portrayed in a concrete historical situation, the conquest of the New World by the Spanish. The ambiguity of the old Caribbean woman puts the relations between Europeans and Indians in a state of ideal innocence where the first sin falls to the Spaniards, who reenact in this new earthly paradise America could have been, the devil's role in the Bible story. The Spaniard himself is, moreover, caught in the very act of cannibalism and attempted rape of Indian women.

More than a simple "vision" of the Indian, the mythic system of the native with sagging breasts appears as an unconscious justification of behavior and practices that characterized the history of colonization in North America: the taboo on interracial marriage, with segregation as the first consequence, whether as Indian "reservations" or as black ghettoes, slavery, or genocide. Moreover, this rationalization set up the basis for the appropriation of Amerindian land not only with respect to the Amerindians themselves, but also with respect to the Spaniards, dangerous competitors.

The mythico-iconographic system of the savage woman thus appears here as complete. To corroborate its interpretation, we must still verify several facts. The system accounting for all variants so far considered rests upon three codes present throughout. These codes form such a logical armature that we cannot meet one code without the other and the system as a whole draws its meaning from the very equivalence of the codes. Is this to say that the Amerindian figure with the aberrant shape of breast can be found only under these conditions? What would be the effect on the system as a whole if one of the codes were to disappear?

As early as part 9 of the *Great Voyages* we see a variant that seems to contain no food code and we put it aside. Later volumes offer other cases. What becomes of the system and the interpretation given of it when one part of its logical and semantic structure seems missing from the outset? Does its absence challenge the validity of all that precedes? These are the problems we must address on taking up the variants that appear in the final parts.

Claribel ≠ Elizabeth

Ferdinand = Henry

Prospero = James

3   Noah's Ark
and the
Bearded Indians

The savage woman appears for the last time later in part 9, in the narrative of the Dutch expedition conducted by Sebald de Weert to Penguin Island, one of the islands in the archipelago near the Strait of Magellan. The inhabitants are probably Alacalufs, that is, Indians of the same group as in the earlier variants of the mother with the raw bird and the woman casting ashes. The figure with which we are now concerned appears three times in part 9: on the frontispiece, in a map of Tierra del Fuego decorated with portraits of some of its inhabitants, and in a third plate (9: frontispiece, 9:0, and 9A:24; illustrations 11, 12, 15, and 16).

The Dutch encountered this woman when a storm ran their boats aground on Penguin Island. The survivors thanked God for their safety, and some set about rebuilding the boats while others explored the island in search of food. These circumstances make up in the background of plate 9:24 (illus. 16). While hunting penguins, who build their nests in underground burrows, the Dutch discovered in one of them "a savage woman, who had been hiding there since the crew came onto the island" (Renneville 1725, 2:332). The engraving, however, shows this woman leaving a cave whose entrance is high enough for men to walk easily through it rather than a burrow where penguins lay their eggs. The next plate, depicting the penguin hunt, shows these burrows as holes dug in a slight hillock above the ground. The Dutch haul out the penguins by means of a pole with a hook attached to one end, and beat them to death with a club. Two of these web-footed birds appear on the frontispiece in the company of the female islander and several other figures.

The narrative explains that the savage woman is the sole survivor of the massacre ordered by Captain Olivier de Noort on the island during his stay some time earlier, in retaliation for the murder of two of his men: "They had killed all of them except for this woman

who nevertheless had been wounded and who let us see her scars"
(Renneville 1725, 2:332). No trace of these scars appears on the
body of the surviving woman; on the contrary, she is portrayed as
being in good health, tall, with a sagging bosom, and her hair
cropped like the other Fuegian women. She wears a woven
loincloth around her hips and a long cape completely covers her
shoulders, arms, and hands. This special garment is worn by most
of the other Indian women portrayed in this volume. The cape
worn by the woman serving fish and by the mother with the raw
bird hangs from a collar of shells, so that it can be arranged to fall
down the back; the women, seen from the front, appear to be
completely naked. This difference between the women from the
northern or the southern part of the Strait is noted in the text: "Her
face was painted and over her body she wore a kind of cloak made
of the skins of animals and birds quite artistically sewn together,
which fell to her knees. Her natural parts were covered with a bit of
animal skin so that the savages of the southern part of the Strait
appear somewhat more modest and tractable than those of the
north" (Renneville 1725, 2:332). As for her appearance: "Her hair
was cut short, whereas the men of both the north and south wear it
exceedingly long, as was seen on the corpse of one of them who
had been killed, who still wore fine feathers on his head and around
his body" (Renneville 1725, 2:332).

The figure in the foreground of the engraving, who lies with his
face on the ground and his hands tied behind his back, wears a
feathered headdress and around his loins a skirt of feathers held
together by a net. He also appears on the frontispiece, paired with
the Penguin Island woman, and this time he holds the attributes of
the hunter: bow and arrows. His hair is long and curly, and he
wears a beard and moustache, whereas most of the Indians portrayed by the de Brys are clean shaven.

If, anatomically, the Penguin Island woman with her sagging
bosom and short hair is indeed a variant of the woman serving fish
and the mother with the raw bird, at first glance it is hard to see
how she fits into the food code, as she does not bring food or eat it,
nor does she "cast filth." She appears armless in these three plates.

She seems indifferent to the figures around her, both to the
Dutch who drag her out of the cave and to the feather-decked
Indian who lies at her feet. Seen sociologically, this variant is a
negative transformation of the other variants. In those variants, the

figure with sagging breasts has shown one of two attitudes: either overly generous toward the foreigner, as for Adam and Eve, the old Caribbean woman, and the woman serving fish; or aggressive, as for the cannibal women and the woman casting ashes. Between these two extremes, the mother with the raw bird holds a middle position: she scorns the foreigners, yet she is generous to her children. The woman of Penguin Island represents a negation of these two different attitudes. Neither aggressive nor generous, she neither gives nor receives and is as indifferent to strangers as to her own kind.

Seen anatomically, the "indifferent beauty" from Penguin Island shows a strong similiarity to the preceding variants: like them, she is nonhybrid and slightly androgynous in her hairstyle and face. However, her cape, which covers her arms and hands, making her look armless, and her loincloth set her apart. Among all the different variants of the female "savage," we can identify two distinctive ways of being unclothed: a half-nudity where the chest is bare and genitals covered, and a more complete nudity where both chest and genitals are exposed.

By relating the various sociological attitudes between strangers and autochthones to the different types of nakedness, one realizes that the figures with sagging breasts wear a covering on their genitals when their relations with strangers are friendly or indifferent, and none when these relations are of refusal or aggressiveness. To be more precise, the latter are unilateral (only one side behaves aggressively toward the strangers or refuses food from them), the former founded on reciprocity, whether in the acceptance of food or in the mutual indifference seen on Penguin Island where no bond is created one way or another. Captain de Weert's men show as much indifference as the savage woman; they don't offer anything, nor do they try to harm her. The text indicates that the woman wished to be taken to the continent, but the Dutch abandoned her alone on her island. To sum up, the presence or absence of a loincloth matches the sociological opposition between reciprocal and unilateral relationships.

So, just as we began to think that the "indifferent beauty" was a negative transformation of the other variants and fell outside the system, it now becomes clear that she broadens the semantic field of nakedness and leads us to view it in the new contexts of the frontispiece and the map of Tierra del Fuego. In the former she stands with a perfect symmetry, on the right of the title page, just opposite the same feathered Indian who, in the plate of Penguin Island, lay bound at her feet, while the dwarf king of Guinea (who offered a frugal meal to Captain de Weert) sits on a wooden throne above the title in the center, flanked by two penguins and just opposite a llama below, in the foreground.

In the map she stands beside a snail (called "muchsel" or mussel in the caption) opposite the same feathered man and along with another "savage" couple, as the caption calls them, a disheveled Indian carrying a harpoon, and the mother with the raw bird (illustrations 11 and 12).

Let us go back to the strange grouping of the frontispiece where two human beings join the "indifferent beauty"—the Indian with the feathered headdress and the dwarf king of Guinea—as well as two animals—a penguin and a llama. These two species of American wildlife crop up in the illustrations from two different texts of part 9: Heynes' narrative of Sebald de Weert's voyage for the penguin, and José de Acosta's *Historia natural y moral de las Indias* for the llama (illus. 15).

Penguins thrived on the islands of the Strait and the Dutch would stop there to catch and store them on their ships for their journey. The plate immediately following the "indifferent beauty" portrays this rather peculiar form of hunting. The Dutch conquerors, armed with long hooked poles, haul their prey out of the burrows where the penguins hide. Then they beat them with clubs and attach them by the beak to the poles, ready to carry them on their backs (illus. 17).

The presence of the llama in South America greatly puzzled the author of the *Historia natural y moral de las Indias*, José de Acosta, a Spanish Jesuit. The Bible does not mention, among the animals of the flood, this member of the camel family. Acosta solves this theological problem by saying that God gives to each part of the earth what best suits it—corn to America and wheat to the Old World. The same must hold true for animals. Acosta distinguishes two different kinds of llama—the guanaco, a wool-bearing animal, and the "short-haired" paco, used as a beast of burden by the Indians. The llamas shown in the frontispiece and in two other plates have an angular hump covered by a cloth. Both represent a caravan of llamas carrying silver ingots from the mines of Potosi for the Spanish.

One of these plates (9A:4, illus. 26) pictures some of the llama's habits, as Acosta reports them: "[The paco] take offense and become stubborn under the load, lying down with it, and no one can make them rise again; they would rather be cut to pieces than move when this mood overcomes them. The Indians' solution is to stop, sit down next to the paco, and pet it until he gets up again, and they are sometimes forced to wait two or three hours until he calms down" (Acosta 1598, p. 205).[1] In the foreground of this plate an Indian fondles the neck of a llama seated in the middle of the path with his load on his back while other llamas graze. In the background a hunter prepares to shoot his harquebus at a capricious llama who has fled with his load: "They suddenly take fright and flee with their loads to the highest rocks so that, as we can not reach them, we are forced to kill them and shoot them with the harquebus for fear of losing the bars of silver they carry" (Acosta 1598, p. 205).

Ethnozoology will be the key to understanding why two such dissimilar animals should pair in the same print in company with our female hero, while their respective "stories" belong to two completely unrelated texts and nothing in the narrative connects them. Once solved, this problem will also cast a light on the relationship between these two animals and the human figures pictured together in the frontispiece along with the Penguin Island woman.

Here she is not portrayed with dead animals used as food, but with live ones hunted by Europeans. Penguins and llamas both relate to the food code through a new opposition between animals—beasts "on the hoof"—and meat. Sociologically, the plates associate these two animal species with three ethnopolitical categories of people involved in the conquest of America: Indians, Protestants (the Dutch) and Catholics (the Spanish). Whereas the bird and the fish were eaten or offered by Indians and considered inedible by Europeans, the llama, a domestic animal used occasionally for food by the Indians in the Andes, is hunted by the Spanish, not for his flesh, but for the silver he is running away with. On the other hand, the penguin is sought for his flesh by the Dutch.

A spatial relationship links the figures of the frontispiece to one another. They fall along a spatial and quasi-geographical axis. In relation to the underground penguin, the high-perched llama and the cave-dwelling woman with the cape, the two male figures appear on the ground level, one seated on a bench, the other standing or lying on the ground. They hold a median position with respect to the llama and the penguin and form an analytic tetrad with them, for, by their way of life and their behavior, they each connote points in space along two axes, that of height (above/middle/below) and that of depth (outside/inside) (fig. 9.1).

	Height	Depth
1. Llama (perched)	above	outside
2. Dwarf (seated) 3. Indian (prone)	middle (ground level)	
4. Penguin (in burrow)	below	inside

Figure 9.1.   Analytic tetrad of the figures of the frontispiece.

With respect to this tetrad, the troglodyte Fuegian woman assumes a synthetic function, as the cave from which she emerges is both above the ground and inside the mountain.

System of Anomalies

The variants of the "indifferent beauty" on the frontispiece and in the other plates set up a system of relations between the initial iconographic motif and the motifs of other figures whose physical traits are out of the norm: the bearded Indian with long hair, the dwarf, and animal species, which, as we shall see, are also full of ambiguity. All of them reveal some form of anomaly. No doubt the dwarf king of Guinea is the most obvious case. The two penguins flanking him on the frontispiece also appear as "shortened" or atrophied figures, if not in their whole body, like the dwarf, at least partially, by their rudimentary wings that are useless for flying, which explains why certain species are called *manchot*, in French, that is, armless or short-armed.

As for the llama, Acosta, in his *Historia natural y moral de las Indias*, combines aesthetic considerations with a providentialist viewpoint while describing the physical peculiarities of this animal unknown in the Bible: "In their body, they greatly resemble the camel, and a good thing it is, for as they are tall and long-legged, they need a neck that long in order not to appear deformed" (Acosta 1598, p. 203).

In contrast to the penguin whose wings are atrophied, the long-necked, hump-backed llama shows physical hypertrophies. How does the native couple of Penguin Island, in the two plates in which they appear, fit into this distinction between atrophied and hypertrophied figures? The man, whose hands are tied behind his back in one of the engravings, appears congruent with the penguin in the appearance of armlessness, though we should note that the penguin's anomaly is constitutional whereas that of the Indian is artificially imposed by the ropes binding his wrists. The woman with the cape once again combines the contradictions setting atrophied figures in opposition to hypertrophied figures: like the bound Indian she evokes armlessness, because her cape hides her arms and hands, and her sagging bosom places her with the hump-backed, long-necked llama (fig. 9.2).

Atrophies		Hypertrophies
by constitution (nature)	by artifice (culture)	by constitution (nature)
penguin (part) dwarf (all)	bound Indian	llama
	Woman in the cape	
	cape (clothing)	sagging breasts (anatomy)

Figure 9.2   Atrophy and hypertrophy of the Penguin Island figures.

The physical peculiarities of both animals and men correspond to different kinds of activities, or, for the atrophied figures, to an inability to perform some action. The penguin, though it looks like a bird, cannot fly; on the contrary, it finds refuge in burrows dug into the earth and appears as an underground figure. Game hunters, seeking to take it for food, must pull it out of its burrow with a pole. The llama, loaded with ingots that should hamper its movements, flees with its burden and the hunter has to shoot it.

These two animal species thus make up an antithetical couple as far as anatomy (atrophy/hypertrophy), movement (slow/rapid), and nature are concerned, one being killed for food, the other to salvage the load it is carrying (edible/inedible). Both represent a fruitful hunt by European hunters: the Dutch killing the penguins; the Spanish shooting the thieving llamas from a distance.

As opposed to these successful hunters, the Amerindian world appears sterile and lifeless. The dwarf king, too small, turns out to be a bad guest as well as a bad host, by offering his guest an inedible meal and by overindulging in the food offered to him. The bearded Indian—who stands in the frontispiece in company with the "indifferent beauty" with hunter's attributes in his hand—brings us back from the plate in which he is seen bound to the paradigm of capture and the prisoner. With his bow and arrows by his side he appears as a slain hunter, reduced to prey for the Dutch. The reappearance of capture as a motif is all the more flagrant here because it is introduced at a purely iconographic level: the text never mentions that the last male survivor of the massacre carried out by de Noort's expedition on the island has his hands bound, but only that he lies still.

Whereas the other variants of the savage woman led, through a series of transformations, to a regressing world doomed to liquefaction and self-destruction, the "indifferent beauty" having lost all initiative in giving, refusing, or eating food—a role held so far by every figure with sagging breasts—confronts us with a static Amerindian world, somehow stricken with inertia and sterility. In contrast, the European world has taken the initiative of hunting and capture, and also condemns the indifferent savage Indian woman to solitude and sterility by doing away with the only surviving male on the island, who, on the frontispiece, joins with her to make a couple.

This reversal in the perception of Indian-European relations brings into sharper focus the problem of how systems of transformations and historical evolution, or, more generally, mythic thought and practice relate. Before tackling this problem, we may now appreciate the gains made in the iconographic analysis by the new syntagmatic chain into which the Penguin Island woman fits.

FROM STATIC STRUCTURES TO DYNAMIC STRUCTURES

The reader may wonder why the "indifferent beauty" opens a new section, "Noah's Ark and the Bearded Indians," whereas, as we have just seen, she is certainly a variant of the Indian woman with sagging breasts and belongs to the system revealed in the analysis. Moreover, like the other Fuegian variants examined earlier, she is found in part 9 of the *Great Voyages*. Its analysis had been temporarily put off, for at first glance, it seemed to contradict, by the absence of a food code, the transformation system accounting for the other variants. This apparent lack in the engraving actually becomes meaningful itself within the food code through negative transformations. From the standpoint of method, this example brings several important new facts to iconographic analysis. These facts should justify this artifice of composition.

The food code appears in each of the other variants of the motif. It is made of two elements: a sign of recognition—the presence of fruits, bird, fish, blood, or ashes—and a function that links this sign to the figure—giving, refusing, eating, or casting ashes. In part 9, the food code reappears in plates other than those in which the woman from Penguin Island is found. Through the engravings of part 9, we can follow the story of the other figures pictured with her on the frontispiece and can build the syntagmatic chain in which the paradigm of the hunt—the hunt for the silver-carrying llamas and for penguins as game—appears. This paradigm brings us back to the food code, with a double transformation: (1) transformation of the sign of recognition that broadens the semantic field of the animal kingdom as shown in figure 9.3; (2) negative transformation of the function assigned to the other variants, for the woman of Penguin Island does not offer, reject, or eat any of these animals. The European now initiates the hunt and the capture.

We are faced with something different from the type of transformation shown for the other variants. Those variants were organized into three groups of transformations set up on the equivalence of three codes—anatomical, sociological, and alimentary. But in

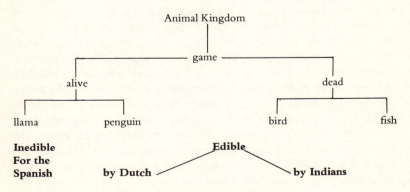

Figure 9.3   New semantic field of the animal kingdom.

fact the food code has played the role of "pivot code." The signs of recognition in this code (fruit, meat, excrement) served as a basis on which the sociopolitical relations between Indians and Europeans, as well as the anatomical variations, have been organized into three groups of transformations: vegetable, animal, and antifood. The function of these signs was to mediate between Europeans and Indians, and their variations led to transformations on the sociological level: prescribed or prohibited alliance and self-destruction.

The situation has now changed. The live animals (llama and penguin) serve no mediating function between Indians and Europeans as was assumed by the other foods and the antifoods. In relation to the Europeans, and thus from the sociological viewpoint, the animal world falls on the same level as the Amerindian couple: relations of hunters to game and of takers to taken (or to captives) replace those of takers to givers and hosts to guests that linked foreigners to autochthones. The relations joining the woman of Penguin Island with the animals are of a very different kind. She does not hold them in her hand as objects to be offered, thrown, or eaten. On the contrary, by her anatomy (hypertrophy, atrophy) and her style of life (as a cave-dweller), she synthesizes the elements expressed analytically both by these zoological examples and by the other natives—the dwarf king and the bearded Indian.

The anatomical code now serves as a pivot, for through it the syntagmatic chain binds animals, Indians, and Europeans together. Further, this change in the function of the codes includes equally aberrant figures—the dwarf and the bearded Indian—in the system. Our iconographic system seems to swing in a broader system of anatomical oppositions, in which height and secondary sexual characteristics—hair and beard, for example—become meaningful.

Thus the "indifferent beauty" brings changes inside the system at the very moment when, on the semantic plane, she brings to a halt the regressive movement to which the Amerindian world seems doomed and immobilizes it, through new structures, in the inertia of a trapped animal or a sterile woman. In relation to the structures of transformations previously shown, she falls logically into the second set: by her physical appearance—young, adorned, ambiguous but not hybrid; by the signs of the food code—the animal kingdom, seen in the llama and the penguin; and finally, by the sociological paradigm that states a refusal of alliance between foreigners and autochthones. In the Penguin Island plate the Indian prisoner is not eaten but left dead; the woman with the cape, hauled out of her cave like a hunted animal, is not violently rejected and execrated but simply forsaken and left alone without any of her kin.

However, as it fits in the second set of transformations, this last variant introduces from within a new type of structure that cannot be placed on the same plane with the others. Put schematically, these developed, as it were, horizontally. But within the second group, one could represent the new type of transformation on a vertical axis, it being understood that the position of the axes has a relative, not an absolute value (fig. 9.4.).

Group 1
vegetable kingdom
	→Group 2
	     animal kingdom
	↓ A. dead game
	          (bird, fish)
		Group 3
		mineral kingdom

	B. live game (llama, penguin)	

Figure 9.4.   Transformations on the vertical axis.

Unlike the first type of structures analyzed, these new ones account for diachronic transformations and bring an evolutionary dimension to the system.

First Variant: The Woman with the Fan
and Neptune

Surrounded by tropical fruit and branches, on a rock
that rises from the water and is covered by a tasseled carpet, a
woman with a fan sits hidden from the background figures under a
heavy plume, her right arm raised over her head (plate 11A:F; illus.
18). Except for her loincloth she is naked; her body, with its full
curves, is marred by misshapen breasts.

At the left, Neptune sits on a sea monster and holds his trident.
Behind him an exotic figure, who exhibits the first "Indian" profile
of the collection, points a harpoon in the direction of a horned devil
hidden by the woman with the plumes. The man with the harpoon
is a variant of the disheveled Fuegian with long hair, beard, and
moustache who appears on the map of Tierra del Fuego in company with the women with capes. The Indian of this frontispiece,
however, has a clean-shaven face, his long hair flattened across the
forehead and braided at the side, and his nose is adorned with two
rings. These two men with harpoons and long hair use their hunting attributes to drive away an intruder.

On the frontispiece, the intruder is the devil in person, recognizable by his horns, his goat's forehead covered with animal
hair and the stick he holds in his hand. The Fuegian man with the
harpoon appears earlier, in another plate, taking a defensive position upon the arrival of the Dutch. As the Dutch sloops approach,
the Indians of the Strait—probably Alacalufs—who have been
fishing from their graceful, gondola-shaped boats, hasten to shore
and throw stones in the direction of the newcomers. Then, "with
their own hands" they pull up "trees that appeared from a distance
to be a span through and used them for retrenchments" (Renneville
1725, 2:331).

The aggressive gesture displayed by the man with the harpoon toward the devil in this frontispiece combines with the defensive posture of the woman with sagging breasts, who hides her fruit under her and escapes the devil's notice by withdrawing behind her large fan. In this scene, the theme of the earthly paradise explicitly reappears. The protagonists in the origin myth are all present: the autochthonous couple, the intrusive devil, and even, one might say, God, in the guise of Neptune, while in the background of the boats of the new conquerors stand against a tempestuous sea. The paradigm of the fruits associated with the savage woman brings us back to the first set of transformations, in which the Spanish conquest enacts in reverse the myth of the fateful gift to humanity. Still, the situation portrayed is clearly quite different from that of the Caribbean variant. It is not a question of reenacting the same story by recasting the parts of autochthones and intruders as in part 4.

On the contrary, we come back to the initial cast of the origin myth: Adam and Eve, the devil and God; it is the very events of the myth that are transformed. The irrevocable transgression is not committed, for our Amerindian Eve does not offer her fruit to the approaching foreigners, but hides them and protects them, while a warrior Adam holds himself ready, weapon in hand, to repulse the intruding devil. At the same time, the devil loses any ambiguity and is unmasked as the devil from hell. The conquerors' ships founder in the waves and a sea monster emerges from the depths prepared to devour them, while Neptune, impassive master of waters and maker of storms, sits triumphantly on the side of the Amerindian world.

The Polynesian variants of part 9 appear in the same context and further clarify this contradiction imposed on the myth of original sin. It is as if the natives, in a situation like that of the first human couple, did not commit the transgresssion. The mythic story is not repeated but turns back on itself.

Second Variant: The Flight of the Women of Traitors' Island

The scene occurs on one of the Polynesian islands, no doubt one of the Tonga Islands,[1] approached by the members of the Dutch expedition led by Le Maire and Schouten in order to lay in supplies (plate 11A:6; illus. 19). The inhabitants try to repulse them with clubs but are unsuccessful. Three "savage" women appear in the midst of the melee. They carry neither fruit nor any other offering in their hands, but their anatomical features here indicate a defensive attitude toward foreigners. One of the women, her arms raised over her head, runs to give the alarm, a second closes her ears, and the third throws herself on the neck of one of the warriors with a club in his hand. These women attract the attention of the narrator, who notes, "Our men saw some of their women, that cryed and claspt their men about their neckes, but knew not what they meant, but thought they did it to get them from thence" (Schouten 1619, p. 33).[2]

The attitudes of the three women on this plate stand in contradiction to Eve's attitude with respect to the devil and to that of the old Caribbean women facing the Spanish. One woman gives an alarm, instead of greeting the intruders or going to meet them, another refuses to hear, instead of listening to deceitful words, and the third drags the man away from danger rather than urging him to be their victim.

THIRD VARIANT: THE FEAST OF KAVA ON HOORN ISLAND

Our heroine, in her Polynesian guise, appears in the foreground while in the background a feast takes place (plate 11A:7; illus. 21). With one hand she holds some fruit, probably coconuts, against her side, and in the other a plant difficult to identify. She openly stands aloof from a group of four Polynesian men busy chatting and from the welcome in the background. The scene portrays a feast of kava, a narcotic drink requiring a whole ceremony on several of the Polynesian islands. This feast is given by the king of the island of Hoorn[3] in honor of his two groups of guests: the Dutchmen, seen performing on trumpets and drums in front of the kings' *belay*[4], and the party of a neighboring king, come to pay a visit. According to the narrator, the feast does not celebrate the arrival of the Europeans but rather the announcement of their departure. On learning that the Dutch were going to weigh anchor in a few days, the king is reported to have jumped for joy and immediately called for the slaughter of many pigs to celebrate the good news.

The background scene portrays a strange kind of greeting exchanged by the two neighboring kings and their subjects when they meet. They throw themselves down, face to the ground, then rise

again. In the center, an intermediate scene shows the two Polynesian kings seated on a mat under the belay. Some of the Dutch stand
in the belay, while the musicians play their music in the open
air—to the king's evident pleasure, according to the narrator. Outside, too, a group of Polynesians prepares the kava by first chewing
a root then spitting it into a basin to which they add water.[5] This
drink is offered to the guests, but the Dutch refrain from drinking:

> After that came a company of peasants, bringing with them a
> quantity of greene herbs, which they called CAVA, such as the
> 300, men aforesaide had about their midles, and all together at
> once began to chaw the herbs in their mouthes, which being
> chawed they tooke it out of their mouthes, and laid it all in a
> wooden vessel, like a tray, or trough, and when they had
> chawed a great deale, they poured water into it, and so stirred
> and prest it together, and gave the liquor thereof to the kings to
> drinke, who dranke thereof with their gentlemen: they also pre-
> sented that notable drinke (as a special and a goodly present) to
> our men, but they had enough, and more then enough of the
> sight thereof. [Schouten 1619, p. 55]

The physical type of the Polynesians of part 11 differs markedly
from that of part 9. The de Brys used new models, of which some
must have been drawn after sketches from life. They come from a
Dutch edition of 1618, the first version of *Australian Navigations
Discovered by Jacob Le Maire*, published under the name of Cornelius
Schouten, though it was written by some crew member other than
Schouten. This text appears in 1618 as an appendix to the report of
Spielbergen's navigations (*Nieuwe Oost ende West Indische Navigation*)
and contains a certain number of plates copied by the de Brys. But
the engravers had introduced several significant changes. In the
Dutch edition, the woman, her breasts sagging "like leather
pouches," sits tailor-fashion and holds a child with one hand a
clump of leaves in the other (illus. 20). The changes are precisely
those linking this figure to the paradigm of the savage woman: the
disappearance of the child removes all connotation of motherhood
and nursing from the anatomical anomaly. The fruits she holds in
her hand have been added, however, and the king has been given
the bunch of leaves or herbs. The other figures have curly hair and
flat noses. Still, from the viewpoint of the anatomical paradigm, the
savage woman, in common with the Fuegian women, has short

hair, which gives her a masculine face; in contrast, the men of this country wear their hair long, arranged either in braids or pulled straight up onto their heads "like hog bristles" (ibid., p. 57).

The narrator of the Schouten voyage also stresses another difference between the men and women of this region, a difference easily seen in the graphic representation of the inhabitants of Hoorn Island. The men are typically tall, with well-proportioned bodies and limbs. The women are short, of an unpleasant appearance both of body and face: "The women were very unsightly both in face and body, of small stature, their hair cut close to their heades, as our mens in Holland, their brests long hanging downe to their bellies like lether satchels" (1619, p. 57). And indeed, the face and body of the woman in the foreground are rather distorted, or at least scarcely pleasant to look at, by contrast with the four men from whom she stands apart and who are tall and handsomely built. The king is conspicuous among them by his feathered headdress and the long braid hanging down his left side, "below his hips." Two of the other three hold sticks on which birds roost. The narrative notes that these birds are sought for their plumage: "The crownes were made of long small white feathers and underneath and above mixt with some red, & greene feathers, for they have many parrots, and some doves, whereof they make great account, for every one of the kings counsell had a dove by him sitting upon a sticke" (ibid.).

FOURTH VARIANT: MONSTROUS COUPLE AND CORNUCOPIA

In the frontispiece for part 13, the savage woman appears in her final apotheosis, accompanied by an Indian hunter; they flank a portal heaped with fruits and leaves spilling from a cornucopia (plate 13:F; illus. 22). The physical appearance of this Indian woman offers all the attributes of the woman monster, with a wealth of new details. This exuberance is also enhanced by symmetrical developments in the Indian hunter standing with her.

1. Both exhibit hypertrophy of the sexual organs. The bosom, in this new variant, attains proportions unseen before. The breasts hang down below the navel and the nipples are unusually long, like cow's teats. In a counterpart to these distorted female features, the impressive portrait of her companion accents his virility. His penis is covered by a sheath, and held erect by a tie around his waist.[6] This is the first time a penis sheath has appeared in the *Great Voy-*

ages, the more remarkable because the de Brys had seen pictures of them earlier in some of their earlier models.

The care with which the anatomical details have been drawn, including the testicles and urogenital meatus, stands in contrast to the conventional modesty apparent in the other portrayals of naked men and women. Obviously, the penis sheath, a new element in the dress of the Amerindian, is more than a covering like a loincloth. Its semantic function is symmetrical to the sagging breasts of the savage woman. Far from concealing, the penis sheath on the contrary emphasizes the attributes of sexuality and sexual differentiation between the Indian man and his female companion.

2. Both figures are afflicted with physical deformity. The two figures, so manifestly naked and without sexual ambiguity, nonetheless share in the monstrous or hybrid nudity seen earlier in the old Caribbean woman, their fingernails and toenails sharpened to resemble claws and their skin piereced by many holes and distorted by the weight of the inserted ornaments. Along with handmade ornaments like the rings, we find natural objects (stones) and dead animals (mice and frogs) hanging from their cheeks, ears, nostrils, and chin. This kind of adornment, compared to the set-in ornaments of the old Caribbean woman, marks a further stage in the expression of the unnatural hybridism, "outside of nature," created by the body ornamentation.[8]

Although the couple on the frontispiece does not reappear in part 13 and relate to no textual narrative, the same is not true of this new kind of set-in ornament. The plate depicting a shamanistic rite among the Powhatan Indians shows the warriors and shamans adorned with other examples of this type of ornamentation (plate 13:6, illus. 23). The scene comes from a narrative of the adventures of Captain Smith, taken prisoner by the terrible Powhatan,[9] chief of the confederation of Algonquian tribes of the same name. During his captivity, Smith attended a series of rites aimed at discovering whether Smith and the English had favorable intentions toward the Indians. These ceremonies preceded the council meeting at which the Indians decided to execute the English captain. Smith oweḍ his life to the intervention of the famous Pocahontas, Powhatan's daughter. She threw herself between Smith and his executioners, thus convincing her father to spare the captain.

The idea that the Indians "worship the devil" and "have conference with him and fashion themselves as neare to his shape as they can imagine" (Smith 1624, pp. 34–35), pervades the whole description of the ritual and its participants. Chief Powhatan's costume and headdress, described by John Rolfe, thus appear to the English as an imitation of the devil. Among the details of ornamentation, otherwise clearly different from the ornamentation of the couple on the frontispiece, the set-in ornaments are most specifically associated with diabolical and idolatrous practices: "In each eare commonly they have 3 great holes, whereat they hang chaines, bracelets, or copper. Some of their men wear in these holes a small greene and yellow coloured snake, near halfe a yard in length, which crawling and lapping her selfe about his neck oftentimes familiarly would kiss his lips. Others weare a dead rat tyed by the taile" (Smith 1624, p. 30).

Let us now consider the attributes held by the two figures on the frontispiece. The female monster holds a sheaf of corn and a branch of leaves in one hand, a web-footed bird in the other. Considered by herself, then, she brings together the terms of two separate series of the food code, vegetable and animal. The man carries a hunter's attributes of bow and arrow. From a sociological viewpoint, the plate as a whole, with the European boats as a reminder in the cartouche at the bottom of the portico, expresses the triumph of the uncivilized Indian couple, keeping for itself the privileges of hunting and gathering.

TRANSITION TO SERIALITY

In all these examples, it is clear, then, that the woman with misshapen breasts reappears in circumstances reversing the events in the myth of the Fall. The autochthonous couple either refuses to welcome the intruders or tries to repulse them with weapons. The only meal offered—by the Polynesian king to the Dutch—is in honor of their departure. Even so, they are offered an antifood, kava, the drink made from a plant they have chewed and then spit out, while the Polynesian woman defensively holds the fruits of the fateful gift close to her chest. The plate portraying the flight of the woman of Traitors' Island, which lacks the food code, expresses the rejection of the European invasion in other ways—by a refusal to hear or by sounding an alarm. In other words, the acoustical code acts here as a substitute for the food code to convey the same message. The last frontispiece is even more explicit. Our heroine herself, in the company of an Indian hunter once again in possession of his full complement of attributes, holds the products of hunting and gathering.

The structures of oppositions which, in terms of food diets, was made up of three groups (vegetable, meat, and antifood), now blend together. Instead of standing in opposition to one another, the elements of the food code combine and, from this point of view, the new variants can be distinguished from one another not by a system of oppositions, but by the addition or subtraction of elements from some one of the earlier structures. Thus the woman with the feather fan corresponds, in terms of the food code, only to the vegetable diet, because of the maize and leaves on which she sits. The Hoorn Island variant concerns both fruits and a premasticated food (the kava): hence, it participates in both vegetable food and antifood. The monstrous couple in the last frontispiece belongs to the first and to the second groups. In the Traitors' Island variant, the food code slips into an acoustical code (the spreading of the alarm, the refusal to hear) to convey the same message. As with the "indifferent beauty," the food code is missing.

The anatomical variations reveal the same interplay of addition and subtraction of the clearly structured elements of the earlier anatomical code (fig. 10.1).

These new variants still contain elements borrowed from one or another of the different groups of transformations, except for the "indifferent beauty," who falls entirely within the second group by her physical appearance. The woman seen in the frontispiece exhibits features of the second group, like the Fuegian women, for, like them, she is young and adorned, but, like the figures of the third group, she lacks any sexual or animal ambiguity. The Fuegian

	Group 1	Group 2	Group 3
1. Hybrid	+	−	−
2. Androgynous	+	−	−
3. Young/old	− or +	−	+
4. Adorned/ not adorned	− or +	−	−

Figure 10.1   Anatomical variations of "serial" variants with respect to previous structures of transformation. Plus (+) and minus (−) signs indicate presence or absence of features in the three groups.

women also belong to the second group by their masculinity and adornments, and to the third group, by their old age. Their short stature, absent from the other examples, is a new feature.

The same problem appears when we compare the variations of the food code and the anatomical code. Elements taken from various groups combine without any systematic regularity. This leads us to the transition "from structure to seriality" described by Claude Lévi-Strauss in *The Origin of Table Manners*: "structure deteriorates into seriality. The deterioration begins when oppositional structures give way to reduplicatory structures: the successive episodes all follow the same pattern." Moreover, "the myth appropriates elements from other myths" (1978, p. 129).

This observation tends to confirm that, beyond cultural differences (between Amerindian and European) and the contents of the symbol, we are reaching essential properties of symbolic thinking. Furthermore, as simultaneously the symbol proliferates and its structure deteriorates, two sets of facts become relevant: (1) the internal evolution of the *Great Voyages* (the process begins with part 9, in 1601) and (2) the historical changes occurring in the process of the American conquest and appearing in the later texts of the collection. This type of question, which is crucial in the present context, does not apply, of course, when one deals with undated oral myths.

To conclude, then, we shall take up again the motif of the savage woman from the diachronic turning point just shown, and demonstrate that this shift from structures to seriality, and the blending of the initial motif with new ones, do not dilute the semantic value of the symbol, but on the contrary, clarify its functions and its *raison d'être*, in the social, political, and economic dynamics of colonization.

some of its features overlap the limits drawn between conceptual categories within a classifactory system. Impurity is disorder. Classification is not simply a reflection about natural or objective differences distinguishing objects or beings from one another, but is also a cultural operation. As Montaigne says, "Whatever road I choose, I must needs break down some barrier set up by custom, so carefully has she blocked all our paths";[1] and again, "We call contrary to Nature what comes about contrary to custom."[2] Thus, according to Mary Douglas's theory, beings and things that participate in two or more categories as fixed by a given culture appear ambiguous and monstrous for that reason, and become instantly burdened with interdictions, horror, and disgust. What is decreed impure, thus execrated and condemned by a culture, is an object out of place, a cause of disorder. The British anthropologist's example of food prohibitions in Leviticus is very convincing: the pig is not forbidden because it is naturally impure or dirty but is considered impure or repulsive, thus inedible, because it exhibits two features contradicting the classification of animals set forth in Deuteronomy—it has cloven hoof but is not a ruminant.

Moreover, another anthropologist Victor Turner, extends this theory of taboo and anomaly to other liminal or marginal situations, not simply to static situations (within a taxinomic system, for example) but to transitory and dynamic ones, as those in which one changes from one state to another. Thus Turner (1967 and 1969) analyzes the symbolism surrounding the neophytes in the rites of passage widespread in Africa, particularly during the liminal period of the ritual. At that time, the neophytes, already separated from the initial state from which the first phase of the rite has taken them, have not yet been integrated into the new role society reserves for them at the final phase of the rite. For a while, then, they stand in the same interstructural position as the abominations of Leviticus: outside any classification, betwixt and between, belonging to several orders simultaneously and to none, outside time, outside society. They become endowed, then, with all the ambiguities of anomalous and monstrous beings and with the ideas of contamination and impurity this kind of situation entails. They are stripped of every sign or attribute that identifies the other individuals of the group according to sex, age, and status; they are treated symbolically as both living and dead, men and women, asexual or androgynous. At the same time, the sacred objects pertaining to the rite (masks, statues, farm tools, bow and arrow, etc.) become characterized by elements that are incongruous, disproportionate, and therefore, monstrous (Turner 1967, pp. 104–5).

Far from interpreting this symbolism as a mere projection of dream, hallucination, or mental deficiency, Turner stresses the fact that the ambiguity and confusion among different species and orders observable in these liminal objects or beings intend to draw the attention of the neophyte and the social group to the different elements of reality as it is conceived in their own culture. Moreover, the symbols representing the liminal person are quite often borrowed from biological phenomena, either from physical processes with negative nuances (death, decomposition, or menstruation), corresponding to the fact that the neophyte no longer belongs to the first classification from which he has been removed, or by symbols modeled on the process of gestation or birth to express that they are not yet born into the world awaiting them. The neophyte is then likened to the embryo or newborn.

Although these analyses bear on cultural facts taken from geographical regions very different from our own, they clearly relate to the conclusions we have reached about the symbolism of sagging breasts. Furthermore, by drawing inferences from studies made by Africanists (Douglas, Turner, and also Rigby) on the symbols accompanying certain rites of transition, we shall be able to understand the paradox mentioned at the beginning of the chapter: from part 9 on, the motif of the sagging breasts appears with increasing frequency and is associated with other ambiguous and aberrant figures just when the structures of transformation seem to be breaking up.

At every point in our analysis, systems of pertinent oppositions have acquired meaning only when attached to a concrete historical situation: the conquest of the Amerindian by the Protestant countries and the attitudes and actions of these conquerors with respect to those they intended to subjugate. This historical situation, of contact, then conquest and colonization, places the Indian successively in two interstructural or, liminal positions.

At first, the Amerindian, by his very existence on a previously unknown continent and the mystery surrounding his origins, introduced chaos into the order of things such as the Europeans imagined it in their own cosmogony, moral code, and ideas on the origin or man.[3] The fact that the Europeans quickly dispelled their

Golden Age formulae

doubts about the Indians' humanity only reenforced the Indians' basic ambiguity in their eyes: they are indeed men with a soul and a mind (for making tools, as de Bry notes in the beginning of the *Great Voyages*), but men *without* God, *without* law, and *without* breeches.[4] It is in relation to these classificatory systems that the Europeans portray the Amerindian, so different culturally, as an anomalous, ambiguous being, in Mary Douglas's sense. In this perspective, the appearance of the Indian woman with the sagging breasts and all her ambiguities, in contrast to the conventional, "normal," portrayal of the Indian, attracts attention to the chaos brought about by cultural differences, which is unacceptable to a classificatory mode of thinking (the *pensée sauvage*) avid for logical order.

But later on, when the colonizing intentions of the Protestants become more specific at the beginning of the seventeenth century, the Amerindian assumes a new liminal position, not with respect to a static system of classification (this problem has already been solved in the images), but with respect to the goal of settling permanently in America. We can understand why the Indian should become fraught with new ambiguities, the motif of the sagging breasts should multiply rather than disappear and finally combine with other symbols of anomaly. For the Protestant conquerors, the Amerindian is in the same situation as the neophyte with respect to the initiator in a rite of passage. In this case, the rite participates in what is known as "cumulative history." As a rite of domination, it consists in symbolically transforming the free, autochthonous Indian, master of his land, into the Indian dispossessed and colonized by his own guests. The more he rebels and challenges an order—not as yet established, but projected by the Europeans—the more anomalous he becomes in their eyes and the more visible the signs of his anomaly. In other words, if the first phase of the symbolism of the Indian woman with the sagging breasts attempted to integrate the Indian into a preexisting order, the second phase, on the contrary, seeks to integrate him into an order yet to come. Seen in this light, the increased frequency of ambiguous and aberrant figures beginning with part 9, and the phenomenon of seriality described in the previous chapter will become clearer.

Before we reexamine the serial variants of the savage woman and the new motifs of ambiguity that accompany it in the light of ritual symbolism, we must take stock of the method that led us to move from the notion of iconographic motif to that of ritual symbol. (By this term I mean, following Victor Turner, that a visual sign—serving as a symbolic vehicle—has the function of provoking an effect, an action, by bringing together representations or images with instances of behavior and actions.) In so doing it is clear that we are far from the notions of pertinent oppositions with which we began. From pertinent oppositions to ritual symbol, we have crossed through different levels, in these sense in which linguists distinguish "levels" of representation between phonemes, monemes, or the transformational level. In addition, as we went along, I have referred quite loosely to the motif of the sagging breasts as a "mytho-iconographic system" made of structures of transformation linking the variants of the figure and the meanings attached to them. This system now appears as the very mechanism by which we move from sign to ritual symbol. For this reason we shall retrace our steps and identify the processes by which we moved from one to the other. This way, it will be possible to grasp a twofold process: first the making of structures ("structuration") which seems to lead to "static" structures (this will be discussed later); then their undoing ("destructuration") under the pressure of external events, a phenomenon that should not be interpreted as a mere loss of meaning, through attrition, but as itself significant.

From Sign to Symbol

At the outset, we selected an iconographic motif, the savage woman with sagging breasts, inherited from a pictorial tradition. This motif consists of an easily recognizable visual or iconic sign we may call an "iconic sememe," as would Umberto Eco, or a "symbolic vehicle," as would Victor Turner.[5] This sign in turn is composed of a series of denotations quickly identifiable by a European (feminine nudity, secondary sexual organ, motherhood, suckling), combined with several connotations: the figure of evil (sorceress, devil, capital sins), ambiguity (hybrid being, vampires, hermaphrodite), decadence, and decrepitude (death, old age, ugliness).

Our whole analysis has shown that these connotations and denotations, which might on occasion be associated with the sign, do not in fact combine with it and that they become meaningful on a first level only by their position and according to a dual process: selection (a choice from among a limited number of possibilities) and combination (an association with other elements).

Thus, for example, the denotative meaning that would most spontaneously come to mind, suckling a child or motherhood, never appears and holds no place in the symbolic system of the sagging breasts. The iconographic motif of the nursing Indian woman, present in certain plates of the *Great Voyages*, shows no deformity of the bosom. Either it is completely hidden, that is, absent on the graphic level, or it is no different from that of other women. Moreover, the engraver sometimes deliberately omits the denotation of suckling directly associated with this iconic sign in the models he chooses (illus. 20). Of the variants examined, only one actually portrayed a mother as giving her children— who are old enough to stand—a bird to eat, a diet the very opposite of suckling. The same holds true of the connotations of old age, decreptitude, and hybridism: they are never given intrinsically in the sign itself (sagging breasts), but only by association with adjoining elements in a given context, plate, or series of plates. This interplay between selection—from a pool of possible meanings, culturally determined, and attached to the representation of the natural biological and anatomical phenomenon of the female breast—and combination with other representational elements determines a level at which pertinent, syntagmatic, and paradigmatic oppositions can be perceived.

From these oppositions, we were able to build transformations relating different variants and set out the laws by which one changes to another. Figure 11.1 shows these processes schematically, at their beginnings, that is, for the variants of the first four parts. This figure though sketchy, at least has the advantage of outlining the genesis of the structures, a process that gives rise to a third level, that of the symbolic system. In fact it is only when the transformation groups are formed (T1 → T2), then [(T1 → T2) → T3], that, in my opinion, one can speak of "symbol" or "symbolic system." The system is composed, then, of all of these transformations. But it is scarcely more than formed when it begins to break up.

In this perspective, there is no contradiction between the fact that the phenomenon of destructuration, affecting the symbolic system from 1601 onward, does not cause the iconic sign or symbolic vehicle to disappear, but on the contrary is accompanied by a proliferation of the signs of ambiguity and anomaly (dwarf king, bearded Indian, and strange animals). In fact, if the structures of transformation arising from this symbolic vehicle are one stage in the formation of the symbol within a given historical cultural con-

Symbolic vehicle (sagging breasts)		

| Reserve of culturally determined meanings: | Denotative meanings:

Connotative meanings: | female sex organ, motherhood, nursing decrepitude, age, ambiguity, hybridism, evil being |

→Syntagm 4, etc.

	Selection	Selection	Selection
Combination →	syntagm 1	syntagm 2	syntagm 3
Code of anatomy and adornment	sagging/firm breasts young/old unadorned/adorned	sagging breasts old adorned hybrid	sagging breasts young unadorned hybrid
Food code	cannibalism blood/flesh fresh/roasted	Offering of fruit ripe	unripe
	Syntagmatic Chain 1	Syntagmatic Chain 2	Syntagmatic Chain 3
Sociological code	Distribution and cooking of prisoner by age and sex divisions	Spanish-Indian relations Spanish conquest	Devil/Adam and Eve intruder/ autochthone relations
	Paradigmatic set 1	Paradigmatic set 2	Paradigmatic set 3
	(T3)	(T2)	(T1)

First transformation structure (T1 → T2) The fateful gift

Second transformation structure ([T1 → T2] → T3) From oblation to holocaust

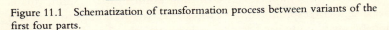

Figure 11.1   Schematization of transformation process between variants of the first four parts.

text, it seems that this vehicle, once having acquired its symbolic value and having assumed sociocultural functions, has no need any more for such solid structures. It may replace them, if need be, by an accumulation of signs having the same function.

I say "if need be," for nothing allows us to say that it should do so by some kind of automatic mechanism. In the present case, on the contrary, external, historical conditions provide the occasion for this change, and as will be shown, there is an internal logic in this dual phenomenon. If, in fact, a symbolic system survives beyond the stage of structuration (but there is no necessity for this to happen), it must then keep the same functions, the same sociocultural properties in relation to the external reality it attempts to organize and to which it gives meaning. If this reality or external situation continues to exist without changing, the system only integrates new content into the same structure. If, on the contrary, the situation changes, the structure must necessarily evolve so that the symbol continues to fulfill the same function and be recognizable and significant.

Thus we shall be able better to identify the dialectic relation set up between external historical facts and the structures in a symbolic system. We shall once again turn to rites practiced among African peoples in order to understand how a symbolic system coming to us from our European ancestors functions.

From Food to Ornamentation

Even in the first transformation structures—those linking the myth of the Fall with the gift made by the Caribbean woman to the Spanish—we are able to identify a set of correlations between the flow of time, evil, and the relations between the sexes (sexual differentiation starting with the hermaphrodite and exchange of women). This correlation becomes better defined later when the structured variants are grouped. The three transformation groups into which the variants fall link types of alliance and kinship relationrelations with a threefold conception of time originating in the Christian myth of the Fall and with it, moral concepts on the nature of man tied to a sense of his history. The three stages are shown in figure 11.2

If part 9 (1601) appears as a turning point in the system, this is because it corresponds to the Protestants' first holdings in America and because, compared to the earlier parts that involved only the Spanish conquerors, it completely reverses the perception of the moral value of colonization. In fact, after the English launched privateering expeditions against the Spanish, the incidents of which are reported in part 8 (1599) in the voyages of Drake, Raleigh, and

Group 1	Group 2	Group 3
Before the Fall	**After the Fall**	
Past	**Present**	**Future**
mythic	of the Protestant	apocalyptic
(Adam and Eve)	conquest	
(Spanish		
conquest)		

Figure 11.2   Tripartite conception of time.

Cavendish, the Dutch in turn launch an attack on the Spanish hegemony, badly battered in the Lowlands, now independent, and in America. From this point on, the volumes of the *Great Voyages* (beginning with part 9) are almost exclusively devoted to these Dutch voyages and to the permanent English settlement in Virginia and New England.

Up to and including part 8, the moral issue of colonization confronting the Protestant conquerors is concealed and transferred to the diabolical Spaniard, whose victory in North America, like a second original sin, stamps later relations between Europeans and Indians with the mark of the Transgression. The English in Virginia do not conquer, nor do the French Huguenots in Florida: they are greeted with open arms by the Indians and enter into amicable relations with them. At least this is the impression given in the first two volumes.[6] In parts 4 through 7, however, the Spanish, though welcomed as warmly as the Protestants, torture, exploit, and destroy the Indians. In part 8, the issue is dodged in another way. The English pirates (Drake, Raleigh, and Cavendish), much too absorbed in seizing Spanish ships, scarcely consider settling on the South American coast. The plates portray, then, only very superficial contacts and landing incidents with the inhabitants. Many of them still express the Indians' good will toward the English. Some Indians offer fruit, others go so far as to crown Drake king.[7] Still, a skirmish between Indians and English appears in this part.

But it is chiefly in part 9 that the facts challenge the Protestant position in the problem of conquest. The populations met by the Dutch are neither cannibalistic, as were the Tupinambá of part 3, nor particularly cordial. They flee at the approach of the newcomers, defend themselves, and repulse the advances made by the Europeans. Or, if they accept the Europeans, it is with scorn and distrust, as witness the incident of the imprisonment of Sebald de Weert after the meal with the dwarf king.[8] The Dutch and the English then find themselves in the same position as the Spanish. They have to use arms to submit the "rebels," sometimes massacring them "in retaliation," as they did the Fuegians of Penguin Island, of whom the indifferent beauty is the last female survivor.

It is clear that this reversal of the situation, and particularly the awareness of the problems it involved, is a blow to the conceptual framework bonding the relations between Indians and Europeans. In part 9 we can thus see a shift of perspective, a shift leading finally to a genuine evolution of the symbolic structures.

The first of these changes affects the ecological aspect of the system. Until now, this framework has governed the oppositional structures of the three systems—fruit-eating, meat-eating, and excremental. In the final variants of part 9 (the indifferent beauty and the map of Tierra del Fuego) it ceases to play this role, and subsequent variants emphasize the phenomenon. This change testifies to the perception of a problem the Protestant conquerors must confront: they can not continue to act as perpetual guests, well or badly received, leaving to the Indians the task of feeding them. They have already denounced this parasitic and ungrateful attitude in the Spanish tyrants. When the Indians reject the role of food-givers and the Protestants increase their effort to build settlements, the Protestants in their turn must brave the natural world of America and become hunters and fishermen.

Not until part 8 do the Protestant conquerors engage in hunting. The members of the Cavendish expedition cudgel the sea dogs to death while a group of soldiers use their harquebuses to drive off a band of Indians who attack with bows and arrows. The sea dogs show all the traits of the ambiguous anomalous monster described by Mary Douglas (1966). Let us examine them more closely (illus. 25): they have the tail of a siren and the head of a dog, a lion's mane, and flippers formed like the claws of a bird. Some are shown swimming, others move upright or crawl on the shore, while in the foreground a female nurses her young, thus showing these amphibians as mammals—part fish, part quadruped, and part bird. American wildlife thus acquires the ambiguities of monsters, and enters the system of anomalies that includes the Indian woman with sagging breasts and the long-haired, bearded Indian.

Furthermore, the ecological framework of the system, whose

transformation structures had assimilated the cultural differences between the Indians and Europeans and the problem of their relationship, loses its *raison d'être* little by little, for hunting and fishing, components of a rustic culture, no longer serve to differentiate the Indian from the Protestant European.[9] It becomes quite understandable that the oppositional structures set up among the three diets should lose their relevance as soon as the problem of subsistence is seen in this new perspective. At the same time, with the system's new structures, the conceptualization of cultural differences also evolves. It bears less and less on food and more and more on ornamentation. This evolution appears in the changes affecting the relations of the ambiguous heroine with the various kinds of wildlife associated with her. Their function shifts from the food code to the code of ornamentation and habitat, and this shift can be traced chronologically through the last volumes of the *Great Voyages*.

The image of the indifferent beauty initiates this shift. In terms of anatomical anomalies and of habitat—an emerging code in this system—a syntagmatic bond links her with two different animals, llama and penguin. The map of Tierra del Fuego and the mother with the bird also associates the snail with two variants of Fueigan women in a triple relation of ornamentation, anatomy, and habitat. In fact, the Fuegians use the snail in making necklaces like the one worn by the woman with the dead bird. This ornamental use is the only one mentioned in the text relevant to his engraving. But on the map of Tierra del Fuego, the snail is associated with the indifferent beauty. It is linked with her insofar as the gastropod, by carrying its house on its back, presents the same congenital or accidential peculiarities as those which in various degrees paralyze the other figures, whether they be armless, bound, or powerless, and shares the characteristics of their habitat, whether underground, aerial, or troglodytic.

The same is true for the variants of parts 11 and 12. In the scene of the kava festival where we see a woman with sagging breasts, the birds, perched on sticks held by the king's counselors, are tended not for their flesh but for their feathers, which will be made into ornaments. Finally, the last frontispiece combines the alimentary with the ornamental functions of the animals: the sea-bird relates to the corn, for the monster woman holds both and they are products of hunting and farming, respectively; the dead frog and rat, strung through the pierced skin of the monstrous Amerindian pair, are used as ornaments. These animals represent a further stage or degree in the changed function of the wildlife. Parts of the snail and the perched birds have been used by the natives for ornamentation, the shell of the one, the feathers of the others, whereas the frog and the rat are used whole, as ornaments directly attached to the skin of the monstrous couple.

This progressive change in American fauna and its role toward the actors in the conquest can be seen more clearly in a summary figure (11.3).

	Fauna	Related to anomalous Indians through:			
		Hunted as game	**Ornaments**	**Anatomy**	**Habitat**
Part 8 (illus. 25)	Seal	+ (by English)	−	+	−
Part 9 (illus. 26)	Llama	+ (by Spanish for silver)	−	+ (hypertrophy	+ (high)
(illus. 15 and 17)	Penguin	+ (by Dutch for meat)	−	+ (atrophy)	+ (low)
Part 11 (illus. 21 and 24)	Birds	−	+ (feathers)	−	+
Part 13 (illus. 22)	Bird	+ (by Indians for food)	−	−	+
	Rat and frog	−	+ (inserted)	−	−

Figure 11.3   The role of American fauna.

THE EFFEMINATE INDIAN AND THE MOTIF OF VOMITING

The presence of a second ambiguous figure, the bearded Indian, next to the savage woman, plays a much more efficient role in keeping the ritual function of the symbolic system at a time when new events shake its structures. In fact, this analysis would be unfinished if we did not seek the semantic value of this male figure through all its contexts, before it comes to join our heroine to make a couple. The Indian man with the long hair is also an anomalous, ambiguous figure, and it is no accident that he is found linked with the savage woman in part 9.

As we shall see, long, disheveled hair constitutes the male counterpart of the symbolic vehicle of the sagging breasts. In fact, it is attached both to the paradigm of sexual ambiguity and to the food paradigm. More specifically, his sexual ambiguity is disclosed by his homosexual or "hermaphroditic" manners, noted in the texts and the illustrations.

Hermaphrodites and Sodomites

As early as part 2, two plates portray "hermaphrodites," as the text calls them, among the Timucua. Their curly, uncombed hair hangs to their shoulders in a way recalling the traditional medieval image of the "sodomite," as Chaucer depicts it in the person of the Pardoner:

> This pardoner hadde heer as yelow as wex
> But smoothe it heeng as dooth a stricke of flex
> By ounces henge his lokkes that he hadde,
> And therwith he his shuldres overspradde.
> But thynne it lay, by colpons, con and con. . . .
> [Prologue of the *Canterbury Tales*]

The effeminate appearance of the hermaphrodites is intensified by their clothing, which is like the women's: a skirt made of the Spanish moss that hangs gracefully from the trees in Florida. By contrast, the scalp-hunting Timucua warriors wear a cotton loincloth draped around their hips and ornaments of copper and animal skin. Their hair is pulled up to the top of the head in a smooth chignon, quite frequently adorned with a fur tail, feathers, or woven rushes. The hermaphrodites' long curly hair and their female attire mark them, then, as an intermediate sexual category, between the Timucua warriors and the women.

A specific social function is attached to this sexual ambiguity. The hermaphrodites carry the ill and the dead on the stretchers and deep baskets full of rations to the public storehouses. Women help in this task (illus. 27).[10] According to the caption, "Each year, at a certain time, they [the Timucua] gather a store of wild animals, fish, and even crocodiles. These are put into baskets and carried by the curly-haired hermaphrodites to the storehouse" (Lorent 1965, p. 81).

Shown among the Timucua as beasts of burden and entrusted with the care and transportation of sick men and of rations, the Indians with the long wavy hair appear again in part 4 in more tragic circumstances. The Spanish conquistadors charge them with sodomy and feed them to a pack of dogs, under the eyes of their executioners, among whom we see Balboa himself, the man responsible for this ignominy. The punishment the Spanish inflict on these effeminate Indians is the reverse of the treatment they receive among the Timucua, as food-bearers; they are themselves reduced to being food for fierce animals, trained by the Spanish and thus agents of their cruelty (illus. 28).[11]

The Patagonian Arrow-swallower

An allegorical plate portrays the triumph of Magellan discoverer of the strait bearing his name (illus. 29). Alone in his boat the Portuguese conqueror enters the strait among a crowd of monsters of sky and sea and mythological figures, among whom is a bearded, disheveled man, a garland of vine leaves girding his loins and a kind of animal-skin mocassin on his feet. In one hand he holds a bow and in the other an arrow that he thrusts down his throat. This figure is a Patagonian, a name which, according to Benzoni, was given to the inhabitants of the Magellan Strait because "for shoes these giants wore animal skins on their feet, making them looks like the paws of a bear of some other wild beast than like men's feet" (Benzoni 1579, 1:139). Benzoni takes his description of the Patagonians from the narrative of Pigafetta, the first chronicler of Magellan's adventure. As for the plate itself, it comes from an old engraving, executed by Jean Galle after a drawing by Jean Stradan, celebrating the arrival of the *Victoria*, Magellan's ship, on its return from the first trip around the world in 1522. The triumphal arrival of boats in unknown lands, celebrated by mythological figures— Tritons, nymphs, or Neptunes—is a common motif in Renaissance iconography. These figures are often portrayed with foliage twisted around their waists, as is our Patagonian, for in the Middle Ages this motif had begun to be one of the attributes of the "savage"[12]

A passage from Pigafetta's narrative explains the strange action of the Patagonian who thrusts an arrow down his throat as if killing himself on the conqueror's arrival. In fact, it was a therapeutic practice of the Patagonians, who scratched the throat with an arrow to induce vomiting. Magellan's expedition must have witnessed this feat performed by shamans, which involved thrusting an arrow down the throat after first removing the point.

This new image of the disheveled Indian man seems at first glance to have none of the sexually ambiguous features of the preceding variants. Moreover, the Indian holds a bow and arrow in his hand, attributes par excellence of the hunter or warrior. On closer examination, however, the way the man uses his weapons—whether we interpret his act as a suicide attempt or an emetic practice—contradicts what we expect from a hunter or warrior.[13] In either case, instead of aiming his bow and arrows at game or a foreign invader, such as Magellan pictured here as a victorious conqueror, he used them either to kill himself or to make himself vomit.

Vomiting, the opposite of eating, belongs to the paradigm of food being offered, eaten, or, as in the present case, rejected by an ambiguous figure.

This motif leads us to link the disheveled Patagonian with all the plates in which Indians are seen vomiting, spitting out food, or scratching their throats with an instrument. The rejection of food, seen as a theme, actually occurs several times under these three aspects.

Vomiting the "Black Beverage"

Before they went scalp-hunting, Timucua warriors gathered in a war council to drink the famous "black beverage," or holly *casina*, a narcotic drink made from a plant with emetic qualities and which was also used to relieve hunger on the warriors' long marches (illus. 30). In the foreground women prepare the beverage, then offer it in a large conch shell to the men. Some of them vomit, thus disqualifying themselves from participation in the warrior expedition. Le Moyne relates that this drink has such powerful effects that whoever drinks it breaks out in a violent sweat: "For this reason no one is considered fit to be given any military responsibility who cannot keep the casina down."[14]

Thus vomiting the casina, as shown in this plate, indicates on the part of men an effeminate behavior unworthy of the warrior.

Zemi Worship

Elsewhere, the Arawak, smooth-skinned and well-groomed, try to induce vomiting by thrusting a little stick into their throat before they enter the temple, bringing a libation to lay at the feet of the idols with sagging breasts, or zemis (illus. 6).[15] This ritual vomiting was intended as an act of purification before one offered a communal meal and shared it with the other members of the group and the idols. Thus it is linked with a food offering, with an ambiguous being, and with food-sharing. As seen earlier, these idols belong to the paradigm of the "fateful gift."

Preparing *Cahouin*

In yet another plate, beautiful young Tupinambá women spit out the roots they have chewed for the preparation of *cahouin*, a fermented beverage drunk by the Tupinambá in the cannibal rites before executing and eating the prisoner (illus. 8).

Preparing Kava

Men from Hoorn Island used a similar method to prepare their kava, which, along with roast pigs, the Polynesian king offered the Dutch (illus. 21). The Dutch guests, finding its preparation repulsive, refused the drink but accepted the meal. One must also remember that in this plate the sexual roles of the figures were inverted: men wear their hair long, in braids or pulled up on the top of the head; women, on the contrary, wear it short and appear masculine.

Figure 11.4 provides a summary of the various plates in which the motif of food vomited or spat out appears.

There are three ways, then, for the Indians to eject food, each corresponding to a different social attitude shown by male Indians to the foreigners: vomiting may be induced by two different emetic techniques, one intentional, using an arrow or stick, the other involuntary, by swallowing a beverage having emetic properties, like the Timucua's casina, which some—the competent warriors—can drink without difficulty and others vomit up.

These two cases of vomiting, whether voluntary or involuntary, indicate that the Indian's behavior is unworthy of a warrior's behavior or its reverse: the Timucua unable to swallow the emetic drink disquality themselves from assuming the role of scalp-hunter. The Patagonian uses his arrow, an attribute of the warrior-hunter, on himself, instead of turning it against the foreign conqueror come to put the country down. The Arawak also make themselves vomit before sharing a meal with the idols with sag-

	Beverage:		Before
Part 2: (illus. 30)	Prepared by women Vomited up by incompetent warrior	Drunk by qualified warriors	Scalp-hunting expedition
Part 3: (illus. 8)	Premasticated by women	Drunk by warriors	Cannibal meal
Part 11A: (illus. 21)	Premasticated by women	Drunk by native men Refused by foreigners	Sharing a meal with foreigner and sending him off
Part 4: (illus. 29)	**Intentional Vomiting** by disheveled man with an arrow	**Reversal** of warrior's behavior	**Upon** Spanish invaders' arrival

Figure 11.4   The vomiting motif.

ging breasts, who, as we have seen, are related to the tempter of the earthly paradise, and to the diabolical Spanish, in the context of the Indian's subjection and fall.

Finally, a third mode of rejecting food, whether vomiting it or spitting it out, results from the preparation of a narcotic drink. Unlike the other two modes, this one reflects a manly, warriorlike attitude of the Indian toward the foreigners. The cannibalistic Tupinambá, before eating the prisoner-of-war, drink the beverage their women prepare by chewing the roots and spitting them out. Compared to them, the Polynesians show an ambiguous attitude, marked by a reversal of the sexual poles in the physical appearance of males and females. Indeed, the men prepare the beverage and they use the same method as the Tupinambá women. The drink, produced from roots chewed up by the men, is drunk by the natives, including the king, but is refused by the Dutch guests. The Polynesians thus exhibit a twofold attitude toward the foreign guest. They offer him an antifood (an undrinkable beverage which is refused), followed by a good meal (which is accepted). The meal consists of roast pig, a product of animal husbandry and not of hunting or fishing like all the other meats offered by the natives. In addition, they offer this meal to celebrate the foreigner's departure, thus politely sending him off.

Consequently, when a new variant of the bearded and hairy Indian appears on the frontispiece of part 9 and for the first time joins the Indian woman with the sagging breasts in a single syntagm, his presence is already laden with sexual ambiguity, associated, like the attitude of the savage woman, with a certain type of attitude toward the foreigner. The paradigm of food, drawn from all the variants of the disheveled man prior to part 9, appears in part 9 as the inverse of the paradigm of weapons, in terms of the social relations between foreigners and autochthones. Indeed, whether he plays the role of food-bearer or uses an arrow to make himself vomit, he engages in tasks and actions opposed to those suitable to the successful warrior or huntsman.

When this figure appears in part 9 in the company of the savage Indian woman, a contrast in physical appearance, especially in dress, sums up their shared quality of ambiguity. The bearded Indian, with his long curly hair, skirt, and feathered headdress, and the Penguin Island woman with the boy's face and cropped hair, clothed in a loincloth and cape, form an inverted couple. We must now explore the function of this new paradigm of the inverted couple and sex role reversal.

Rite of Passage: The Inverted Couple and the Ruin of the Indies

By following the appearances of this couple from part 9 to part 13, we can see that the play of sexual ambiguities and transvestism between the two figures varies in accordance with the relations between Amerindians or Polynesians and Protestant conquerors.

Considered sociologically, the inverted Fuegian couple displays the following traits: the Indian man with the feathered skirt who holds a bow and arrow on the frontispiece lies bound at the feet of his female companion on Penguin Island, and, the height of paradox for a hunter, is himself treated as game by the Dutch who have taken him prisoner. Joining this unlucky hunter or vanquished warrior, the indifferent beauty is the first variant of the savage woman to break with the food code. Physically, she retains all the traits of the women of the second transformation group: young, adorned, and, with her masculine appearance, androgynous. This inversion of sexual roles remains present in the variants of the subsequent parts, as long as the Indian is vanquished by Protestant conquerors. But when the woman's partner successfully uses his weapons against the invader, she loses her sexual ambiguity, which introduces other changes.

In the picture of the woman with a fan, the Indian with the long braid points his harpoon at a new intruder, the devil in person, with his horns and goat's forehead, while in parallel fashion the woman with sagging breasts, young and adorned but without sexual ambiguity and with her long hair loosened, protects her fruits at the approach of the European vessels, which are swallowed up in the waves.

In the Traitors' Island variant, the Polynesian women, whose cropped hair gives them a masculine look, are surrounded by men wearing their hair in long braids or pulled up on their heads; women give the alarm at the arrival of the Dutch and encourage them to flee; men try to defend themselves with their clubs, but in vain, for the Dutch disembark. The paradigm of the inverted couple persists, but new differences can be seen between the Polynesian women and men: the women are dwarfish compared to the men, and their faces show more age than in the Fuegian variants of part 4.

This is also true in another plate, where the savage woman holds her fruit close to her body, while the men with their long hair tied up or braided—among whom we see the king with his feathered headdress—offer kava to the Dutch (illus. 21). Kava is classifiable as an antifood because it is a waste that has been spat out. The woman still retains a masculine and rather aged look and a short stature. However, the fruits she protects and the food waste (the spat-out beverage) she offers to the Dutch at the beginning of the meal show an attitude of distrust, to say the least, toward the guests, who will still be entertained with a meal.

These conflicting attitudes toward the strangers are associated with variations in the respective sexual appearance of male and female natives and their relationships. Women keep their manly, sexually ambiguous look; the Polynesian males with their hair braided or tied up take on somewhat more of their manhood. Indeed, even in the frontispiece of part 11, the man with the braid and the harpoon has regained all hs manliness as he faces a savage woman without sexual ambiguity, thanks to this aggressive attitude toward the intruders, an attitude met with success, for the European boats are shipwrecked. But, among the Polynesians (illus. 21), the main difference between men and women is that of height and age: men are tall, robust, and well formed; women are short, almost dwarfish, and their faces appear old. In addition, the subsequent plate (illus. 24) leaves no doubt about the heterosexual tastes of the Polynesian king with the braid and the feathered head-dress; it shows the second part of the meal he offers the Dutch. The pigs killed in honor of their departure are served in a formal cere-mony that emphasizes the Polynesian king's prestige and power over his "subjects": "Those people yeeld great reverence and respect unto their kinges, for all the meate which they brought before their king, . . . they laid it upon their heads, and kneeling on their knees, set it downe before the king" (Schouten 1619, pp. 55–56).

In the foreground, the king, seated on a mat, watches little girls dancing to the beat of a drum under the eyes of two Dutchmen. In Schouten's text, as well as in the caption, this scene takes place away from the meal at another time. One moonlit evening, a member of the Dutch crew, returning from fishing, comes upon this extraordinary spectacle: the "old king" watches ("not without pleasure," the caption adds; *"sine voluptate,"* in the Latin edition) a group of "young wenches," dancing "after their maner, very finely and with a good grace, according to the measure of the noyse of the instrument" (Schouten 1619, p. 54).

Actually, the dancers mentioned in the English texts as "wenches" or *"puellae"* in the Latin, are under the age of puberty in the engraving. In addition, there is something provocative about their nudity, to say the least. Their sexual parts are drawn in detail, thus breaking the graphic convention respected in all the female nudes in the *Great Voyages*.

In this context, the king with the long braids appears as the reverse of the dwarf king of Guinea, who, a poor host no less than a poor guest, gives an impression of helplessness because he has to be carried to bed after the meal. The anatomical variations we have observed between the Polynesian variant of the savage woman and the king can thus be explained as partial transformations of both the anatomical code and the sociological code. Sociologically, in fact, the king of Hoorn Island displays a doubly ambiguous attitude: on the one hand, toward his foreign guests, he offers both a food waste (the spat-out beverage) and a good meal; he honors them with this meal to celebrate their departure, a departure that pleases him; on the other hand, toward his own, he is neither helpless like the impotent dwarf king, nor effeminate like the disheveled, long-haired Indians; he has well-defined heterosexual tastes, but they fall outside sociological norms, for he prefers prepubescent little girls to women. This gives rise to partial transformations, both anatomical and sociological (see fig. 11.5).

	Women with sagging breasts		Royal host	
Age: Height: Sex:	young normal androgynous	old dwarf androgynous	adult dwarf diminished	old normal heterosexual
Attitude toward foreigner	dismissed (offering refused by foreigner)	distrustful (holds fruit close to her)	**Host** frugal copious meal abusive + table companion antifood **Foreigner** made prisoner dismissed politely	

Figure 11.5   Partial transformations of savage woman and king motifs.

The figure of the king of Hoorn Island thus marks a new stage in the evolution of the image of the long-haired Indian. Sexually and sociologically he holds an intermediate position between his (chronological) predecessors on the one hand, who are markedly effeminate as hermaphrodites or sodomites, helpless hunters or warriors who join the Indian woman with sagging breasts and masculine air to make an inverted or transvestite couple, and, on the other, the male monster in the last frontispiece. The clearly differentiated sexual features of the monster couple recall, in turn, the hybrid monsters before the Fall (the devil in paradise and the old Caribbean woman).

The portrayal of the Indian couple in the last frontispiece ostentatiously develops the attributes that differentiate man and woman sexually. With the anatomical signs of his manhood, the savage woman's companion regains the status of skillful hunter: he holds a giant bow and arrow, taller than himself, while his companion holds the products of his hunt (a web-footed bird), and, for the first time, an agricultural product (an ear of corn). But when the native couple regains its autonomy from the European conquerors and, at the same time, loses its sexual ambiguity, it becomes more monstrous than ever, and its hybridity is enhanced by the dead animals, rats and frogs, attached to their skin for ornamentation, and physical deformity (hypertrophy of the sexual organs, stretching of the earlobes, hair length and shape of the nails sharpened like claws, etc.) (illus. 22).

Figure 11.6 sums up the simultaneous variations in the anatomy of the ambiguous couple and its sociopolitical relations with Europeans.

Ambiguous couple	Relation with the foreigner
1. "The Indifferent Beauty" and Indian Man (illus. 15 and 16) Inversion of sexual traits: (inverted couple) —effeminate man —masculine woman	hunter } warrior } overcome by foreigner
2. "The Woman with a Fan" (illus. 18) Sexual differentiation —man with braid holds harpoon —woman (sagging breasts) loses sexual ambiguity	Repulses the intruder Protects her fruits
3. "Feast of Kava" (illus. 21) Masculine woman man (king); braid, female connotation	Protects her fruits (from foreigner/offers antifood and meal to foreigner
4. "Monster Couple" (illus. 22) Exaggerated sexual differentiation hypertrophy of male and female sex organs monstrosity of adornment (hybird features)	Successful hunter and farmer (holds products of the hunt and corn) Free Indian; foreigner absent

Figure 11.6   The anatomy of the Indian couple and its relation to the foreigner.

Considered semantically, the "serial" variants relate to each other no less systematically than the first variants, organized as transformation structures. In the serial variants, in fact, the two ambiguous figures assume the aspect of an inverted or transvestite couple each time the Amerindian world appears vanquished by the Protestant conquerors. But their sexual inversion, which would entail the sterility and extinction of the Amerindian, gradually disappears as they successfully resist and drive off the conquerors. Finally, the two figures lose their sexual ambiguity altogether, and their portrait even overstates their sexual attributes. They fall into the category of monstrous hybrid, the most "outside nature"—that of the monster before the Fall (the devil of paradise on earth and the old Caribbean woman with the Spaniards). In the plate where this reversal occurs, the Indian man also reassumes his value as a hunter and, in what must be the height of paradox for the Protestant, is implicitly recognized as a farmer, because for the first time in the *Great Voyages* an ear of corn, the sign par excellence of indigenous agriculture, finds a place as an Indian attribute.

Thus the ritual function of the symbol is unquestionable through the variations of its components (sexual ambiguity, hybridity, food offering, hunting, and so on), it fluctuates with the changing events of the Protestant conquest described in the *Great Voyages*. To portray the coveted Indian world as a sexually ambiguous, inverted couple amounts to condemning it to sterility and thus to extinction. This symbolism occurs at the time of the first battles between Indians and Protestants, when the Protestants triumph and engage in massacres and reprisals. As opposed to this, when overgrown, monstrous hybrid elements, outside of nature, replace sexual ambiguity and inversion, the Protestants become clearly aware of new developments in their relations with Indians. The *Great Voyages* close with the complete deterioration of these relations, in Virginia and New England for the English, and in Tierra del Fuego, among the Yahgans, with the Dutch expedition of Jacques Lhermite. In the last volume, we see for instance the battles of the Virginia colonists with the terrible Powhatan chief, who appears in several engravings in all his power.[16] During this period, the English are forced to draw treaties with the Algonquian confederation of the Powhatans. We see these unpleasant dealings as early as part 10. For the first time in the entire collection, one of these plates depicts the Indians as a political group with whom the English must deal. It shows the Chickahominy, one of the confederated tribes of the Powhatan, surrendering to Captain Argol and concluding a treaty with him.[17] But these relations worsen in part 13 and the English position appears more precarious and threatened by the Indians' resistance. Captain John Smith is taken prisoner by the Powhatan, portrayed as terrifying and diabolical. They condemn him to death and he is saved only *in extremis* by Pocahontas. Next is the Virginia massacre of 1622: the Algonquians use knives for their attack on the English colonists. For the English, this historical massacre was the signal for open war against the Indians and would later be constantly recalled as justification for the expropriation of the Indians.

RITUAL SYMBOLISM AND THE MEANING OF HISTORY

It is clear then that European iconography at the turn of the sixteenth century and the seventeenth century derives from mental processes identical to those that produced certain forms of primitive art intimately connected with rituals. In both cases, certain themes or motifs, borrowed from natural categories—biological phenomena, qualities of matter, divisions of space—are organized by the same type of unconscious logic, while expressing quite different kinds of content. The functions of this symbolism, which longs to accomplish in fact what it signifies, are not simply "magical" and thus "null," as one might be tempted to believe. They also serve to detach and reenforce systems of classification linking the cosmic order to the social and political order, and, at the same time, as far as they imply a system of values, governing the behavior and actions of a social group toward the new event it must confront.

In fact, just as Leviticus, by marking certain animals with the seal of abomination, brings out the natural order as conceived in Deuteronomy, while at the same time dictating the appropriate conduct for dealing with such creatures (the abstention from eating them), likewise the image of the Indian woman with sagging breasts and the image of the disheveled Indian, by the very fact that they depart from the conventional norm, call attention to deeper differences and anomalies—those challenging the Europeans' system of values, beliefs, and knowledge at that period—and at the same time dictate the appropriate conduct for dealing with them (exchange, segregation, and dispossession). It took some time before this new object of knowledge—the Amerindian world, unknown to the Sibyls, as Montaigne says—was incorporated into a first coherent system, and this in relation to the Spanish conquest. When this system is again shaken by the awareness of the problems raised by Protestant expansion in America in part 9, two phenomena occur. On the one hand, certain variants are caught up in the transformation system of the symbolism of the sagging breasts; on the other hand, the other variants fall away, becoming understandable only when joined to other motifs, and introduce a series of diachronic structures linking together the variants of the last parts in a serial way. After we account separately for these two phenomena—the structures of transformation and the evolution of the serial variants—the explanation for the evolution will lead us retrospectively and in conclusion to reconsider the dynamics of the symbolism of the sagging breasts, not based on the antinomy between "static structures" and "dynamic structures," but as a single continuous process.

Ths antinomy rests on the widely held idea that "structure" means "stability," at least as used in the social sciences, by contrast with other fields, such as history and biology. We have first taken up this terminology to define the structures of transformation identified in the symbolism of the "savage woman." These structures indeed impose a time of logos upon chronologically distinct events, which seemed implicitly to deny time its irreversible flow, for the sake of a vision of human history conceived in terms of the myth of the Fall.

However, other factors should prompt us to reevaluate this sharp distinction between "static" and "dynamic." First, the serial movement initiated in part 9 develops at a time when the structures of transformation are still going on and the engravers witness the same external events. Conversely, the Fuegian variants, while combining with the organizing schema of the myth of the Fall, also enrich the symbolic content of the motif with new meanings and transform it to take external events into account. Only when these variants complete the three groups of well-structured transformations does the moral position of the Protestant colonizers become clear. It measures itself against two facts, both previously known and included in the symbolic system.

One of these is the martyrdom of the innocent Indian under the Spanish conquest, and the other his cannibalistic mores, already described and interpreted in part 3. But the a priori justification for segregation is completely absent at that time. It appears for the first time only with the Fuegian variants, well ahead of the actualization of this political ideology and even before it could have been realizable or expressed consciously.

If the function of the initial iconographic motif is to resolve the moral contradictions raised by the conquest for a mind peculiarly sensitized to the notion of justice, as was that of the Protestants persecuted for their religious faith, one cannot say without distorting the facts that the structures giving rise to this symbolism are in this case a mechanism for negating time, history, or praxis, as one might be tempted to think. On the contrary, far from being an a posteriori justification for previously confirmed facts, these structures precede action. The Protestant ideas of justice and sin interpret infrastructures and give form to plans for action. Given the Protestants' conviction that human nature was essentially corrupted by original sin, to the point that, according to Luther, "free will can do only evil and sin," it is understandable that, unconsciously, the Protestant should constantly seek signs reflecting the merciless decree of predestination. Prosperity on earth and success, obligations for the one who knows he belongs to the elect of God, may at the same time appear as material evidence of a favorable predestination; conversely, misfortune, failure, and inferiority in any respect whatsoever, are interpreted as the sign of culpability before God.[18] This sums up the theology governing the ethics of men and men's relations to one another.

From this perspective, cultural differences between Indians and Europeans, and notably those concerning techniques of subsistence, appear at a certain time as the mark that the Indian is damned by God. Hence the importance for the symbolic system of the ecological framework supported by the infrastructures of European society. Through this framework, the theological conception of sin and merit is able to fashion an ideology accounting for cultural differences between Indians and Europeans and to dictate one's behavior towards them. As seen earlier, it is not by accident that the savage woman appears in part 9 in a context in which the food she offers shocks the culinary tastes and customs of the Europeans (an uncooked bird with all its feathers; inedible smoked fish); cannibalism, the supreme abomination, then appears as the unavoidable consequence of these shameful signs of inferiority attached to the culturally degraded Indian, whereas in the first parts, the view of the cannibals, like that of the generous Indian martyred by the Spanish, flows directly from the notion of a corrupted human nature and the Fall of man.

Thus the woman serving fish and the mother with the raw bird, while combining with previous transformation structures and with the organizing schema of the Fall of man, nonetheless bring about an evolution in the content and ideas of the symbol. The implicit justification for the Protestant colonization it reveals with its alternative—complete destruction or separation (through a taboo on interracial marriage and segregation)—is entirely absent from the first transformational system that brings together the Fall of Adam and Eve, the Indian's "fall" into the hands of the Spaniards, and the natural process of degeneration implicit in cannibalism. Yet reciprocally, we can understand the development of the symbol within these structures of transformation only by using the components already present in the earlier structures.

This phenomenon may thus be termed a "genesis" or even, borrowing a biological term, an "epigenesis";[19] and, as in biology, this structural analysis of an iconic symbolism leads us to the conclusion that "no preformed and complete structure preexisted anywhere; but the architectural plan for it was present in its very constituents" (Monod, 1971, p. 87). This is worth stressing, for it invites us to view the symbolic structures that proved to be organized according to unflinching rules, not as the outcome of a blind determinism, but as the work of combinative logic where adaptability to environment and events, and hence human initiative, constantly come into play by means of a dialectic between structure and event.

The same is true of the movement of seriality that starts to take shape at the same time in part 9. As a phenomenon of destructuration (for the meanings attached to the signs have no further need to generate one another through transformation structures), this concatenation becomes laden with new semantic values based on the components of the earlier structures and adds something new to them. The mechanism of this evolution can here be seen in action. The evolution does not result simply from the pressure of external events nor from an internal necessity that would force any structure to move into a later stage. Rather, it is the work of a dialectic between the logic of an internal structure and the awareness of problems resulting from external events.

In this sense, the dual developmental process of doing and undoing of structures seems to reveal the emergence of consciousness in a symbolic system. By a lengthy hidden process—whose growth has been seen in the transformational structures—sign becomes symbol. At this stage, the signs, heavy with these symbolic values, have no need to generate new structures: their meaning comes increasingly close to the surface. As a result, we have been able to follow this slow evolution historically, as it works silently on the conquerors' perception of the problems raised by the conquest. In the present case, this move from unconscious to conscious, from deep structures to surface structures, brings us directly to the problem of political action and efficacy of symbols. How does this shift occur?

By preceding practices, the symbolic system has shown a certain disequilibrium between the plan, unconscious, and its realization, to be accomplished later. The Amerindian world is, at the same time, laden with an increased ambiguity apparent in the proliferation of anomalies. It becomes ambiguous, then, not in terms of previous beliefs about man's origin and fall, but also in relation to the place one wishes to assign to the Indian and the place it actually holds. The problem therefore is to remove him from his actual position (that of a legitimate master of the land, now refusing to feed the parasitic European), to throw him into a projected reality (projection which takes the form of two possible alternatives, destruction or apartheid). As a rite of passage in so-called primitive societies, we find the same liminal situation. The same processes of symbolization are at work: when the structures are shaken by a necessary passage from one state to another—as, for example, that from childhood to adulthood in a puberty rite—they become reenforced by symbolic signs. What happens then is that the incidence of anomalous signs spreads to American wildlife and the Indian man.

Finally, we make the parallel even more precise by comparing the motif of the inverted couple, brought into focus in part 9, with the widespread rituals that consist in temporarily reversing the sex roles in a society. This comparison, at a level at which the essential, sociocultural properties of symbols are affected,[20] is made possible by Peter Rigby's important research on similar rites among the Gogo, Bantu tribes of Tanzania (1968).

From time to time, Gogo society temporarily ceases to function normally. The women take on the men's role and adopt an aggressive and obscene behaviors that apes and mocks the stereotype of masculinity. Conversely, the men take a passive position and are subjected to the women's sarcasms. Sexual relations are forbidden. The women take their meals to the bush, men's territory, associated with the hunt; men, on the other hand, remain in the fields, usually worked by the women. Rigby explains that the purpose of this ritual role reversal between men and women is to manipulate time. In fact, the Gogo have a dualistic conception of time that reflects a dualistic classification of all kinds of symbolic values. Time alternates between two states, one "good" and one "evil." When a catastrophic event occurs for the group, a famine or a disease among the livestock, for example, the Gogo say that "the years have turned about" (Rigby 1968, p. 171). Reversing the roles assigned to the two sexes is thus a way to establish the normal flow of time and of purifying it of any evil element.

To return to the European conquerors, their conception of time and history was also attacked when events occurred to contradict their classifactory system of values and knowledge. It is understandable that, for them, by the same logic, the iconographic motif of sex reveral failed to reestablish by itself the normal flow of time, conceived as tripartite and not as dualistic, and that other symbols of anomaly must be used: those affecting the Amerindian fauna, syntagmatically associated with the protagonists of the drama of the conquest. The problem, then, is not to reverse the poles of time (one good, the other evil), as it is for the Gogo, but of once more to set up an equilibrium (conceived as a third term: the present of the conquest) between an "ideal" pole—"good," innocent, but irrecoverable (the pole of the time before the Fall associated with the innocence of the garden of Eden)—and a catastrophic pole of food waste, cannibalism, war, and the Apocalypse—toward which all of mankind is inescapably drawn by the Amerindian world, reduced after the common Fall to hunting and fishing, signs of a rustic culture.

Thanks to an almost "microscopic" analysis, realized according to Lévi-Strauss's technique of structural analysis, we feel sure we have grasped the invariants of symbolic thought, whether expressed in oral myths or iconic signs, whether among tribal societies like the Bantu or among the pioneers of cosmopolitan captialism. Recognition of these invariants reveals a singular affinity of the unconscious logic with the logic of life, which has been deciphered from the genetic code by biologists, notably by François Jacob:

> The processes that take place at the microscopic level in the molecules of living beings are completely indistinguishable from those investigated in inert systems by physics and chemistry. Only at the macroscopic level of organisms do special

properties appear, imposed by the necessity of self-reproduction and of adaptation to certain conditions [Jacob 1973, p. 299]

In the same way, the characteristic properties of cultural systems, so diverse in their forms through time and space, appear at a "macroscopic" or "surface" level, so to speak, but they also rest on a combinative system of invariable elements. At this "microscopic," deeper level, we saw the same unconscious logic at work in Amerindian myths, Jewish food taboos, Bantu rituals, and European iconography. This did not prevent us from grasping through it an ideology and ethic specific to the social groups, precisely defined in time and space, who elaborated these representations. What ultimately results from the iconographic analysis of the *Great Voyages* is indeed the knowledge that the Protestant conquest of America and the direction of American history itself would have taken a different turn if it had been managed by other peoples. Even if urged by the same desire to settle in America and the same economic motives, other peoples could have reached different political solutions to the problem if they had viewed differently the Indians and their cultures and their own role as settlers toward the native inhabitants.

Strangely enough, at the conclusion of this complex analysis, the many ramifications of a symbolism that fed on odds and ends and incongruous classifications find their organizing principle in a three-part division of time (a past before the Fall, and, after the Fall, a present, and an apocalyptic future). This threefold division is indeed far from Dumézil's theory of three functions in Indo-European ideology. It is true, however, that, like Dumézil's, our three groups of transformations are organized hierarchically, from an ideal and superior state to a catastrophic state, but their content has changed. Our structures belong to a tripartite division of land in which agriculture and animal husbandry, the third "function" in Dumézil's hierarchy, hold an intermediate, and if we are to believe our systems of transformation, a quasi-redemptive place for the European after the corruption brought by the Fall. Farming stands as a middle term between the enclosed garden, which, like paradise, brings to mind idealistic notions of permanent fertility, innocence, union with God, and understanding among men, and, on the other hand, hunting and fishing, which, in the context of the American conquest, carry negative connotations of cultural inferiority and barbarism. As shown earlier, this stage of rustic nature is conceived as inferior to agriculture, which is notably absent from the transformations underlying the vision of Amerindia. This lack serves as grounds to justify an ideology of domination over the Indian; lacking this "superior" mode of subsistence, the more rustic techniques inevitably lead to war and self-destruction.

If we were to carry the parallel further, this system would indicate, then, a nearly complete reversal in the hierarchy of the functions Dumézil describes, at least with respect to the last two. At best, the first has a mystic and religious aspect that attaches it to the myth of the earthly paradise, but the hierarchical positions of agriculture and war are interchanged.

Before we can draw other conclusions with any certainty, we should examine carefully, and with a fund of erudition comparable to Dumézil's, the avatars of this three-part distribution up to the sixteenth and seventeenth centuries. Such research, however, would lie beyond the scope of our study. The point here is simply to remark the degree to which the two systems coincide—all the more surprising in that nothing suggested it at the outset—and to venture a few hypotheses. First, the comparison tends to suggest that, if, as Dumézil's work has shown, these "functions" (or "structures") outlive the social structure they might originally have reflected, this process may last longer than we have ever imagined. In this case, however, the time comes when it is accompanied by deep transformations. Ideology adapts itself to new ecological or sociopolitical facts, but does so within the same scheme dating from time immemorial. When does this occur? Is it a new fact in the sixteenth century, or is its source found as early as the Middle Ages? What pressures give rise to it? The field is open for questions. What remains certain is that the comparative structural method has proven it could grasp the specificity a system of representation in spite of, or rather thanks to, the permanence of invariants in symbolic thought, and above all, the transformational aspect of the method.

In this respect, mythic or "undomesticated" thought, far from being limited in our societies to marginal domains or to relics (popular beliefs, folklore, art, neurosis, etc.), must be sought in the whole of social life and its means of communication. Unless part of mankind one day undergoes a mutation in the genetic meaning of the term (rather than the sociological or political one), by some chemical or nutritional influence, we must accept the fact that our supercivilizations can not escape from the "savage mind" on the pretext that the development of technology and science has brought with it de facto a greater rationality in man, whether this rationality be analytic or dialectic. The *Great Voyages*, the epic of the Protestant conquest, provide the proof. At the close of the sixteenth century and the beginning of the seventeenth century, science and technology bring men the material power to arm a fleet able to cross oceans, the power to overthrow nascent empires with gunpowder and a cavalry that terrified the conquered peoples. But at the same time, this relative superiority carried in its wake a wealth of contradictions, all the greater as the effect of this material progress was sudden and undeniable—just as the effect of the atom bomb at Hiroshima in our time—and brought with it no system of values to replace the one it necessarily shook. Our investigation of the *Great Voyages* has repeatedly shown how a system of values builds up again at the unconscious level around newly perceived events. It is at the unconscious level also that plans for action take form. The imagination acts on the unconscious with no other control than its own laws, which the conscious mind ignores. Now, this kind of thinking, revealed unfettered behind the symbolism of sagging breasts, is not passive or cut off from consciousness. On the contrary, it draws from consciousness the events that foster it and, in turn, aspires to create in reality what it signifies. It does not always succeed, but when it does, it can leave its mark on institutions and on the social and political structure, as it has done in North America for several centuries.

If our conclusions are correct, they suggest that the greater the demands of rationality, the greater the likelihood that the real contradictions offered to consciousness will be repressed by the conscious. If myths, in the strict sense of the word (fabled stories), have lost their sociocultural importance in our societies, pictures, in compensation, have taken their place. As the product of an ever more precise technology of electronics and cybernetics, they have taken on a overwhelming importance in communication, not only through the illustrated press and advertising, but through photography, television, and cinema. The *Great Voyages*, one of the first examples of mass communication through pictures in Europe, give us an overview of the semantic richness and insidious power of iconic signs.

Unlike speech, which is controlled by a rational logic, pictures stem from the unsaid. As a result, they contain a wealth of implicit, thus virtual and ambiguous, meanings. Consciousness loosens the demands of rationality. The communicative power of pictures at the level of the unsaid is unleashed precisely because of technological development: on the one hand through the technical perfection attained at present in the reproduction of events and the physical world, and on the other, because the words accompanying the picture confer on it a deceptive stamp of authenticity.

Montaigne, confronting men intoxicated with their conquests, with their own limits, reminds us that "there is no sect that is not constrained to permit its sage to conform in a number of things that are not understood, or perceived, or accepted if he wants to live" (*Essays* 2.12). And at the close of the seventeenth century, Nicole perceives behind the actions of men and especially their rules of justice "imperceptible thoughts . . . entwined and confused in men's minds with other objects that take the place of direct objects," for

> so little do we know our thoughts that, on the contrary, most of them are unknown to us, and they do not fail to be in our mind and make themselves felt, guide us, lead us to draw precise conclusions and make an infinity of resolves, urge us and determine our decisions, without our having a clear and distinct idea of them, without our being able to express them immediately, and to discover them except through much reflection, of which the majority of men are incapable. [*Traité de la grâce générale*, in Chinard 1948, p. 123]

Now that anthropology and the comparative study of myths have opened up new vistas for understanding the *pensée sauvage* or the "undomesticated" mode of thinking at work in our own societies, will modern man refuse to know himself, under the false pretense that he has gone beyond this "infantile" or "primitive" stage? Or will he submit to the evidence that his conquests over nature do not place him above its laws and that he cannot, without jeopardizing man's destiny on a planetary scale, draw from science, at his convenience, the results that satisfy his vanity, and reject the lessons it offers that threaten his arrogance?

1. Execution and cutting up of a prisoner by the Tupinambá. Child holding severed head

2. Quartering of the prisoner, boiling of intestines and head.

3. Distribution of boiled parts to women
and children.

4. Grilling of limbs and trunk. Old women with sagging breasts.

5. Detail of illustration 4.

6. Zemi worship.

7. Zemi worship, Indians, and sailing vessels.

8a. The Indian women from Cumana province.

8b. Preparation of the *cahouin*.

9. Adam and Eve.

10. The woman with uncooked bird.

11. Map of Tierra del Fuego.

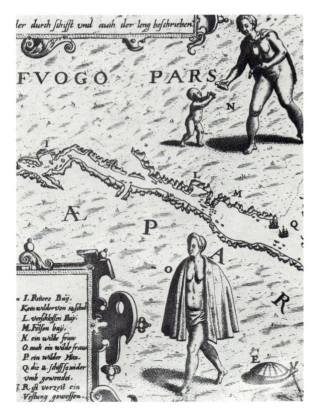

12. Detail of illustration 11.

13. Woman serving fish (right-hand detail).

14. The Old Hag and Pandora's box (left-hand detail).

AMERICÆ
Nona & poſtrema Pars.

QVA DE RATIONE ELEMEN-
TORVM: DE NOVI ORBIS NATV-
RA: DE HVIVS INCOLARVM SVPERSTITIOSIS
cultibus: deq; forma Politiæ ac Reipubl. ipſorum copiosè per-
tractatur: Catalogo Regum Mexicanorum omnium, à primo
vſq; ad vltimum Moteçumam II. addito: cui etiam ritus eo-
rum coronationis, ac ſepulturæ annectitur, cum enu-
meratione bellorum, quæ mutuò
Indi geſſerunt.

HIS ACCESSIT
DESIGNATIO ILLIVS NAVIGATIONIS, QVAM
5.naues Hollandicæ Anno 1598. per fretum Magellanum in Moluc-
canas inſulas tentarunt: quomodo nimirum oborta tempeſtate Ca-
pitaneus SEBALT de WEERT à cæteris nauibus diſpulſus,
poſtquam plurimis menſibus in freto infinitis ærumnis miſerè iacta-
tus fuiſſet, tandem infecta re poſt biennium An. 1600. domum re-
uerſus ſit.

ADDITA EST TERTIO
NAVIGATIO RECENS, QVAM 4. NAVIVM PRAE-
fectus OLEVIER à NOORT proximè ſuſcepit: qui freto Ma-
gellanico claſſe tranſmiſſo, triennij ſpatio vniuerſum terræ orbem
ſeu globum mira nauigatione ſorte obiuit: annexis illis, quæ in itine-
re iſto ſingularia ac memorabilia notata ſunt.

Omnia è Germanico Latinitate donata , & inſuper elegantiſſimis
figuris æneis coornata editaq; ſumptibus

THEODORI de BRY p. m. Viduæ & binorum filiorum.

FRANCOF. Apud MATTH. BECKERVM. 1602.

15. Indifferent beauty; Indian with feathers;
penguin and llama.

16. Indifferent beauty and bound Indian man.

17. Dutchmen hunting penguins.

18. Woman with a fan and Neptune.

19. Flight of the women of Traitors' Island.

20. De Bry's model for 11A:7 (illus. 21):
    Spielbergen's voyage, 1618.

21. Kava festival on Hoorn Island (detail).

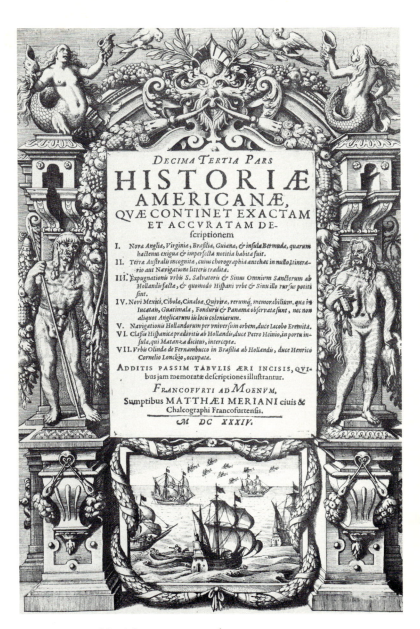

DECIMA TERTIA PARS

HISTORIÆ
AMERICANÆ,
QVÆ CONTINET EXACTAM
ET ACCVRATAM DE-
scriptionem

I.   Novæ Angliæ, Virginiæ, Brasiliæ, Guianæ, & insulæ Bermudæ, quarum hactenus exigua & imperfecta notitia habita fuit.

II. Terræ Australis incognitæ, cuius chorographia antehac in nullo Itinerario aut Navigatione litteris tradita.

III. Expugnationis vrbis S. Salvatoris & Sinus Omnium Sanctorum ab Hollandis factæ, & quomodo Hispani vrbe & Sinu illo rursus potiti sint.

IV. Novi Mexici, Cibolæ, Cinaloæ, Quiviræ, rerumq́; memorabilium, quæ in Iucatan, Guatimala, Fonduris & Panama observatæ sunt, nec non aliquot Anglicarum iis locis coloniarum.

V.   Navigationis Hollandorum per vniversum orbem, duce Iacobo Eremita.

VI. Classu Hispanicæ prædivitis ab Hollandis, duce Petro Heinio, in portu insulæ, qui Matanzæ dicitur, interceptæ.

VII. Vrbis Olindæ de Fernambucco in Brasilia ab Hollandis, duce Henrico Cornelio Lonckio, occupatæ.

ADDITIS PASSIM TABVLIS ÆRI INCISIS, QVI-
bus jam memoratæ descriptiones illustrantur.

FRANCOFVRTI AD MOENVM,
Sumptibus MATTHÆI MERIANI ciuis &
Chalcographi Francofurtensis.

M DC XXXIV.

22. Monstrous couple.

23. Shamanic ceremony among the Powhatan.

24. Ballet of little girls before the king
of Hoorn Island.

25. English hunting sea dogs.

26. Llamas carrying silver bars.

27. Timucua hermaphrodites carrying
food supplies.

28. Indians accused of sodomy thrown to the
dogs on orders from Balboa.

29. Triumph of Magellan; Patagonian arrow-swallower.

30. Preparations of the "black drink";
    beverage ingredient spat out by native warriors.

Appendix 1
Description of the Plates
in the *Great Voyages*

PART 1. WIGWAM LIFE AMONG THE ALGONQUIAN (1590)

Frontispiece	Idol; sorcerer; priest; hunter; woman with a gourd, etc.
Map	The Virginia coast: cartographic landscape; figures; fauna (dolphin).
1:0	Adam and Eve before and after the Fall.
1:0	Portraits of Picts and Britons.
1:1,2	Arrival of the English in Virginia; cartographic landscape; village, fauna, flora.

Portraits with Landscape Backgrounds

1:3	A Weroan or great lord of Virginia.
1:4	A noble lady of Secota village.
1:5	Priest.
1:6	Noble Indian girl of Secota.
1:7	Great lords of Roanoke.
1:8	Noble Indian Lady of Pomeiock and baby girl with a toy.

Festivities (Religion and Leisure Activities)

1:17	Prayer, songs, and dances around a fire.
1:18	Dance and festivities.

Buildings and Dwellings

1:19	Pomeiock and its agriculture.
1:20	Secota and its agriculture.
1:21	Temple of the idol Kiwa.
1:22	The tombs of the Weroans: a priest guards the mummies.
1:23	Totemic marks of the chiefs of Virginia.

PART 2: THE TIMUCUA SCALP-HUNTERS (1591)

Frontispiece   Timucua chief with four male attendants; two warriors; cartouche with Indian queen borne on litter.

Map   Florida and Carribbean islands; ships, landscapes, whale.

Navigation of the French along the May River up to Port-Royal

2:1–7   Timucua welcome; fauna, flora, villages.

2:8   Native worship of a column erected by Laudonnière; offerings.

2:9,10   Construction of a fort by the French.

War among the Timucua

2:11   Saturiba: preparatory ceremony.

2:12   Outina tribe: preparatory ceremony.

2:13   Staged battle between Outina and Potono.

2:14   Marching order of the Outina army.

2:15   Treatment of prisoners: scalp and trophies.

2:16   Dance and music around trophies of victory.

2:17   Hermaphrodites used as beasts of burden.

2:18   War widows petitioning Chief Outina.

2:19   Widows mourning at the warriors' tomb.

2:20   Caring for the sick; medical techniques.

Subsistence

2:21   Agriculture: plowing and harvesting.

2:22   Public storehouses for keeping rations.

2:23   Hermaphrodites carrying rations.

2:24   Smoking and drying meat.

2:25   Stag hunt: luring the animal.

2:26   Alligator hunt: technique of baiting.

2:27   Timucua family equipped for travel.

2:28   Banquet preparations: leaching acorns.

War and Political Organization

2:29   War council; drinking of the black drink, *cassina*.

2:30   Fortified village with sentries.

2:31   Village set on fire.

2:32   Punishment of careless sentries.

2:33   Declaration of war: path strewn with arrows.

Religious Worship
2:34   Sacrifice of firstborns.
2:35   Sun worship; offering of a stag.
2:36   Games and sports.
2:37   The queen-elect borne on a litter.
2:38   Royal marriage and reception by the sovereign.
2:39   King and queen taking a walk.
2:40   Funeral ceremony honoring a chief or priest.
2:41   Extraction of gold from river.
2:42   Murder of the Frenchman François Gambié by a
               Timucua.

Part 3. The Tupinambá in the Sixteenth Century (1592)
Frontispiece   Tupinambá cannibalism; worshipping a maraca.
Map   South America: Brazil, Peru; fauna (whale).
3:1   Tamaraka; guerilla tactic; cannibalism.
3:2   Naval battle between Europeans; sea tortoises,
               native village.
3:3   Arrival of the Europeans; meeting with native
               pirogues.
3:4   Shipwreck near St. Vincent.
3:5   Shipwreck, marine life (whale, swordfish).

Captivity of Hans Staden among the Tamaio
3:6   Staden captured and stripped of his belongings.
3:7   Battle between the Tamaio and the Tupinikin sup-
               ported by the Portuguese.
3:8   Staden kept in the village by the women.
3:9   Women dancing around Staden.
3:10   Attack on a village by the Tupinikin.
3:11   Arrival of Europeans in a village.

Tupinambá Customs
3:12   Burial and death ritual.
3:13   Meals, preparing food, dancing, resting in ham-
               mocks.
3:14   Execution of the prisoner; quartering and cooking.

3:15	Staden's attempted escape toward French ships.
3:16	Naval battle between two tribes.
3:17	The cutting up, cooking, and eating of the prisoner of war.
3:18	Sacrifice of the prisoner; view of fortified village.
3:19	Preparation of the *cahouin*, an intoxicating beverage; dances.

Ritual Eating of the Prisoner

3:20	Women painting the face of the prisoner and the club used to execute him.
3:21	Ritual execution.
3:22	Cleaning the corpse.
3:23	Quartering the body and cooking the parts.
3:24	Women and children eating: head, viscera, and bouillon.
3:25	Men, women, and children eating: roasted limbs and trunk.

Léry's Voyage

3:26	Flying fish eaten by other fish.
3:27	View of the Tupinambá hell.
3:28	Another view of the Tupinambá hell.
3:29	Shamanic tobacco dance.

PART 4. BENZONI'S VOYAGES TO THE SPANISH COLONIES (1594)

Frontispiece	Indian worship of an idol and greeting of the Spanish vessels.
4:0	Triumph with mythological figures.
4:1	Loading of boats in port before leaving for the Indies.
4:2	Flying fish.
4:3	Cumana Province on the Pearl Coast: Benzoni watches the wife of a cacique offer fruit to Pierre Errera.
4:4	Amaracapana: Indians used as beasts of burden by the Spanish under the command of Pierre de Calyce.
4:5	The Arawak of Borichen, Puerto Rico, throw a

Spaniard into water to test his immortality.

4:6 Columbus, discoverer of the West Indies: triumph with mythological figures.

4:7 Episode of Columbus's voyage; anecdote of the egg.

4:8 Columbus's first departure.

4:9 Columbus's meeting with a cacique in Marien Province, Haiti.

4:10 Civil war among Spaniards; a hanging.

4:11 A cyclone in the West Indies; flight of Spaniards and Indians.

4:12 Columbus's third voyage; pearl fishers in Cubagua on Pearl Island in the Gulf of Paria.

4:13 Columbus, a prisoner, is sent back to Spain with his brother, Bartholomew.

4:14 Fourth voyage of Columbus; battle in Jamaica against Francisco Poraz.

4:15 Discovery of the Strait of Magellan; a Patagonian thrusts an arrow down his throat.

4:16 Carib revolt at Cumana against Dominican monks.

4:17 Hanging, by the order of Diego Ocampa, of rebellious Caribs.

4:18 The Spaniards set fire to a native village.

4:19 Construction of caravels by the Spaniards.

4:20 Punishment inflicted on the Spanish by the Indians, who pour gold into their mouths before dismembering and roasting them.

4:21 An adventure of Balboa, near Panama, during a baptism of the Indians; the Pacific Ocean in the background.

4:22 Balboa orders Indians accused of sodomy to be eaten alive by dogs.

4:23 Collective suicide of the Indians of Hispaniola.

4:24 Zemi worship among the Arawak of Hispaniola.

PART 5. EPIC OF THE CONQUISTADORS (1595)

Frontispiece The Indians' martyrdom and their way of the cross.

Map New Spain with natives and examples of fauna: bison, parrots pecking tree branch.

5:0 Surrounding a portrait of Christopher Columbus,

an herbarium of flowers and butterflies, insects, and snails; two monkeys, their tails shaped like flowers, hold an apple.

Slave Trade in the Caribbean Islands

5:1   Blacks of Guinea working the mines of Hispaniola.
5:2   African slaves used to harvest sugar cane.
5:3   Tortures inflicted on slaves.
5:4   Revolt and repression of slaves.

Battle between French and Spanish in the Caribbean Islands

5:5   Capture of a French boat by the Spaniards.
5:6   The French drive the Spanish out of Havana.
5:7   The French seize Chiorera.
5:8   Ransom asked in Huana City.
5:9   Indian canoes sent by the Spaniards to attack French vessels on the island of Cubagua; pearl fishers in the background.

Battle between Conquistadors and Indians

5:10   Native market in Cartagena, in present-day Columbia.
5:11   Caribs of Tunia Valley at war.
5:12   Night attack on native village by Spaniards.
5:13   Caciques of Cartagena Province bringing gold to Governor Diego Gottirez; turtle fishing by Spaniards.
5:14   Meal offered by Diego Gottirez to caciques before inquiring where to find gold.
5:15   Gottirez puts the caciques in chains and demands a ransom.
5:16   The Indians' revenge: they attack the Spaniards and kill Gottirez.
5:17   Torture of Florida Indians by De Soto.
5:18   Native dance, in Mexico, interrupted by a Spanish attack led by Alvarade.
5:19   Revolt of Yucatán Indians against Montijo.
5:20   Benzoni received at the home of a cacique in Nicaragua.
5:21   Dance by Nicaragua Indians.

5:22   Defeat of Pierre Alvarade at Zaliscan by Indians
              using ingenious guerilla tactic.

PART 6. DISCOVERY AND CONQUEST OF PERU (1596)

Frontispiece Opening cut into the mountainside by Indians
              working the mines; in the foreground, Atahualpa,
              last of the Incas, borne on his litter; in the back-
              ground, landing of the Spaniards.

6:0   Map of the city of Cuzco; in the foreground, Indian
              acrobats and jugglers.

Map   North and South America surrounded by portraits
              of four conquerors: Columbus, Magellan, Vespucci,
              Pizarro.

6:1   Pact relative to Peru concluded at Panama in 1524
              between Almagro and de Luques.

6:2   Pizarro landing at Tumbes, Peru.

6:3   Consultation between Pizarro and Almagro on the
              means of subduing the country.

6:4   Oath between Pizarro and Almagro in the presence
              of Father de Luques in 1536.

6:5   Meeting between De Soto and Atahualpa near
              Cajamarca.

6:6   The Cajamarca ambush: Atahualpa borne on his lit-
              ter to place of meeting with the Spanish.

6:7   Attack on Atahualpa and his fall from his litter.

6:8   Bathing Indian women raped by the Spanish.

6:9   Atahualpa, prisoner of the Spaniards.

6:10   The Indians bringing gold ransom to free
              Atahualpa.

6:11   Execution of the Inca by garrotting.

6:12   The taking and pillaging of Cuzco by the Spanish in
              1533.

6:13   Indian revolt organized by the Inca, Manco Capac,
              brother of Atahualpa; defeat of Cuzco by Almagro.

6:14–19   Civil war between Pizarro's and Almagro's troops.

6:20   Indians used as beasts of burden by the Spaniards.

6:21   Almagro led to his death (strangulation and be-
              heading).

6:22   Civil War among the Spanish at Panama; massacre
              of prisoners.

6:23	Gorgona Island: natives ensconced in trees defend themselves against the Spanish army.
6:24	The Spaniards fell the trees where the natives hide.
6:25	Episode in Peruvian history: the mountain-pass of Guayanacapa.
6:26	The mode of burying princes and "satraps" in Peru.
6:27	Gold-melting and gold-working among the Incas near Puna.
6:28	Canary Islands: the tree that produces water.

PARTS 7 AND 8. DISCOVERY OF LA PLATA AND ENGLISH NAVIGATIONS

Frontispiece	Tupinambá cannibalism; worship of a maraca.
7/8:1	Famine among Spaniards and cannibalism: horses are clubbed to death and eaten; men who have been hanged are cut up on the gallows, boiled, and eaten.
7/8:2	Indian ambush; in the foreground, the Spaniards burn Indians alive in retaliation.
7/8:3	Reception of the Spaniards by the king of the "Scherves," probably the Guarago of Paraguay.

Drake's Voyage

7/8:4	Indians stealing Drake's hat near Rio de la Plata.
7/8:5	Drake on the coast of New Albion, California; Miwok ceremony of welcome to the dead.

Maps with Fauna Motifs

7/8:6	Map of St. Joseph, Guinea; flying fish.
7/8:7	Ste. Dominique, Hispaniola; iguana.
7/8:8	Cartagena; iguana.
7/8:9	St. Augustine; fish and sea turtles.

Voyage of Cavendish

7/8:10	Porto Désiré: Seal hunt conducted with clubs by the English.
7/8:11	Watering place and woodpiling on the coast of Maramorena; native dwellings and pirogues.
7/8:12	Ladrone Islands: shooting by the English of natives who have come in pirogues to greet them with offerings.

7/8:13   Capture of Don Antonio de Berrero, Spanish Governor of St. Joseph, Trinidad, by Raleigh.

Voyage of Raleigh in Guyana

7/8:14   Arboreal dwellings of the Tinitive during the flooding of the Orinoco; funerary rites.

7/8:15   The Inca of Manoa, emperor of Eldorado, adorned with gold spangles on a feast day.

7/8:16   Reception of Raleigh by the king of Arromaia.

7/8:17   Indians sorting gold nuggets on the lake shore; making gold statues.

7/8:18   Indians repossessing gold objects stolen by the Spaniards.

PART 9. PRECOLUMBIAN HISTORY OF THE PERUVIANS AND MEXICANS (1601)

Frontispiece   Fuegian couple from Penguin Island: man with feathered headdress and skirt, woman with loincloth and cape; dwarf king of Guinea; penguins and llama.

Peru

9A:1   Strange fish, Indians, and whale hunt.

9A:2   River crossing.

9A:3   The Potosi mines.

9A:4   Llamas carrying silver on their backs.

Mexico

9A:5   Death rituals.

9A:6   Sacred hunt.

9A:7   Penitent priests.

9A:8   Human sacrifices on the pyramid.

9A:9   Festival of Xipe Toltec; another human sacrifice.

9A:10   Public confession of the Xambuxi, Japanese pilgrims.

9A:11   Mexican acrobats.

9A:12   Legend of the founding of Mexico; discovery of the Tunal and floating garden.

9A:13   Fatal banquet offered the Indians of Cuoyacan by their neighbors from Culhuacan, Mexico.

9A:14   Suicide of Montezuma I.

Voyage of Sebastian de Weert

9A:15   Strategy map of the Gulf of Paria.
9A:16   Another strategy map of the Gulf of Paria.
9A:17   Battle against the Dutch.
9A:18   Reception of de Weert and his men by the king of Guinea.
9A:19   Meal preceding the imprisonment of the Dutch.
9A:20   Map with battle scene.
9A:21   Amabon Island.
9A:22   The Dutch meeting fierce men who tear trees out by their roots in the Strait of Magellan.
9A:23   Native mother giving uncooked bird to her children to eat.
9A:24   Shipwreck of the Dutch on Penguin Island; Indian, bound up and dead, and "woman with cape."
9A:25   Penguin-hunting by the Dutch.
Map   Tierra del Fuego and Strait of Magellan with figures and examples of fauna.

OLIVIER DE NOORT'S VOYAGE

9B
Frontispiece   Two native figures flanking an inset portrait of Olivier de Noort.
Map   Tierra del Fuego.
9B:1   View of Portuguese and Dutch Camp.
9B:2   Rio de Janeiro.
9B:3   San Sebastian.
9B:4   Santa Clara.
9B:5   Porto Desire.
9B:6   Dutchmen fighting the cave-dwelling inhabitants of the Strait of Magellan.
9B:7   Mocha Island, Chile.
9B:8   Ladrone Island with three natives.
9B:9   The Dutch using cannons to drive off natives who have come in pirogues bearing offerings.
9B:10   Inhabitants of La Baye, near Manila.

9B:11   Japanese warriors, looking like priests, in procession.

9B:12   Naval battle between Dutch and Spanish, near Manila.

9B:13   Map of Borneo.

PART 10. VESPUCCI, VIRGINIA AND NEW ENGLAND (1619)
Navigations of Amerigo Vespucci

Frontispiece   Figures in a cartouche: in the background, the shipwreck of European vessels.

10:1   Customs of the Indians of Paria: sexual hospitality, abandonment of the dying in the forest; burial of the dead.

10:2   Care of the sick.

10:3   Surprise attack on the lake city of Aruba.

10:4   Dragons chained for later roasting.

10:5   Fighting the invaders; a woman among the warriors.

10:6   Vespucci's adventure on the Island of Giants, Curaçao.

Narratives by Ralph Hamor and John Smith

10:7   Pocahontas deceitfully handed over to the English.

10:8   Pocahontas's brothers coming to reclaim their sister.

10:9   Chickahominy surrendering to Captain Argol.

10:10   Ralph Hamor is sent to Powhatan to ask for the hand of his daughter Pocahontas on behalf of John Rolfe.

10:11   English hawking and fishing in Virginia.

10:12   Captain John Smith taken prisoner by the French during a storm at sea.

PART 11. VOYAGES IN THE SOUTH SEAS (1619)

11A
Frontispiece   Figures in a cartouche; in the background, the shipwreck of European vessels.

11A:1   The conquerors of the Strait of Magellan.

11A:2   Map of Tierra del Fuego and the Strait of Magellan.

11A:3   On the high seas, Dutch firing on a Polynesian craft.

11A:4   Invasion of flies along Uligen Island.
11A:5   Coco Island and Thieves' Island.
11A:6   The Dutch fending off natives by rifle shots.
11A:7   Kava festival on Hoorn Island.
11A:8   Reception given by the king of Hoorn Island.
11A:9   Bay of Hoorn Island.

B. Navigations of Spielbergen

11B:1   Map of St. Vincent, Brazil.
11B:2   Strait of Magellan and Tierra del Fuego: inhabitants
             and fauna.
11B:3   Man and woman of Mocha Island with a guaco.
11B:4   Map of Ste. Marie Island, off Chile; wild horses, the
             Dutch fleet.
11B:5   Concepción Island, Chile; inhabitants and wild
             horses.
11B:6   Two warriors in the Bay of Valparaiso.
11B:7   Native family and wild horses from Quintero Bay.
11B:8–11   Sea battles; ocean maps.
11B:12   Monstrous bird from the Bay of Payta.
11B:13   Bay of Acapulco, Mexico; giant fish.
11B:14   Bays of Santiago and Nativida; fight between Dutch
             and Spanish.
11B:15   Ladrone Island: sailing ships and canoes with out-
             riggers.
11B:16   Port of Manila in the Philippines.
11B:17   Macon Island and Bacian Island.
11B:18   Solor Island; two natives.
11B:19   The islands of Amboyna and Nera; volcano of
             Ganapus; two natives.
11B:20   Porto Desire: sepulcher of the giant Patagonians;
             fauna (sea lions, ostriches, penguins).

PART 12. HISTORY OF THE MEXICANS (1623–24)

Frontispiece Pantheon of Mexican gods reproduced from the
             codex Maglia Becchamo; full-length portraits of
             Magellan and Pizarro flanking a cartouche sym-
             bolizing America.
12:1   Map of Cuzco with acrobats.

12:2   Election and triumph of a Mexican king.

12:3   Chichimeca giants overpowered during a meal by
        the Tlascala.

12:4   Foreboding signs of Montezuma's fall.

12:5   Volcanic eruptions and fantastic animals; maps and
        geographical reliefs without figures or wildlife.

PART 13. ENGLISH COLONIZATION IN NORTH AMERICA
AND VOYAGES TO TIERRA DEL FUEGO (1634)

Frontispiece Portal with figures and animals.

Map   The two Americas with the names of Indian tribes;
        map of Tierra del Fuego with figures.

History of New England by John Smith

13:1   The English greeted by sirens while the natives flee.

13:2   English and Indians exchange knives and necklaces.

13:3   Indian techniques of fishing and stag-hunting.

13:4   Map of Virginia with effigy of an Indian and por-
        trait of Powhatan in a wigwam.

13:5   Portraits of Algonquians: Indians around Smith;
        sorceror; idol.

13:6   Religious ceremony and scene of shamanic exor-
        cism; Smith saved from death by Pocahontas.

13:7   Massacre of 1622 by Algonquians.

13:8   Tierra del Fuego; woman with a bird; gathering of
        pearl oysters; transporting the wounded; dwellings
        and pirogues.

13:9   Execution of a prisoner; cannibalism; fantastic
        figures: man covered with animal fur, man with
        angel's wings.

13:10   Map of Olinda with figures of natives.

Appendix 2
Order of Publication of the
Great Voyages

Date Volume

1590   1   English expedition to Virginia under the command of Sir Richard Grenville in 1585.

1591   2   French Huguenot expedition to Florida under the command of Captain Laudonnière in 1565.

1592   3   Voyages to Brazil: Hans Staden, 1549–55; Jean de Léry (Villegaignon expedition), 1555–58.

1594   4   Voyage of Girolamo Benzoni to the Spanish possessions, 1541–56.

1595   5   Epic of Christopher Columbus and the early conquistadors, 1492–1520.

1596   6   Conquest of Peru by Pizarro and fall of Atahualpa, 1519–20.

1599   7   Voyage of Ulrich Schmidel and expedition of Pedro de Mendoza (Gran Chaco, Paraguay, La Plata), 1535–55.

1599   8   English Voyages: Drake (Strait of Magellan, Pacific Coast, California), 1577–80; Cavendish (around the world), 1586–88; Raleigh and Keymis (Guyana), 1595–96.

1601   9   Precolumbian history, Mexicans, Peruvians, before 1492. Voyages of Sebald de Weert and Olivier de Noort, 1598–99.

1619   10   Voyage of Vespucci, 1499–1504; history of Virginia and New England, 1607–16.

1619   11   Voyages in the South Seas. Various Dutch Navigations.

1623   12   *Historia natural y moral de las Indias* (the first part of volume 9 is repeated here).

1634   13   Virginia and New England (Captain John Smith), 1607–22. Voyage of Jacques Lhermite to Tierra del Fuego; discovery of the Yaghans, 1624.

Notes

Introduction

1. On the relationship between Panofsky and structuralism, see Recht 1968 and Lévi-Strauss 1973, pp. 322–25.

Chapter One

1. See the complete listing of the plates in appendix 1.

2. This news is composed of business correspondence received and kept by the Fuggers; pamphlets printed in Germany and sold by peddlers in the streets (Neu-Zeitungen); and information furnished by an agency to its subscribers, among whom were the Fuggers.

3. See Denis 1851 and Chinard 1911. A trace of what was called the "American revels" can be found in a bas-relief preserved in the Departmental Museum in Rouen and discovered in that city above a hotel portal. See Hamy 1908.

4. This letter is included in Conway 1889, p. 101.

5. For more complete information on the images of the New World in the sixteenth century, see Hunnewell 1890.

6. Translated from the preface of *Icones quiquagenta virorum illustrium* (Frankfort 1597), illustrated by de Bry. For further details of de Bry's life, see Giuseppi 1917, Hind 1963, Lorant 1965, and Zulch 1935.

7. The narrative of Schmidel appears in part 7 of the *Great Voyages*; that of Vespucci in part 10. List of topics and dates of the volumes are given in appendix 2.

8. For more information on the art public at that period, see Hauser 1951, Symonds 1960, and Wright 1958.

9. See Pirenne 1942, vol. 2.

Chapter Two

1. Facsimile edition of John White's watercolors conserved in the British Museum, accompanied by a study of the artist and a detailed analysis of the ethnological elements in these drawings by William C. Sturtevant (1964).

Chapter Three

1. The quotation comes from a letter addressed by de Bry to his book-seller Raphalengis on 1 September 1575. One anecdote recounts how the conquistadors caught by surprise some Indian women bathing in the river. Plate 6:8 depicts their abduction and rape. Plate 6:5 portrays Atahualpa's composure when De Soto's horse charged him.

2. These first two stages are, first, what Panofsky calls "pre-icono-graphical description," which bears on "the primary or natural subject matter" "constituting the world of artistic motifs" (1962, p. 14), and sec-ond, the iconographical analysis proper, dealing with "secondary or con-ventional subject matter, constituting the world of images, stories, and allegories" and supported by a knowledge of literary sources (ibid.).

3. For descriptions of London's Globe Theatre, see Watkins 1964, and for the Italian theater, Sypher 1955.

4. The image of naked young children fighting is used as an icono-graphic theme of the New World throughout the seventeenth century. In particular, it can be seen in Antoine Jacquart's *Album du Nouveau Monde*.

Chapter Four

1. For a discussion of the depiction of Africans, see Snowden 1969 and Baudet 1965. Baudet notes that the African has been "canonized in our culture," both literary and iconographic, long before the Amerindian. This is due, in part, to the tradition of the Magi, among whom Gaspar, the Ethiopian.

2. These watercolors are conserved in the British Museum. Some of them were first published in 1946 in the first edition of Stefan Lorant's *The New World*, by the publishers Duell, Sloane & Pearce. See Lorant 1964.

3. One of the few paintings we still have by Le Moyne is at the New York Public Library, and is reproduced in Lorant 1964.

4. In commenting on this exotic world of color, Léry, for example, describes the fruit of the *génipa*, from which the Tupinambá make a dye with which they paint the sacrificial club.

5. Dürer tells of having seen in the museum, "things that have been brought back to the king from the new land of gold (Mexico): a sun a span in width, all in gold, and a silver moon of the same size; also two cases full of war costumes of the people there and all kinds of marvelous weapons, harnesses and traces, strange articles of clothing, beds, and all sorts of marvelous objects useful to man and far more interesting to see than prodigies" (Conway 1889, p. 247).

6. The Indians' brown and copper-colored skin is noted in the texts, often accompanied by the idea that the Indians are not born with colored

skin but acquire it through their customs of walking naked in the sun and anointing their bodies with oil.

7. I am using the terms "metaphor" and "comparison" in the most traditional sense of classical rhetoric and not in the sense Jakobson gives them. A comparison is an image expressing a relation of similiarity by means of a grammatical tool ("as," "like," "resembling," and so forth). Metaphor sets up a similarity by a total substitution of one term for another.

8. Thus, in part 1, the narrator praises the Indians and complains about the English in these terms: "They eat with moderation and thus avoid illness; would to God that we followed their example. We would be freed of all the evils from which we suffer as a consequence of our sumptuous and too-frequent banquets where we delight in a great variety of indigestible sauces, intended to stir up our insatiable and greedy appetites."

9. The theme of blood and the child can be seen as a leitmotif in the collection, notably in the plates concerning the cannibals.

10. A single plate escapes this convention and by contrast takes on a mildly erotic character: it portrays some little girls, with clearly drawn sexual parts, performing a ballet for a Polynesian king (plate 11:8).

Ariadne's Thread

1. "Le Dedoublement de la representation de l'Asie et de l'Amérique," *Renaissance*, vols. 2 and 3 (1944–45):168–86. This paper is republished as chapter 13 of *Structural Anthropology*.

Chapter Five

1. To avoid repeating "sagging breasts," I shall use the shortened form of "savage woman" or simply "savage" to designate the Indian women typified by this physical feature in the *Great Voyages*.

2. Two texts appear in part 3: (1) Hans Staden, *Warhaftige Historie und Beschreibung einer Landschaft der wilden, nacketen, grimmigen Menschenfresser Leute in der neue Welt Amerika gelegen*, first published in Marburg in 1557. A French translation appeared in the following year with the title, *Histoire d'un pays situé dans le Nouveau Monde* (Marburg, 1558); (2) Jean de Léry, *Histoire d'un voyage fait en la terre du Brésil* (La Rochelle: A. Chuppin, 1578), translated into German and Latin by the de Brys. The quotations are drawn from the original edition.

3. An example of this motif in the iconography of the capital sins appears in an engraving by Cornelius Bos who depicts Envy in this way and with dog's ears (Metropolitan Museum, New York).

4. This theological text from the early twentieth century simply repeats

basic Church doctrine concerning the theology of sins as it was codified by the Scholastics and reiterated by the Council of Trent. One can cite, for example, the Jesuit Roberto Bellarmine, who expresses the same idea in Latin: "Saepe etiam ex gula luxuria procedit, quae omnes suas quoque filias comportet" (Bellarmine 1619, p. 234).

5. *Gula est appetitus* inordinatus, *quae* inordinatio (Bellarmine 1619, p. 234).

6. In fact, the Tupinambá certainly did not grill their meat on a bonfire as shown in the engravings; the wooden platform or "boucan" they used would have quickly caught fire and the meat would have burned. On the contrary, their cooking was done with a very slow fire and was much more like smoking (Métraux 1963). This distorted view of cannibal cooking as hellfire speaks for itself.

7. For the sake of brevity, I shall use the term "blood" instead of "juices of roasted human flesh." Blood and melted fat (which compose the "juices") have the same differentiating function with respect to meat flesh (solid/liquid; container/contained; whole/part) and, from the point of view of cooking, both are presented in a less cooked or more raw state than the roasted meat from which they escape, unlike the broth prepared from the cooking water.

Chapter Six

1. The first edition of Benzoni's text was published in Venice in 1565 in Italian as *Historia del mundo nuevo*, but the de Brys used a French translation: *Histoire du Nouveau Monde* (Genève: Vignon, 1598). Quotations come from this edition, as many elements of the prints match with this particular edition.

2. De Bry, a Huguenot, was run out of Liège, his home town (then under Spanish domination) for his religious opinions and must have witnessed the religious persecution ordered by the duke of Alba.

3. In the *Navigationi* by Ramusio (1556), for example, but chiefly in the *De civitatis orbis terrarum* by Braun and Hogenberg (1537), from which de Bry borrows a view of Cuzco. From this book he also draws the royal litter carrying Atahualpa and many details of the Peruvians' dress, which he also used in part 4 to depict Indians from Hispaniola.

4. Cf. the engraving by Agostino di Musi, *Le Squelette* (1518). It portrays Death seated on the carcass of an antediluvian monster, with the same male robustness and musculature, contrasting with the same sagging and emaciated bust, that can be seen in the de Bry engraving.

5. "The Bible does not specify the serpent's sex. Medieval artists made it female, Freud might have argued for a male; the structural argument suggests hermaphrodite qualities" (Leach 1970, p. 58).

6. It is striking to note how a moral lesson drawn from a late sixteenth-century mythic system echoes, albeit partially, Marcel Mauss's "gift theory" (1966) or even notions familiar to the readers of *The Elementary Structures of Kinship*. These concepts, as we can see, have deep roots in the Judeo-Christian tradition.

Chapter Seven

1. Although the term "Fuegians" does not reflect a true ethnographic distinction, it is used, as in the time of the discovery of these regions, to name the nomadic Indian peoples, "hunters and fishers, who inhabited Tierra del Fuego and the ring of islands that stretches from Chiloé Island to Cape Horn" (Emperaire 1955, p. 70).

2. For method, see Lévi-Strauss (*From Honey to Ashes*, pp. 160–71). I remind the reader that the double arrow (⟵⟶) means that a condition must be met for a transformation to be produced (if and only if).

3. "Relation d'un voyage de cinq vaisseaux de Rotterdam partis le 27 de Juin de l'an 1598 pour aller au détroit de Magellan d'où le capitaine Sebald de Weert qui montait le vaisseau la Foi prit la voile pour le retour le 21 de Janvier 1600 et rentra dans la Meuse le 13 de Juillet de la même année 1600," first French translation of the voyage of Sebald de Weert, edited by René Augustin de Renneville in his *Recueil des voyages qui out servi à l'établissement et au progrès de la Compagnie des Indes orientales* (Amsterdam: Pierre Cailloux, 1725).

The ship's log of Captain de Weert was first published in Dutch, edited by Zacharias de Heynes from notes written by Jantz Barent Potgierer, the ship surgeon, under the title *Journal van't geene vijt Schafen von Rotterdam in't Jaer 1598, na de Straet Magelanes* (Amsterdam, 1600).

The German and Latin translations of the text for the *Great Voyages* were made from the Dutch text.

4. It was not the technique of smoking itself that displeased the Dutch—they were familiar with this method of cooking and appreciated it—but the particular manner of preparing the smoked fish offered by the native king.

Chapter Eight

1. This is true not only in French but also in English, "that which remains after sifting, the lees, refuse," and in German, "Auswurf," literally, "that which is rejected."

2. "Les figures hiéroglyphiques de Nicolas Flamel ainsi qu'il les a mises en la quatrième arche qu'il a bastie au cimetière des Innocents," in *Le livre des figures hiéroglyphiques*, edited from the 1612 edition by Maxime Priard (Paris: Denoël, 1970), p. 82.

3. For a discussion of this iconographic motif, see Panofsky 1962.

4. The word "paradise" comes from the Persian *pairidaéza*, which originally meant "parcel of land surrounded by a circular wall," and very early applied to royal parks (Hughes 1968). Hughes supports this observation with many illustrations and stresses the fact that the image of paradise remains imbued with ideas of order and domesticated nature: "They were images executed in grass, flowers and vegetables of the power which consciousness had over brute nature in all its spontaneous irrationality.... Gardens became ideal symbols of order, for in them nature is subdued and made to conform with a humanized, rational scheme which is not its own" (1968, p. 47). As such, paradise is the opposite of hell, which is chaos above all. For the Arabic concept of oasis, see Tennant 1968.

5. "For a season therefore these strips seemed, like the cultivated 'tofts' of the village, to be the territory of individual owners. But after the harvest, signs and fences were removed, and the strips returned for a time to pastoral use, and were reincorporated into the larger areas where access to animals was free. To a greater or lesser extent then . . . the arable appeared as a limited and temporary extension of the cultivated 'toft' area and thus private property, at the expense of the wild area which was left to collective use" (Duby 1968, p. 10).

6. These preternatural gifts are intuitive knowledge, the mastery of the passions, immortality of the body (which constitute the "gift of integrity"), and sanctifying grace (see Tanquerey 1924).

7. It should be noted that, even in these examples, the Indians' techniques of farming are often distorted, because they were misunderstood, and seem inconsistent. One plate in particular portrays the Indian technique of planting kernels of corn in the ground with a digging stick, but at the same time it shows a woman in the process of sowing the kernels broadcast, thus making the native technique seem absurd.

8. It is remarkable that in the entire collection, with the exception of the first two volumes, aimed at attracting colonists to the new "promised land," the Indian is never portrayed as *homo artifex*, except as a goldsmith or blacksmith: he is shown holding and using tools and weapons, feeding himself, wearing fabric clothing, but never shown weaving, or cultivating the land, or engaged in any of the arts such as pottery-making or basket-weaving, though pots and baskets are shown.

9. Even at the end of the seventeenth century, Locke in his *Two Treatises on Government* (1690), advocates measures to force hunters to become farmers. For more on these ideas and other justifications for the dispossession of the Indians, see Washburn 1959.

10. This comes from Bacon's treatise, *De dignitate et Augmentis scientiarum* (book 2, chap. 2, published in 1623), but these ideas were already partly expressed in *The Advancement of Learning* (1605).

11. In fact, this division is not new. Pliny gives an equivalent in his *Historia naturalis*: the history of generations in book 2, which deals with

celestial things, the four elements, the shape of the earth, volcanic phenomena, and so forth; the history of pretergenerations which deals with the history of monsters; and finally the history of arts. As Emile Bréhier points out "Bacon deserves credit, not for bringing the study of abnormal conditions and the arts into natural history, but for stating that such study constitutes an indispensable part of natural science and is not merely an appendage of curious facts. Monsters and technics bring to light forces that were less obvious in natural generation—*natura omnia regit*" (Bréhier, p. 28). It does not seem necessary to note, as Margaret Hodgen does, that the collectors of monstrosities and curiosities over the course of the seventeenth century were "Baconian" without knowing it; they simply inherited their ideas from Pliny.

12. Mehl 1966, p. 123. Cf. Lenoble 1969, p. 288: "Protestant thought begins by scorning nature, which, neither in the rational demonstrations of theology nor in sacramental life needs no longer be the mediator of God and man: grace does not come through nature. But, for this very reason, Protestant thought will be better prepared for the new state of science, which will see nature as a soulless mechanism and for physics, which will no longer be a contemplation of forms, but a tool for exploitation."

13. The texts mention several times that Europeans other than the Spanish mistreated the Indians. Léry shamelessly recounts how the Tupinambá slaves in Brazil had to be whipped before they would wear clothing: "And in fact this animal [the Tupinambá woman] takes such great delight in this nudity that, not only do the Tupinambá women, remaining on the mainland in full freedom with their husbands, brothers, and relatives obstinately refuse to be dressed in any manner whatsoever, as I have said, but also, though we forced clothing on the female prisoners of war whom we had bought and held as slaves to work in our fort, as soon as night fell, they secretly slipped out of their shirts and the other rags that had been given to them: for their pleasure and before they went to bed, they had to walk around naked on our island. In short, if it were up to these poor miserable creatures, and if we had not forced them to dress by whipping them, they would have preferred the scorch and heat of the sun . . . to enduring any clothing over their bodies" (Léry 1578, p. 127).

Chapter Nine

1. The German and Latin translations of Acosta for the *Great Voyages* come from a Dutch translation based on Acosta's Spanish text, *Historia natural y moral de las Indias* (Seville: Juan Leon, 1590).

Chapter Ten

1. The island in question was very probably Nina-Tobutabu, or Keppel Island, one of the most northerly of the Tonga group.

2. The original edition in Dutch appeared under the title *Journal ofte Beschryvinghe van de wonderlicke reyse ghedaen door Willem Cornelisz Schouten, van Hoorn, in de Jaren 1615–1616 en 1617* (Amsterdam: Willem Jansz, 1618). The quotations are taken from the English translation, *The relation of a wonderful voyage made by W. C. Schouten* (London: Nathanael Newbery, 1619). A facsimile was published by World Publishing Company, Cleveland, Ohio in 1966, with notes and introduction by A. L. Rowse and Robert O. Dougan.

3. This island, still called Futuna, is one of the Wallis Island group. The Dutch thought they were in the Solomons, trusting the descriptions of Quiros. The incident concerning the king of Hoorn Island took place in May 1616.

4. The "belay" is open on the sides and its roof is made of palm fronds.

5. They used the root of the plant called *Piper methysticum* to prepare the kava. For its preparation, see R. Levy 1971. For the ceremonial, see Sahlins 1958.

6. This type of penis sheath was fairly common in South America, particularly among the peoples of the Amazon. The drawing by the original author shows an interest in ethnographic accuracy. For the distribution of this ornament, see Ucko 1970.

7. They probably saw the penis sheath earlier particularly among the vignettes illustrating the Venitian edition of Benzoni's *History of the New World* (1565). In one of them, which was precisely the one de Bry used as a model for the plate, a man was shown wearing a penis sheath. The engravers suppressed this detail.

8. In the medieval iconography of the Renaissance, we should note that the motif of the sagging breasts is sometimes associated with the insertion of dead or living animals into the skin. Grünewald, in the fourteenth century, depicts the damnation of lovers (Museum of the Strasbourg Cathedral) in this way, with the couple's skin shown pitted and rotting. The woman, skinny and with flabby breasts, has snakes threaded into her skin and a toad placed on her genitals.

9. The term "Powhatan" is applied both to a cultural area and to a political division of the Algonquian tribes established along the Atlantic coast in the eastern part of Virginia south of the Potomac as far as the North Carolina border. Chief Powhatan was so named by the English.

Chapter Eleven

1. *Essays* 1.36 (Frame translation): "Of the custom of wearing clothes."

2. *Essays* 2.30 (Frame translation): "Of a monstrous child."

3. Until the eighteenth century the problem of the origin of the Indians was indissociable from the general problem of the origin of man in spite of certain isolated attempts. For example, Acosta tried to calculate the time

and migration routes of the first Indians; Paracelsus proposed the hypothesis of a multiple creation of man (the polygenetic theory). See Huddleston 1967.

4. Paul III issued a papal bull in 1537 stating that the Indians are men and thus creatures of God, capable of understanding the Catholic faith. This bull, *Sublimus Deus*, also defends the Indians' right to property against the plundering carried out by the conquistadors.

5. Turner's term, "symbolic vehicle," seems to be preferable in this case, for it is freer from the linguistic model and lets us grasp the mythic or symbolic thought regardless of the medium through which the visual message is transmitted (gesture, disguise, body paintings, drawings).

6. The relations between Indians and Europeans are generally amicable. One plate of part 2, however, portrays the murder of a Frenchman by two Indians using a hatchet. In the caption, Le Moyne explains that he placed this plate at the end of the volume in order to keep the sequence intact.

7. In fact, Drake's "coronation," an incident that occurred when he discovered New Albion, that is, present-day California, did not have the meaning given it by the Englishman. As Heizer has shown, the strange rites occasioned by the arrival of the English on the California coast must have been a ceremony celebrating the return of the dead. Through misinterpretation on both sides, the Miwok took the newcomers for the phantoms of their ancestors, and the English saw their reaction as the clear sign that the Indians were granting them kingship over the country.

8. The reader is reminded that the incident involving the dwarf king actually occurred on the coast of West Africa, but that in the illustrations it was transposed to America and enters the continuum of the other plates dealing with the Fuegians.

9. Reduced to famine, the Spaniards fish for turtles. Elsewhere they eat their horses, then eat one another. Texts and illustrations present these calamities befallen the Spaniards as punishment for their diabolical cruelty. By exterminating the Indians, they are faced with starvation, then they regress to the state of cannibalism.

10. From an ethnographic viewpoint, it is quite true that among the Timucua and other North American tribes before the conquest, there was a category of man called "berdache," who dressed as women and worked at special tasks. Two hypotheses about their selection have been suggested. One, supported by A. Requena, presumes that the berdaches were chosen as children to become beasts of burden and were drawn to sodomy from childhood, in order to keep them in an inferior position. Or the change of status might have taken place at puberty. Some of them were not homosexuals, but "individuals with weak sexual instincts," who, from fear of being ridiculed by the women, deliberately chose the berdache role. They enjoyed a certain social prestige.

11. The episode of the Indians cast to the dogs, which Benzoni tells, was

first reported by Peter Martyr and passed on by Oviedo. It took place in the isthmus of Panama, in Quaraco province, in September 1513. Balboa attacked and forced the Indians of this province to surrender. These must have been Cueva Indians, who spoke a Chibcha language (of whom the present-day Cuna are the descendants). In fact, the chiefs were surrounded by transvestites, and Peter Martyr records that the Spaniards cast twenty of them alive to a pack of bulldogs. There is no evidence that the Cuna were particularly given to homosexuality, nor that they kept a class of sodomites to guard their king. The Spaniards must have interpreted in this way the role of the albinos, who, according to Stout (1963), comprised about seven percent of the population. They were kept in a state of inferiority and did not have the right to marry.

12. A reproduction of a seventeenth-century fountain in Bamberg, showing the same motif, appears in Bernheimer 1952.

13. As the plate's caption gives no explanation of the Patagonian's action, the reader who does not know the source of this illustration might see it as an act of self-destruction; still, Stradan's engraving had been widely circulated since 1522, with different captions, and Pigafetta's narrative and his anecdotes were well known.

14. This explanation of the utility of the "black beverage" is translated from the caption for plate 2:29. For this drink, see. E. M. Hale, "Ilex cassina, the aboriginal of North America tea," U.S. Department of Agriculture, Division of Botany, Bulletin 14 (Washington, 1891).

15. See chapter 6, pp. 70–72.

16. Powhatan appears most notably on the illustrated map of Virginia, which shows portraits of several Algonquians and of the Indian chief, inspired by White's drawings. The plates also give a terrifying and diabolical image of the Indians of Virginia. These pictures come from the English edition of Captain John Smith's text.

17. This engraving stresses the fact that the English conquerors must deal with the representatives of a group organized politically in a mode essentially different from Europeans. The chiefs with whom they deal are the representatives of a people seen in the background of the scene of the Anglo-Chickahominy treaty. One of the chiefs speaks to his people and conveys to them the terms of the treaty.

18. The same argument is found in the story of Job who, being righteous, is scandalized at God's burdening him with earthly ills that he did not deserve, but whose friends, using his misfortune as their argument, accuse him of sinning.

19. Epigenesis is a process by which new forms appear in the developing living being that were not present in the seed or egg.

20. It is important to stress the fact that such a comparison is possible only at a more or less "microscopic" level of analysis, when the properties

of the symbols in a given society have been identified, and not at a level of signs or themes. Nothing proves, for example, that the motif of the transvestite has the same function in other societies; the chances are great, in fact, that it would not.

Bibliography

Acosta, José de. 1598. *Histoire naturelle et morale des Indes tant orientales qu'occidentales*. Paris.

Adhémar, Jean. 1947. *Frère André Thevet*. Paris: Editions franciscaines.

Arents, George. 1937–52. *Tobacco: Its History Illustrated by the Books, Manuscripts, and Engravings in the Library of George Arents, Jr.* With an introductory essay, a glossary, and bibliographic notes by Jerome E. Brooks, editor. Vol. 1. New York: Rosenbach.

Ariès, Philippe. 1960. *L'Enfant et la vie familiale sous l'Ancien Régime*. Paris: Plon. English translation by Robert Baldick, *Centuries of Childhood: A Social History of Family Life*. New York: A. Knopf, 1962.

Aubigné, Théodore Agrippa d'. 1969. *Oeuvres*. Paris: Gallimard, Editions de la Pléiade.

Bacon, Francis. 1852. *Oeuvres*. Paris: Charpentier.

Baudet, Henri. 1965. *Paradise on Earth: Some Thoughts on European Images of Non-European Man*. Translated from the Dutch by Elizabeth Wentholt. New Haven: Yale University Press.

Beaglehole, John Cawte. 1947. *The Exploration of the Pacific*. 2nd edition. London: Adam & Charles Black.

Beidelman, T. O. 1968. Some Nuer Notions of Nakedness, Nudity, and Sexuality. *Africa* 48:113–32.

Bellarmine, Robert. 1619. *De officio principis Christiani libri tres*. Cologne.

Benzoni, Girolamo. 1579. *Histoire nouvelle du Nouveau monde*. Translated from the Italian by Urbain Chauveton. Geneva: Vignon.

Bernheimer, Richard. 1952. *Wild Men in the Middle Ages: A Study in Art, Sentiment, and Demonology*. Cambridge: Harvard University Press.

Bible oecuménique. 1965. Paris: Editions Planète.

Bird, Junius. 1963. The Alacaluf. In *The Handbook of South American Indians*, edited by Julian Steward, volume 1, pp. 55–79.

Boaistuau, Pierre. 1560. *Histoires prodigieuses*. Reprinted, Paris: Club du livre, 1961.

Boas, George. 1948. *Essays on Primitivism and Related Ideas*. Baltimore: Johns Hopkins University Press.

Boissard, Jean-Jacques. 1596. *Theatrum vitae humanae*. Frankfort: Theodori Bryi.

Boisset, Jean. 1964. *Calvin et la souveraineté de Dieu*. Paris: Seghers.

Bourne, Edward Gaylord. 1904. *Spain in America, 1450–1580*. New York: Harper & Bros. Reprinted, New York: Barnes & Noble, American Nation Series, 1962.

Braun, Georg, and Hogenberg, Franz. 1572–1618. *Civitates orbis terrarum*. 6 vols. Cologne.

Bréhier, Emile. 1934. *Histoire de la philosophie*. Vol. 2. Paris: F. Alcan. English translation, *The History of Philosophy*. Volume 3, *The Middle Ages and the Renaissance*, translated by Wade Baskin. Chicago: University of Chicago Press, 1963.

Brun, Robert. 1930. *Le livre illustré en France au seizième siècle*. Paris: F. Alcan.

Bucher, Bernadette. 1975. The Savage European. A Structural Approach to European Iconography of the American Indian. *Studies in the Anthropology of Visual Communication* 2:80–86.

Burrage, Henry, editor. 1959. *Early English and French Voyages Chiefly from Hakluyt, 1534–1608*. Original Narratives of Early American History. Reprint of 1906 edition. New York: Barnes & Noble.

Cabeza de Vaca, Alvar Nuñez. 1922. The Journey of Alvar Nuñez Cabeza de Vaca, 1528–1536. Edited with an introduction by Adolph Francis Bandelier. American Explorers Series. New York: Allerton.

Camus, Armand. 1802. *Mémoire sur la collection des Grands et Petits Voyages*. Paris: Baudouin.

Cate, Chester. 1917. De Bry and the Index Expurgatorius. *Bibliographical Society of America Papers* 11:136–40.

Chinard, Gilbert. 1913. *L'Amérique et le rêve exotique dans la littérature française au dix-septième siècle*. Paris: Hachette.

———. 1914. *L'Exotisme américain dans la littérature française au seizième siècle*. Paris: Hachette.

Cirlot, Juan Eduardo. 1962. *A Dictionary of Symbols*. Translated from the Spanish by Jack Sage, foreword by Herbert Read. New York: Philosophical Library.

Conway, William. 1889. *Literary Remains of Albrecht Dürer*. Cambridge, Eng.: At The University Press.

Cooper, John. 1917. *Analytical and Critical Bibliography of the Tribes of Tierra del Fuego and Adjacent Territories*. U.S. Bureau of American Ethnology Bulletin no. 63. Washington, D.C.: Government Printing Office.

―――. 1963. The Chono. In *The Handbook of South American Indians*, edited by Julian Steward, volume 1, pp. 47–54.

―――. 1963. The Patagonian and Pampean Hunters. In *The Handbook of South American Indians*, edited by Julian Steward, volume 1, pp. 128–68.

―――. 1963. The Yaghan. In *The Handbook of South American Indians*, edited by Julian Steward, volume 1, pp. 82–106.

Davy, Marie Magdeleine. 1964. *Initiation à la symbolique romane*. Paris: Flammarion.

Denis, Ferdinand. 1851. *Une fête brésilienne célébrée en 1550, suivie d'un fragment du seizième siècle roulant sur la théogonie des anciens peuples du Brésil et des poésies en langue tupique de Christovam Valente*. Paris: Techner.

Douglas, Mary. 1966. *Purity and Danger*. London, Routledge & Kegan Paul.

Duby, Georges. 1962. *L'Economie rurale et la vie des campagnes dans l'Occident médiéval*. 2 vols. Paris: Aubier. English translation by Cynthia Postan, *Rural Economy and Country Life in the Medieval West*. Columbia: University of South Carolina Press, 1968.

Dumézil, Georges. 1968. *Mythe et epopée*. Paris: Gallimard. English translation by Derek Coltman, *From Myth to Fiction*. Chicago: University of Chicago Press, 1973.

Eco, Umberto. 1970. Sémiologie des messages visuels. *Communications* no. 15. Paris: Seuil.

―――. 1972. *La Structure absente: introduction à la recherche sémiotique*. French translation by Uccio Esposito-Torrigiani. (Original title, *La Struttura assente*.) Paris: Mercure de France.

Emperaire, José. 1955. *Les Nomades de la mer*. Paris: Gallimard.

Estienne, Henri. 1566. *Conformité des merveilles anciennes avec les modernes*. Paris.

―――. 1911. *The Frankfurt Book Fair*. Original Latin text with English translation and notes by James Westfall Thompson. Chicago: The Caxton Club.

Etiemble, René. 1956–57. *L'Orient philosophique au dix-huitième siècle*. 2 vols. Paris: Centre de documentation universitaire.

―――. 1963. *Comparaison n'est pas raison*. Paris: Gallimard.

Evans-Pritchard, E. E. 1966. *Theories of Primitive Religion*. Oxford: Clarendon Press.

Febvre, Lucien, and Martin, Henri-Jean. 1958. *L'Apparition du livre*. Paris: A. Michel. English translation, *The Coming of the Book*. Translated by David Gerard and edited by Geoffrey Nowell-Smith and David Wootton. London: NLB, 1976.

Flamel, Nicolas. 1612. *Le Livre des figures hiéroglyphiques*. Reprinted from the original edition. Paris: Denoël, 1970.

Flandrin, Jean-Louis. 1975. *Les Amours paysannes*. Paris: Gallimard.

Fox, Robin. 1967. *Kinship and Marriage*. Baltimore: Penguin.

Friedländer, Max. 1963. *Landscape, Portrait, Still-life: Their Origin and Development*. Translated from the German by R. F. C. Hull. New York: Schocken Books.

Gaffarel, Paul. 1874. *La Découverte du Brésil par Jean Cousin*. Paris.

Giuseppi, Montague Spencer. 1915–17. The Works of Theodore de Bry and His Sons, Engravers. *Proceedings of the Huguenot Society of London*, volume 2, pp. 204–26.

Glacken, Clarence. 1967. *Traces on the Rhodian Shore: Nature and Culture in Western Thought from Ancient Times to the End of the Eighteenth Century*. Berkeley: University of California Press.

Goldmann, Lucien. 1970. *Marxisme et sciences humaines*. Paris: Gallimard.

Gomara, Francisco Lopez de. 1552. *Historia general de las Indias*. Saragossa.

Goody, Jack. 1971. Incest and Adultery. In *Kinship*, edited by J. Goody. Harmondsworth, Penguin.

Goudet, Jacques. 1965. L'Arbre de l'Eden, la gourmandise et la haine. In Dante et les mythes. *Revue des études italiennes* n.s. 11:162–78.

Griaule, Marcel. 1966. *Dieu d'eau: entretiens avec Ogotemmêli*. Paris: Fayard. English translation, *Conversations with Ogotemmêli*. Oxford: Oxford University Press, 1975.

Hakluyt, Richard. 1589. *The Principal Navigations, Voiages and Discoveries of the English Nation*. London: G. Bishop & Ralph Newberie.

Hamy, E. T. 1908. Le Bas-relief de l'Hôtel du Brésil au musée départemental d'antiquités de Rouen. In *Journal de la société des Américanistes de Paris* n.s.

Hanke, Lewis. 1937. Pope Paul III and the American Indian. In *The Harvard Theological Review* 30:65–102.

————. 1949. *The Spanish Struggle for Justice in the Conquest of America*. Philadelphia, University of Pennsylvania Press. French translation by François Durif, *Colonisation et conscience chrétienne au seizième siècle*. Paris: Plon, 1957.

————. 1959. *Aristotle and the American Indians: A Study in Race Prejudice in the Modern World*. Chicago: Henry Regnery.

Hauser, Arnold. 1951. *The Social History of Art*. Vols. 2 and 3. New York: Vintage Books.

Hauser, Henri. 1962. *La Naissance du Protestantisme*. Paris: Presses universitaires de France.

Heizer, Robert Fleming. 1947. Francis Drake and the Californian Indians, 1579. *University of California Publications in American Anthropology and Ethnology* 42:251–302.

Heulhard, Arthur. 1897. *Villegaignon, roi d'Amérique: un homme de mer au seizième siècle*. Paris: Leroux.

Hind, Arthur. 1923. *A History of Engraving and Etching from the Fifteenth Century to the Year 1914*. Boston. Reprinted, New York: Dover, 1963.

Hodge, Frederick Webb, ed. 1959. *Handbook of American Indians North of Mexico*. U.S. Bureau of American Ethnology Bulletin no. 30. 2 vols. Washington, D. C.: Government Printing Office.

Hodgen, Margaret T. 1964. *Early Anthropology in the Sixteenth and Seventeenth Centuries*. Philadelphia: University of Pennsylvania Press.

Holmyard, Eric John. 1957. *Alchemy*. Reprinted, Baltimore: Penguin, 1968.

Holt, Elizabeth G., ed. 1957. *A Documentary History of Art*. 2 vols. New York: Doubleday.

Huddleston, Lee Eldridge. 1967. *Origin of the American Indians: European Concepts, 1493–1729*. Latin American Monographs, no. 11. Institute of Latin American Studies. Austin: University of Texas Press.

Hulton, Paul, and Quinn, D. B. 1964. *The American Drawings of John White, 1577–1590*. 2 vols. London: Trustees of the British Museum.

Hunnewell, James. *Illustrated America, 1493–1889*. Proceedings of the American Antiquarian Society. Worcester.

Hymes, Dell, ed. 1972. *Reinventing Anthropology*. New York: Random House.

Jacob, François. 1970. *La Logique du vivant*. Paris: Gallimard. English translation: *The Logic of Life*. Translated by Betty E. Spillman. New York: Pantheon. 1973.

Jones, Howard M. 1964. *O Strange New World*. New York: Viking Press.

Journal d'un bourgeois de Paris à la fin de la guerre de cent ans, 1405–1449. 1963. Presented and adapted by J. Thiellay. Paris: Union générale d'éditions.

Korn, Francis. 1973. *Elementary Structures Reconsidered*. London: Tavistock.

Las Casas, Bartolomé de. 1552. *Brevissima relacion de la destruycion de de las Indias*. Seville: Sebastian Trugillo.

———. 1598. *Der Spiegel der Spanische Tyrannie*. Illustrated by de Bry. Frankfurt.

Laudonnière, René Goulaine de. 1856. *L'Histoire notable de la*

Floride. Edited by Martin Basanier. Paris: Guillaume Auvray.

Leach, Edmund. 1964. Animal Categories and Verbal Abuse. In *New Directions in the Study of Language*, edited by E. H. Lenneberg. Cambridge, Mass.: Massachusetts Institute of Technology Press.

————. 1969. *Genesis as Myth and Other Essays*. London: Cape Edition.

————. 1970. Lévi-Strauss in the Garden of Eden. In *Claude Lévi-Strauss: The Anthropologist as Hero*, edited by Nelson and Tanya Hayes, pp. 47–60. Cambridge, Mass.: Massachusetts Institute of Technology Press.

Lempertz, Heinrich. 1853–65. *Bilder-Hefte zur Geschichte des Bücherhandels*. Cologne.

Lenoble, Robert. 1969. *Histoire de l'idée de nature*. Paris: A. Michel.

Le Roy, Louis. 1575. *De la vicissitude ou variété des choses en l'univers*. Paris: Pierre L'Huillier.

Léry, Jean de. 1578. *Histoire d'un voyage fait en la terre du Brésil*. La Rochelle: Antoine Chuppin.

Lévi-Strauss, Claude. 1958. *Anthropologie structurale*. Volumes 1 and 2. Paris: Plon. Reprinted, 1973. English translation, *Structural Anthropology*. Volume 1 translated by Claire Jacobson and Brooke Grundfest Schoepf; volume 2 translated by M. Layton. New York: Anchor Books, 1967.

————. 1960. *Race et histoire*. Paris: UNESCO. English translation, *Race and History*. Paris: UNESCO, 1968.

————. 1962. *La Pensée sauvage*. Paris: Plon. English translation, *The Savage Mind*. Chicago: University of Chicago Press, 1966.

————. 1964–71. *Mythologiques*. 4 volumes. Paris: Plon. English translation, *An Introduction to a Science of Mythology*. Translated by John and Doreen Weightman. 4 volumes. New York: Harper and Row, 1969–.

Levy, R. 1971. Ma'otti Drinking Patterns in the Society Islands. In *Polynesia*, edited by R. Howard, pp. 301–18. Scranton, Pa.: Chandler.

Lorant, Stefan, ed. 1965. *The New World*. 2nd edition. New York: Duell, Sloane & Pearce.

Lothrop, S. K. 1963. Indians of Paraná Delta and La Plata Littoral. In *The Handbook of South American Indians*, edited by Julian Steward, volume 1, pp. 177–90.

Lovejoy, Arthur; Boas, George; et al. 1934. *Primitivism and Related Ideas in Antiquity*. Baltimore: Johns Hopkins University Press.

Lussagnet, Suzanne, ed. 1953. *Les Français en Amérique pendant la seconde moitié du seizième siècle*. 2 volumes. Paris: Presses universitaires de France.

Luther, Martin. 1937. *Traité du serf arbitre*. Paris: Je sers.
————. 1969. Extraits. In *Luther,* by Theobald Süss. Paris: Presses universitaires de France.
Lyell, James P. 1926. *Early Book Illustrations in Spain*. London: Grafton.
Mac Cary, B. C. Indians in Seventeenth Century Virginia. In *Virginia 350th Anniversary Historical Booklets*, no. 18., edited by Earl Gregg Swenn. Jamestown, Va.
Maier, Michael. 1617. *Atalanta fugiens, hoc est, Emblemata nova de secretis naturae chymica*. Illustrations by Theodore de Bry. Oppenheim. Facsimile edition, Cassel-Basel, 1964.
Mandrou, Robert, 1961. *Introduction à la France moderne: essai de psychologie historique, 1500–1640*. Paris: A. Michel
Martinet, André. 1960. *Eléments de linguistique générale*. Paris: A. Colin. Reprinted, 1967. English translation, by Elisabeth Palmer, *Elements of General Linguistics*. Chicago: University of Chicago Press, 1964.
————. 1969. *La Linguistique: guide alphabétique*. Paris: Denoël-Gonthier.
Matthews, George T. 1959. *News and Rumor in Renaissance Europe: The Fugger Newsletters*. New York: Capricorn Books.
Mauss, Marcel. 1966. Essai sur le don: forme et raison de l'échange dans les sociétés archaïquies. In *Sociologie et anthropologie*. 3rd edition. Paris: Presses universitaires de France. English translation by Ian Cunnison, *The Gift: Forms and Functions of Exchange in Archaic Societies*. Introduction by E. E. Evans-Pritchard. Glencoe, Ill.: Free Press, 1954.
Mehl, Roger. 1966. *La Théologie protestante*. Paris: Presses universitaires de France.
Métraux, Alfred. 1963. Ethnography of the Chaco. In *The Handbook of South American Indians,* edited by Julian Steward, volume 1, pp. 197–370.
————. 1963. The Tupinambá. Ibid. 3:95–133.
————. 1967. *Religions et magies indiennes d'Amérique du Sud*. Paris: Gallimard.
Metz, Christian. 1970. Au-delà de l'analogie, l'image. *Communications* 15:1–10.
Monod, Jacques. 1970. *Le Hasard et la nécessité*. Paris: Seuil. English translation, *Chance and Necessity*. New York: Random House, 1972.
Mooney, James. 1907. The Powhatan Confederacy, Past and Present. *American Anthropologist* n.s. 9:129–52.
————. 1910. Pamunkey. *Bureau of American Ethnology Bulletin*, no. 30, part 2, pp. 197–99.

————. 1910. Powhatan. Ibid., pp. 299–302.

Mounin, Georges. 1970. *Introduction à la sémiologie*. Paris: Editions de Minuit.

✓ Münster, Sebastien. 1554. *Cosmographia universalis*. Basel: Heinrichum Petri.

Murray, Margaret A. 1921. *The Witch-Cult in Western Europe*. Reprint. Oxford: Clarendon Press, 1962.

Nader, Laura. 1972. Up the Anthropologists: Perspectives Gained from Studying up. In *Reinventing Anthropology*, edited by Dell Hymes, pp. 284–311. New York, Random House.

Nuttall, Zelia, editor. 1903. *The Book of the Life of the Ancient Mexicans, Containing an Account of Their Rites and Superstitions*. Facsimile reproduction of the Hispano-Mexican manuscript, with introduction, translation, and commentary by Zelia Nuttall. Part 1: Introduction and facsimile. Berkeley: University of California Press.

Oliver, Douglas. 1961. *The Pacific Islands*. New York: Doubleday.

Ovid. 1564. *La Métamorphose d'Ovide figurée*. 2nd edition. With 178 woodcuts by Bernard Salomon. Paris.

Panofsky, Dora and Erwin. 1965. *Pandora's Box: The Changing Aspects of a Mythical Symbol*. 2nd edition, revised. New York: Harper and Row.

Panofsky, Erwin. 1955. *Meaning in the Visual Art of the Renaissance*. New York: Harper Torchbooks.

————. 1962. *Studies in Iconology: Humanistic Themes in the Art of the Renaissance*. New York: Harper Torchbooks.

✓ Paré, Ambroise. 1964. *Des monstres, des prodiges, des voiages*. Paris: Club français du livre.

✓ Parks, Brunner G. 1928. *Richard Hakluyt and the English Voyages*. American Geographical Society Special Publications, no. 10.

✓ Pearce, Roy H. 1967. *Savagism and Civilization*. Baltimore: Johns Hopkins University Press.

Perrisin, Jacques. See Jean Tortorel.

Piaget, Jean. 1970. *Le Structuralisme*. Paris: Presses universitaires de France. English translation, *Structuralism*. Translated and edited by Chaninah Maschler. New York: Basic Books, 1970.

Pichois, Claude, and Rousseau, A. M. 1967. *La Littérature comparée*. Paris: A. Colin.

Pigafetta, Antonio. 1888. *Premier voyage autour du monde sur l'escadre de Magellan, par Vincenzo* [sic] *Pigafetta, 1519–1522*. Paris: C. Delagrave.

Pirenne, Henri. 1946. *Les Grands Courants de l'histoire universelle*. Paris: A. Michel.

Ramusio, Giovanni. 1556. *Delle navigationi e viaggi*. Venice.

Read, John. 1957. *Through Alchemy to Chemistry*. London: G. Bell. French translation, *De l'alchimie à la chimie*. Paris: A Fayard, 1959.

Recht, Roland. 1968. La Méthode iconologique d'Erwin Panofsky. *Critique* 24:315–23.

Requena, Antonio. 1945. Noticias y consideraciones sobre las anormalidades sexuales de los aborigenes americanos: sodomía. *Acta venezolana* 1:44–73. Caracas.

Renneville, René A. de. 1725. *Recueil des voyages qui ont servi à l'établissement et aux progrès de la Compagnie des Indes orientales*. Volume 2, *Voyages de Sebald de Weert*. Amsterdam: J. F. Bernard; Rouen: P. Cailloux.

Ricoeur, Paul. 1963. Structure et hermeneutique. *Esprit* n.s. 31:596–627.

Rigby, Peter. 1968. Gogo Rituals of Purification. In *Dialectic in Practical Religion*, edited by E. Leach, pp. 153–78. London: Cambridge University Press.

Ripa, Cesare. 1766. *Iconologia del cavaliere Cesaro Ripa*. 6 vols. Perugia.

Rouse, Irving. 1963. The Arawak. In *The Handbook of South American Indians*, edited by Julian Steward, volume 4, pp. 507–46.

Rowe, John H. Ethnography and Ethnology in the Sixteenth Century. *Kroeber Anthropological Society Papers*, no. 30, Spring.

———. 1965. The Renaissance Foundation of Anthropology. *American Anthropologist* 67:1–20.

Rowse, A. L., and Dougan, Robert O. 1966. Historical introductions by A. L. Rouse and bibliographical notes by R. O. Dougan for *The World Encompassed by Sir Francis Drake 1628* and *The Relation of a Wonderfull Voiage by William Cornelison Schouten, 1619*. Bibliotheca Americana. Cleveland: The World Publishing Co.

Ruwet, Nicolas. 1967. *Introduction à la grammaire générative*. Paris: Plon.

Sahlins, Marshall. 1958. *Social Stratification in Polynesia*. Seattle: University of Washington Press.

———. 1972. *Stone Age Economics*. Chicago: Aldine-Atherton.

Sauer, Carl O. 1966. *The Early Spanish Main*. Berkeley: The University of California Press.

Schouten, Willem Cornelis. 1619. *The Relation of a Wonderfull Voyage Made by W. C. Schouten of Horne*. London: Nathanael Newbery. Facsimile edition. Cleveland: World Publishing Company, 1966.

Schuler, Rudolph. 1924. The Oldest Known Illustration of the South American Indians. *Journal de la société des Américanistes de Paris*. N. s. volume 16.

Serres, Olivier de. 1619. *Le Théâtre d'agriculture et le mesnage des champs*. Rouen: Jean de la Mare.

Seznec, Jean. 1961. *The Survival of the Pagan Gods*. Translated by Barbara F. Sessions. New York: Harper & Row. Original French title: *La Survivance des dieux antiques*. London: Warburg Institute, 1939.

Smith, John. 1624, *The Generall Historie of Virginia, New-England, and the Summer Isles*. London: M. Sparkes.

————. 1967. *Captain John Smith's America: Selections from His Writings*. Edited by John Lankford. New York: Harper and Row.

Snowden, Frank M. 1969. *Blacks in Antiquity*. Cambridge: Harvard University Press.

Speck, Frank G. 1928. Chapters on the Ethnology of the Powhatan Tribes of Virginia. *Indian Notes and Monographs* 1:227–455. Publications of the Museum of the American Indian, Heye Foundation.

Spencer, Robert, editor. 1969. *Forms of Symbolic Action*. Proceedings of the 1969 Annual Spring Meeting, American Ethnological Society. Seattle: University of Washington Press.

Spielbergen, Joris van. 1906. *East and West Indian Mirror: Being an Account of Joris van Spielbergen's Voyage around the World and the Australian Navigation of Le Maire*. Translated, with notes and an introduction, by J. A. J. De Villiers. Works issued by the Hakluyt Society, second series, no. 18.

Staden, Hans. 1557. *Wahrhaftige Historie und Beschreibung einer Landschaft der wilden, nacketen, grimmigen menschenfresser Leute in der Neue Welt Amerika gelegen*. Marburg.

Stern, T. 1952. Chickahominy. *Proceedings of the American Philosophical Society* 91:157–225.

Stevens, Henry. 1924. The de Bry Collector's Painful Peregrination Along the Pleasant Pathway to Perfection. *Bibliographical Essays: A Tribute to Wilberforce Eames*, pp. 269–76. Cambridge, Mass.: Harvard University Press.

Steward, Julian, editor. 1963. *The Handbook of South American Indians*. 7 vols. New York: Cooper Square.

Stout, David B. 1963. The Cuna. In *The Handbook of South American Indians*, edited by Julian Steward, vol. 4, pp. 257–68.

Structuralisme et Marxisme. 1970. Paris: Union générale d'éditions.

Sturtevant, William C. 1964. John White's Contribution to Ethnography. In *The American Drawings of John White*, edited by Hulton and Quinn, pp. 37–47. London: Trustees of the British Museum.

Süss, Theobald. 1969. *Luther*. Paris: Presses universitaires de France.

Symonds, John A. 1960. *The Renaissance in Italy*. 2 vols. New York: Putnam's Sons.

Tanquerey, A. 1924. *Précis de théologie ascétique et mystique*. Paris: Desclée & Co.

Taylor, C. R. H. 1963. *A Pacific Bibliography: Printed Matter Relating to the Native Peoples of Polynesia, Melanesia and Micronesia*. Oxford: Clarendon Press.

Tennant, F. R. 1968. *The Sources of the Doctrine of the Fall and the Original Sin*. New York: Schocken Books.

Thevet, André. 1558. *Les Singularités de la France antarctique*. Paris.

Thomas Aquinas. 1963. *Somme théologique*. Paris: Desclée & Co.

Tiele, Pieter, 1867. 1867. *Mémoire bibliographique sur les journaux des navigateurs néerlandais réimprimés dans les collections de de Bry et de Hulsius*. Amsterdam: Muller.

Toledo, Francisco de. 1649. *Summa casum conscientiae absolutissima*. Book 8. *Peccatis mortalibus*. n.p. Petrum Hennigium.

Tortorel, Jean, and Perrissin, Jacques. n.d. *Premier volume, contenant quarante tableaux ou histoires diverses qui sont mémorables touchant les Guerres, Massacres, et Troubles advenus en France en ces dernières années, 1559–1570*. n.p.

Trubetskoi, N.S. 1967. *Principes de phonologie*. Translated by J. Cantineau. English translation by Christiane A. M. Baltaxe, *Principles of Phonology*. Berkeley: University of California Press, 1969.

Turner, Victor. 1967. *The Forest of Symbols: Aspects of Ndembu Ritual*. Ithaca: Cornell University Press.

———. 1969. *The Ritual Process*. Chicago: Aldine.

Ucko, Peter. 1970. Penis Sheaths: A Comparative Study. *Proceedings of the Royal Anthropological Institute of Great Britain and Ireland for 1969*, pp. 27–68.

Van Lennep, J. 1966. *Art et alchimie*. Brussels: Meddens.

Vespucci, Amerigo. 1926. *The Letter of A. Vespucci Describing his Four Voyages in the New World, 1497–1504*. San Francisco: The Book Club of California.

Washburn, Wilcomb. 1959. The Moral and Legal Justification for Dispossessing the Indians. In *Seventeenth-century America: Essays in Colonial History*, edited by James Morton Smith, pp. 15–32. Chapel Hill: Published for the Institute of Early American History and Culture at Williamsburg, Va., by the University of North Carolina Press.

———. 1971. *Red Man's Land/White Man's Law: A Study of the Past and Present Status of the American Indian*. New York: Scribner's.

Watkins, Ronald. 1965. *On Producing Shakespeare*. New York: Citadel.

Wegener, Richard. 1925. Frankfurt Anteil an der Rassen und Völkerkunde: die Indianerzeichung Porträt des Th. de Bry. *Festschrift der Anthropologische Gesellschaft Frankfurts*. Frankfurt.

Weitzmann, Karl. 1947. *Illustrations in Roll and Codex: A Study of the Origin and Method of Text Illustration*. Studies in Manuscript Illumination. vol. 2. Princeton: Princeton University Press.

Williamson, J.A. 1965. *The Age of Drake*. New York: The World Publishing Company.

Willoughby, Charles. 1907. The Virginia Indians of the Seventeenth Century. *American Anthropologist* 9:57–86.

Witthoft, J. 1949. Green Corn Ceremonialism in the Eastern Woodlands. Occasional Contribution from the Museum of the University of Michigan. *OCMA* 13:31–77.

Wolf, Eric. 1972. American Anthropologists and American Society. In *Reinventing Anthropology*, edited by Dell Hymes, pp. 251–63.

Worth, Sol. 1972. Towards an Anthropological Politics of Symbolic Forms. Ibid., pp. 335–65.

Wright, L. B. 1958. *Middle-class Culture in Elizabethan England*. Ithaca: Cornell University Press.

Zulch, W. K. 1935. *Frankfurter Künstler, 1223–1700*. Frankfurt.

Index

Abbéville, Claude d', 58
Acosta, José de, 9, 19, 20, 22, 23, 86, 124, 125, 126
Adam and Eve, 110; and Dutch captain, 93; and Fuegians, 88–89; Garden of Eden variant of, 72; and original sin, 109; and Polynesian women, 134; as sexually differentiated figures, 76–77; and Spaniards, 79–81, 117; and Eve's creation, 62. *See also* Myth of the Fall
Age, as pertinent opposition, 52–53
Ages of life: depiction of, 52; and distribution of body parts, 58–59; and gift of fruit, 83; and types of food, 61–63
Alacalufs, 86, 121, 132, and chap. 9 passim
Alchemical symbolism, 20–21
Alchemy in European thought, 55, 64, 99, 100–102
Alexander III (pope), 6
Algonquian, 13, 37, 46, 163; body paintings of, 34; illustrations of, 14
Alliance, 102–4, 130–31. *See also* Sexual relations
Amor, Ralph, 22
Analysis of motifs, method of, 43–45
Analytic codes: categories of, 31–32, 96; constancy of, 74; pivotal, 129–30. *See also* Food code
Anatomy, human, and cosmic time, 54–55. *See also* Physical features
Androgyny: of Christian devil, 73, 75; of Caribbean woman, 66, 75; of Fuegian woman, 89; of idols, 69–70; and myth, 77–78; of Penguin Island woman, 123

Animal kingdom, 124–31, 150–52
Animal meat and cannibalism, 57
Animals: of Fuegians, 88–91; illustrations of, 20–21; ornamental functions of, 151–52; of Penguin Island, 124–31
Anomalous figures, 38–39, 47; bearded Indian, 126, 128, 130, 152–58; Christian devil, 73, 74–79, 132; dwarf king, 91–93, 94, 124, 126, 128, 130, 150, 160; Fuegian women, 88–93, 94–96; Indian man with harpoon, 86–87, 132; inverted couple, 158–69; king of Hoorn Island, 134–36, 159–61; long-haired Indians, 152–58, 160–61; transformations of 88–89, 91, 93, 95
Anomaly, 141–45, 164; in Fuegian women, 89–90, 91, 151; of monstrous couple, 136–37; in Penguin Island figures, 122, 126–27; and liminal situations, 142–44, 168; of old Tupinambá, 49
Antifood. *See* Food code
Antiochus of Athens, 55
Aquinas, Thomas, 62
Araucanian, 86, 109
Arawak, 17, 73, chap. 6 passim, 155–56; and vomiting, 156
Ashes and defilement, 94–96
Astrology in European thought, 55
Aubigné, Théodore Agrippa d', 97, 101
Autochthony, 77–81
Aztec, 19, 34, 86

Bacon, Francis, 113
Bearded Indians, 126, 128, 130, 152–58
Benzoni, 10, 22, 34, 65, 116, 154
Bible oecuménique, 69